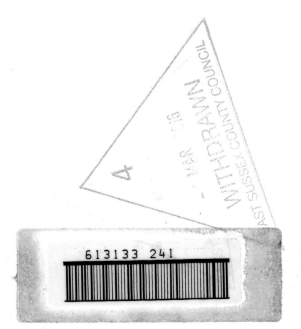

# The Early Industrial Revolution

BRITAIN IN THE EIGHTEENTH CENTURY

# The Early
# Industrial Revolution

BRITAIN IN THE EIGHTEENTH CENTURY

## *Eric Pawson*

Department of Geography, University of Canterbury
New Zealand

Batsford Academic

*For John Patten*

ABBREVIATIONS USED
(Standard form of abbreviation given in brackets)

| | |
|---|---|
| Ag.History (Ag.Hist) | Agricultural History |
| Ag.Hist.Rev. (Ag.H.R.) | Agricultural History Review |
| Ec.H.R. | Economic History Review |
| Expln.in Econ Hist (EEH) | Explorations in Economic History |
| Geog.Jnl. (GJ) | Geographical Journal |
| Hist.Jnl (Hist J) | Historical Journal |
| Jnl.Hist Geog (JHG) | Journal of Historical Geography |
| Scottish Geog Mag (SGM) | Scottish Geographical Magazine |
| T.I.B.G. | Transactions of the Institute of British Geographers |
| Trans Newcomen Soc | Transactions of the Newcomen Society |
| Trans Royal Hist Soc (TRHS) | Transactions of the Royal Historical Society |
| Yorks Bull of Econ and Soc Res | Yorkshire Bulletin of Economic and Social Research |

First published 1979

© Eric Pawson, 1978

ISBN  0  7134  1625  4 (Hardcover edition) ✓
ISBN  0  7134  1626  2 (Limp edition)

Photoset, printed and bound
in Great Britain by
REDWOOD BURN LIMITED
Trowbridge & Esher
for the publishers
B. T. Batsford Ltd
4 Fitzhardinge Street
London W1H 0AH

# Contents

# List of Figures

# List of Tables

# List of Photographs

# Acknowledgements

The Author and Publishers wish to thank the following for permission to reproduce the illustrations appearing in this book: Academic Press Inc (London) Ltd, figs. 6:2, 6:3, 6:5 and 8:2 (from E. Pawson, *Transport and Economy: The Turnpike Roads of Eighteenth Century Britain*, 1977); British Waterways Board, pl. D1 and D2; British Library, pl. A1 and B2; Cambridge University Press, fig. 3:2 (from H.C. Darby, *A New Historical Geography of England*, 1973), fig. 3:3 (from A.R.H. Baker and R.A. Butlin (eds.), *Studies of Field Systems of the British Isles*, 1973) and fig. 4:1 (from P. Deane and W.A. Cole, *British Economic Growth*, 1967); Clive House Museum, Shrewsbury, pl. B1; Derbyshire County Library, pl. B3; Crescent Museums, Scarborough, pl. F2; Institute of British Geographers, London, fig. 3:1 (from *Trans.* no. 51, 1970) and fig. 8:4 (from *Trans.* no. 41, 1967); Museum of English Rural Life, University of Reading, pl. A2, A6, E1 and E2); Dr. P.J. Perry, pl. F3; Radio Times, pl. A3 and B5; Royal Commission on Historical Monuments, pl. B4 and E3; Science Museum, London, pl. C2, D3 and D4; Scottish Tourist Board, pl. B6 and F4.

# Preface

Recent years have seen a flood of research publications of all sorts, the historical subjects being swept along with everyone else. The experience, of course, is exciting and necessary for the more dedicated (which usually means other researchers), but for the rest (and this must cover many teachers and most students) it is often both confusing and frustrating. My aim has therefore been to produce a book for 'the rest', summarising the more illuminating and worthwhile findings about one major historical theme: the acceleration of economic and geographical change in eighteenth century Britain, the formative century of her industrialisation.

It has been written primarily for students of historical geography, a field that in Britain at least has been singularly devoid of such books (Darby's renowned edited collections being only partial exceptions). That most historical geography courses have to rely heavily on texts written by and for economic historians is not wholly satisfactory, although it goes almost without saying that geographers can learn much from their colleagues. However, in the late 1970s, many of these economic history texts, having been published some years ago, are themselves rather out-of-date. I hope, therefore, that this book will also be of use to economic historians, both as a synthesis of recent research and for its own geographical slant.

There are, no doubt, advantages in undertaking projects such as this after a lifetime of scholarly reflection, but there are also very good reasons for doing them considerably sooner. All the same, I am very grateful to those who have saved me from some of the blunders of youth. Professor Gary Hawke read the draft and made many perceptive suggestions. Dr Peter Perry had the unenviable task of ploughing through the hand-written version yet still managed to offer much constructive criticism. Dr Dick Bedford was particularly helpful with the second chapter. Their comments have immeasurably improved the manuscript, but all remaining blemishes are of course my responsibility alone. Mrs Nanette Mann produced the typescript with great care, the Department of Geography at the University of Canterbury generously assisted with the cost of the photographs and its cartographers drew all the maps. To all of them my thanks, and to Harvey and to many more besides.

Canterbury, New Zealand

# 1 The Industrial Revolution

Historians have long recognised many apparent breaks in the continuity of history. The Fall of Rome, the Norman Conquest, the Renaissance, the Reformation, the French Revolution: all conspicuously claim attention as symbolic turning points. Yet none has had such far-reaching effects on the pattern of human existence as the Industrial Revolution that began in Europe in the eighteenth and nineteenth centuries. It is this great economic discontinuity, rather than the political and cultural upheavals littering history, that holds the key to the understanding of progress, to the increase in the wealth of nations.

The undisputed leader in this transition from a traditional rural to an urban-industrial society was Britain, in the late seventeenth century two Kingdoms[1] of no great importance off the coast of Europe – a position, in fact, not unlike the one she seems to seek to re-enter in the late 1970s. But it was Britain (rather than England alone, for Wales and Scotland contributed fully) that of all the countries of Europe, became the first industrial state: a place that she held unchallenged until the rise of America as a great economic power in the last quarter of the nineteenth century.

## The Industrial Revolution

The Industrial Revolution in Britain was, however, rather more than just the rise of industry. It was a whole transformation from the relative economic and social stability of preceding centuries into a new experience of sustained economic growth and social change. Population and towns grew, production and trade grew, incomes grew. There was expansion within all the economic sectors, agriculture, industry and the services, bringing not only a rise in output, but with the increasingly efficient use of resources, rising per capita output as well. Accompanying this expansion was a relative shift of importance between sectors. Out of an agricultural economy, with small-scale craft industries and few basic services, emerged a new structure dominated by mass-industry and overseas trade, with a wide range of service functions and a flourishing stratum of professional activities. Alongside these shifts in economic structure came important social changes. A rural society gave way to an urban one, and with this, the age-old division between the landed and the landless was replaced by the now familiar consciousness of the urban middle and working classes. These four basic trends: per capita economic expansion, structural change, the transition from rural to urban, and the emergence of a new social order, are the essential facets of the period labelled the Industrial Revolution. They brought fundamental alterations in the way of life, as well as a long-term rise in the standard of living that has been continuous and pervasive. The Industrial Revolution had many casualties, far too many to be dismissed so callously, but as a process of *sustained economic growth*, it generated increasing wealth and opportunity for more and more people, to the eventual immense benefit of all.

*Timing*

The problem of dating the Industrial Revolution has most frequently been analysed in terms of its starting point. There are two common, but essentially complementary interpretations of this. The 1780s have traditionally been regarded as the key decade of economic acceleration, a point of view associated particularly with the economic historian T.S. Ashton, and sealed 20 years ago in the famous take-off theory of W.W. Rostow. This is however an oversimplification of the evidence, although it is undeniable that the 1780s and 1790s were the period of most rapid change in the eighteenth century. Deane and Cole, the most assiduous collectors of quantitative information relating to Britain's industrialisation,[2] have shown very clearly that the upturn is earlier, with sustained growth beginning in the 1740s, slowing in the 1770s with financial crisis and the American War, then being re-invigorated in the 1780s. The best available estimates of agricultural and industrial output, and graphs of population, foreign trade and urban growth support this two-phase pattern. Some important elements of change, in particular the introduction of certain agricultural and transport innovations, the seeds of scientific advance, the expansion of trading links and the growth of London, can be traced further back still, into the seventeenth century. There was no simple or stark take-off, but a long period of gradual preparation, that was translated in the 1740s into sustained growth, with a notable acceleration in the years after 1780.

But if the Industrial Revolution has its origins in the eighteenth century, and its roots even earlier, the period of most rapid change is nevertheless the nineteenth century. Britain in 1800 was certainly different to Britain in 1700. Industrial activity in a whole range of spheres had begun to grow rapidly. The spatial pattern of industry had shifted: away from the south to the Midlands and north of England, and into south Wales and central Scotland. A significant number of provincial towns had expanded to a considerable size. Yet two-thirds of the population still lived in the countryside in 1800, and agriculture remained the most important economic sector. In the nineteenth century however, the mechanisms of change moved altogether into a higher gear. Britain in 1900 was not just different, but vastly different to Britain in 1800. This is summarised quite plainly by the raw data in table 1:1.

TABLE 1:1   *The Changing Structure of the Economy, 1700–1900.*

|  | 1700 | 1800 | 1900 |
|---|---|---|---|
| % GNP – Agriculture | 40+ | c33 | 6 |
| – Industry | c20 | c24 | 40 |
| – Services | c35 | c44 | 54 |
| % Urban | 22–3% | 28–33% | 75% |

*Sources:* The GNP figures are adapted from Deane and Cole (1967). They are essentially rough guides, given problems of estimation and definition (e.g. many farmers were also involved in service activities). 'Industry' covers manufacturing, mining and building. Trade and transport come under 'Services'.

Two important points follow from this brief discussion. Firstly, the extent of change in the eighteenth century must be kept within the perspective of the massive transformation in the nineteenth. Problems studied in isolation invariably assume an exaggerated importance, which is why it is necessary to set them in context, and consider their general interrelationships with adjacent problems or periods. But, secondly, the eighteenth century nonetheless is of considerable interest per se. It well repays close study. It is the period of transition from the relative stability of pre-industrial life to a growing, industrialising economy, the century when the essential nature and direction of change were worked out. The eighteenth century in Britain can realistically be labelled the Early Industrial Revolution.

*Causes*

There has been considerable variation in emphasis on the possible causes of the Industrial Revolution. A whole range of factors from fortunate resource endowments to scientific advance and the growth of foreign trade, as well as less concrete qualities such as 'inventive genius' and 'the will to industrialise' have been singled out as prerequisites or even prime-movers. Another drawback of the take-off theory is that it also unduly emphasises one factor – a rise in the rate of capital investment. Yet it can be said with certainty of the process of growth that it is highly complex and any single or simple prescription (as the experience of many Third World countries has shown) is false. Growth is multi-causal, depending on change and interaction between all factors on both the demand and supply side of the economic equation.

Rising demand was, of itself, of considerable importance. It was not, however, simply a matter of growing numbers. Rapid population growth has certainly not brought industrialisation of its own accord in the Third World today, but this is because so much of the population is self-subsistent, divorced from the wage-economy and market. This was not true of the state of England in 1700, and it became steadily less true of Scotland and Wales as the eighteenth century progressed. Britain's relatively undeveloped pre-industrial economy was nonetheless characterised by short (and some long) distance exchange within agriculture, craft industry and the urban service sectors. Because of this, the rising demand of a growing population was widely felt throughout the economy, and likewise the benefits of this rising demand, in terms of increasing returns, were equally widely felt. There was a slow but general rise in the level of real wages, the evidence of this being the increasing and widespread consumption of a growing range of foodstuffs (both home-produced and imported), simple industrial goods (such as cotton textiles and small items of metalware), as well as basic and professional services. It was the middle-income groups (in particular the farmers, traders, merchants and members of the professions) which led the way, but rising demand in the early Industrial Revolution was very broadly based.

Rising demand on its own, however, was insufficient to generate economic growth. To bring benefits, it had to be met by responsiveness from supply inputs. Had the economy not attained a sufficient degree of advancement in the eighteenth century to produce this responsiveness, then Britain might well have entered a Malthusian trap (if population had continued to grow quickly), or become heavily reliant on the products of overseas trade to satisfy the demands of middle and higher income groups. But neither happened. Britain possessed both a plentiful supply of resources and the means to exploit them with increasing efficiency, so as to produce a gradual rise in output per capita over time.

The country was well endowed with natural resources, such as good farming land, minerals, waterways and harbours. The effective supply of these could be boosted by bringing into production those unused or under-used. The area of cultivated land expanded considerably in the

eighteenth century, for example. Some basic materials of industrialisation had to be imported – cotton being the obvious case – but
these were earnt by trade. The country was not short of labour, and its
supply increased as population grew. There was also sufficient capital
available to sustain the economy, deriving essentially from agriculture,
trade and the profits of new enterprise, i.e. the pooled savings of an economy operating above subsistence level. Yet an expanding supply of these
resources, with a growing population, need have done no more than
merely sustain production per head. Economic growth, or development,
meant a rise in per capita production, which only came about by increasing efficiency in the use of the resources, or supply inputs, available. This
was achieved in three ways: by innovation, by improving organisation
and by the conquest of space.

Eighteenth century Britain was extremely innovative, both in respect
of the classic series of technical changes traditionally associated with the
Industrial Revolution and of the less obvious innovations in commerce
(such as the wider use of the mortgage and other instruments of credit),
education and administration. Innovations enabled a higher scale of production to be achieved by increasing the efficiency of men themselves, or
the equipment with which they worked, and permitted an increasing
division of labour. The innovations underlying the change from organic
to inorganic sources of raw material (such as the introduction of coke-
smelting in the iron industry and coal-generated steam as a means of
power) removed low ceilings to production thus greatly raising its
potential. Innovations in agriculture which were both technical (new
crops and better rotations, for example) and structural (enclosure) underlay a rise in food production that not only fed the growing population,
but enabled it to be fed better. The series of technical changes in the textiles industries so cheapened the final product, by expanding supply to
ever increasing levels, that cheap quality cloth was available to nearly all
the population by 1800.

The exact source of this upsurge of innovation is impossible to pin-
point, however. It was obviously encouraged by the general economic climate; by experimentation, argument, discussion in the firms and towns
of the day; by education, and not least, by Britain's overseas links, which
provided ideas and skills as well as goods and markets. It was associated
with rising capital accumulation, although the economy's requirements
were modest and per capita investment levels did not rise dramatically in
the eighteenth century. As a means of increasing efficiency in the use of
resources, this particular concept – rising per capita investment – is more
applicable to the nineteenth century.

The organisation of enterprise, or entrepreneurship, is one of the least understood aspects of the development process. To a certain extent, all producers can be regarded as entrepreneurs, but the early Industrial Revolution was certainly characterised by the emergence of a type of bold, successful organisers, particularly in industry and trade. These entrepreneurs played a critical role, harnessing the other factors of production and directing their collective efforts towards the exploitation of markets, thereby bringing supply and demand forces together. Again, the exact reasons for this emergence are obscure: it is difficult to be any more specific than for the sources of innovativeness. But the role of protestantism, proposed by R.H. Tawney in a famous work *Religion and the Rise of Capitalism*, was of less direct significance than once thought, although it is undoubtedly true that some groups, bound by ties of kinship and belief, did produce clusters of successful businessmen. The Quakers are the best example.

The conquest of space was the third source of increasing efficiency. Improving transport and communications (an important aspect of capital accumulation) permitted an increasing amount of exchange within the economy. It allowed entrepreneurs to assemble raw materials from a wide area, and enabled them to break out of local markets, so encouraging specialisation in agriculture, industry and the services: rational specialisation being one of the most potent forces of economic advance. Better transport cut real costs of movement, whilst better communications, channelling flows of information, were fundamental to the extension of markets, to the organisation of large scale enterprises, and to services such as banking and insurance. The conquest of space thus not only improved the efficiency of supply factors, but was another necessary link between them and rising demand.

It is apparent, therefore, that a whole range of factors must be considered as causes of the Industrial Revolution. Individually, many of these factors were necessary, but none were sufficient. Assessing the relative importance of each is difficult, if not impossible, which is why as often as not they are listed in seemingly random and unconnected order in the texts, if they are explicitly identified at all. It is however, possible to group these causes into three broad, and interrelated, categories: firstly, rising demand; secondly, an increasing supply of resources, or factors of production; and thirdly, increasing efficiency in the use of those resources.

## Britain in 1700

Enough has been said already to indicate that Britain in 1700 was not, in the modern sense of the term, an underdeveloped country. She had already attained a certain degree of advancement, sufficient to produce a self-generated economic revolution over the next two centuries. However, there were marked spatial variations in the level of development in 1700. Much of England was in productive farmland (although large acreages of upland still lay in waste), agriculture was specialised to a degree by region, and well-served by a web of market towns. There were a number of loose concentrations of industrial activity, whilst London, as a centre of trade and services, was the biggest city in Europe. Wales and Scotland were considerably different. There were no towns of any size in Wales, its agriculture was poor, the upland farms producing only sturdy black cattle for outside markets. And Scotland even described itself as 'a country the most barren of any Nation in these parts of Europe', in a petition sent to Westminster in 1720. This was largely true. Highland agriculture was merely subsistent, and the medieval routine of lowland agriculture had hardly changed. There was little industry, except for some poor domestic linen-working. Even so, the country was not completely barren. The seeds of advance were planted. Glasgow was slowly extending its trading links, Edinburgh had an embryonic banking system (which became a factor of the greatest importance in Scottish development). Coal mining had long been an activity along the Firths of Forth and Clyde. The Scottish educational system was reacting positively to the needs of commerce. It was from such seeds that Scotland transformed itself, probably more rapidly than any other part of Europe, over the next century.

But if Britain as a whole provided some indicators of a fair level of development in 1700, it also exhibited many of the characteristics of underdevelopment. Firstly, the economy was relatively unspecialised, being mainly dependent on agriculture. Secondly, most industrial production was concerned with very basic goods. Wool textiles were the staple, accounting for over a third of all industrial output, and the bulk of exports. Thirdly, economic activity, although widespread, was dominated by London, a great primate city. There were no provincial towns that came anywhere near it in size or influence. It did, however, prove to be an engine of growth rather than a drain or sink-hole in the eighteenth century economy: as a wealthy market and source of enterprise, it was able to contribute much. Fourthly, by today's standards Britain was a poor country, even though both Gregory King, the late seventeenth century statistician, and Adam Smith, the great classical economist, considered it was the second richest in Europe. But King estimated that 850,000 families in England and Wales (or 60 per cent of the total) had an annual income of £15 or less in 1688. This was low, but his tabulations also show that the subsistence sector was small too. In other words, the essential condition of participation in the market economy was present as well. Fifthly, Britons in 1700 were still subject, to a considerable degree, to the vagaries of nature. Disease, dearth and natural hazards loomed large in life to an extent that is inconceivable today. A major check on pre-industrial population growth was epidemic disease; it was also a heavy risk in agriculture. The lack of a close link between crop and animal husbandry, until the extensive spread of rotations and fodder crops, put farmers at the mercy of long, hard winters, and could induce serious food shortages. The Scottish famines of the 1690s were the last major instance, although there were many hard years after this, including those at the turn of the nineteenth century throughout Britain. Industrial activity, reliant to a large degree on water-wheels, was governed by the seasonal variation in stream-flow. And not least, the risk of fire in towns was so great that most suffered a major conflagration every few generations. Man was, of course, no closer to controlling nature's course in 1800 than in 1700, but he had developed considerably more resistance to her ways: he was far more his own master.

In 1700, therefore, pre-industrial Britain was quite advanced in some respects, and relatively underdeveloped in others. But if only because a high proportion of her population, particularly in England, was participant in a market economy, she could not be regarded as an underdeveloped country in the Third World sense of the term. Many other seeds of advance were already apparent. They grew to fruition over the succeeding two centuries, in so doing bringing about a complete transformation of economy and society. The succeeding chapters explore the first half of this transformation, the Early Industrial Revolution in Britain. Change within, and changing relations between each of the sectors of the economy are discussed, and the role and growth of towns examined. The obvious starting point, however, is with the acceleration of population growth that accompanied the whole process.

## NOTES

1  The Act of Union with Scotland was passed in 1707. The Union had some important economic results, for example, it brought Scotland inside the sphere of the Navigation Acts, it encouraged a freer flow of ideas, particularly in agriculture, and gave limited state assistance to the linen industry. These topics are dealt with in the appropriate chapters below. See also Rae (1974).

2  Deane and Cole's *British Economic Growth, 1688–1959* was published in 1962, rev. 1967. It was a path breaking work of quantitative economic history, and along with its companion volume *An Abstract of British*

*Historical Statistics* (ed Mitchell and Deane), contains a wealth of statistical reconstructions. Their interpretations of this material have been the subject of much stimulating debate, and in this respect, the work should be handled with care.


## FURTHER READING

Nearly all the good books on the Industrial Revolution have been produced by economic historians, and most are a little out-of-date given the tide of recent research. Well worth consulting however are T. S. Ashton: *An Economic History of Britain: the Eighteenth Century* (1955); E. J. Hobsbawm: *Industry and Empire* (1968); P. Mathias: *The First Industrial Nation* (1969) and the relevant chapters of H. C. Darby's *A New Historical Geography of England* (1973). These books are preoccupied with England; for Scotland, see H. Hamilton: *An Economic History of Scotland in the Eighteenth Century* (1963), R. H. Campbell: *Scotland since 1707* (1965), and T. I. Rae (ed.): *The Union of 1707: Its Impact on Scotland* (1974). There are also two new works which show the contribution of the 'new' economic historians and geographers respectively: R. C. Floud and D. N. McCloskey (eds.): *The Economic History of Britain since 1750* (forthcoming), and R. A. Dodgshon and R. A. Butlin (eds.): *An Historical Geography of England and Wales* (1978).

There are several important studies of the Industrial Revolution as a process of growth: R. M. Hartwell: *The Industrial Revolution and Economic Growth* (1971); Allan Thompson: *The Dynamics of the Industrial Revolution* (1973) and Phyllis Deane and W. A. Cole: *British Economic Growth, 1688–1959* (1967, 2nd edn.). This latter reference contains the most comprehensive collection of economic indices relating to this period. See also M. W. Flinn: *The Origins of the Industrial Revolution* (1966); R. M. Hartwell (ed.): *The Causes of the Industrial Revolution* (1967), which reprints several of the important articles on this topic and T. S. Ashton: *Economic Fluctuations in England 1700 to 1800* (1959). Mention should also be made of W. W. Rostow's two provocative works, provocative because they stimulate, but rather oversimplify the process of growth. The famous work was *The Stages of Economic Growth: a non-communist manifesto* (1960) which found the answer in a rising rate of productive investment and his more recent contribution *How It All Began: Origins of the Modern Economy* (1975), which finds it in the scientific revolution of the seventeenth century.

On the pre-industrial period, there are several suitable references: L. A. Clarkson: *The Pre-Industrial Economy in England, 1500–1750* (1971), B. A. Holderness: *Pre-Industrial England: Economy and Society 1500–1750*

(1976) and D. C. Coleman: *The Economy of England, 1450–1750* (1976). Books which place the British experience in a European perspective include: H. J. Habakkuk and M. M. Postan (eds.): *The Cambridge Economic History of Europe*, vol. VI (1965), C. M. Cipolla (ed.): *The Fontana Economic History of Europe: The Industrial Revolution* (1973), A. Milward and S. B. Saul: *The Economic Development of Continental Europe, 1780–1870* (1973) and David S. Landes: *The Unbound Prometheus* (1969).

A useful statistical source is the *Abstract of British Historical Statistics*, (eds.) B. R. Mitchell and Phyllis Deane (1962). Daniel Defoe's *Tour through the Whole Island of Great Britain* (Everyman's Library 1962) is well worth reading as a contemporary picture of early eighteenth century Britain. Useful printed collections of documents can be found in: R. H. Campbell and J. B. A. Dow: *Sourcebook of Scottish Economic and Social History* (1967).

# 2 The Growth of Population

'This keeping the People together, is indeed the sum of the whole matter, for as they are kept together, they multiply together; and the Numbers, which by the way is the Wealth and Strength of the Nation, increase!'

Daniel Defoe, 1728.

Pre-industrial Britain had certainly known lengthy periods of population growth, but they had been neither rapid, nor – in the long-term – sustained. There had been a steady expansion of numbers after the Norman Conquest, through the twelfth and thirteenth centuries, but it was terminated by epidemic disease, culminating in the infamous Black Death, and a substantial fall in the population in the mid-fourteenth century. It took a hundred years or so for growth to reassert itself, and when it did, numbers increased steadily again till about 1600. Yet the seventeenth century saw a repetition of the widespread epidemic outbreaks (of which the Great Plague of London was only one), and consequent stagnation. However, the population surge that then began in the eighteenth century was on an unprecedented scale and, despite the grave forebodings of the Reverend Thomas Malthus, has proved to be of sustained force. In 1700, the estimated population of England, Wales and Scotland was under 7 million, by 1800 – about 10.5 million, and by 1900, no less than 37 million (fig. 2:1).

Set in its own historical context, the British demographic experience in the eighteenth and nineteenth centuries was therefore impressive. The rate of population increase rose from about 0.4 per cent per annum between 1700 and 1750, to over 0.8 per cent between 1750 and 1800, reaching its maximum of nearly 1.5 per cent between 1800 and 1850. These rates were impressive by general European standards too: the continental population was increasing by only 0.7 per cent per annum from 1800 to 1850, and no more than 0.8 per cent from then until 1900. However, they are by no means exceptional. Some parts of the continent, such as Siberia, Bohemia and Hungary, recorded consistently higher rates. The population of the new United States shot up at between 2.5 and 3.5

per cent per annum for most of the nineteenth century. And in the Third World today, similarly high rates are commonplace. Notions of a 'demo-

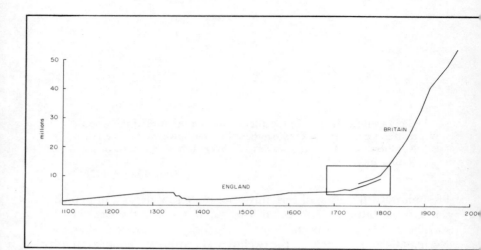

Fig. 2:1   *The Long Term Course of Population Change in Britain. Source*: Pre-1700 figures from Chambers (1972). Post-1700 figures: see text.

graphic explosion' in industrialising Britain must therefore be kept firmly in perspective. So too must the actual size of the British population. In 1800, there were twice as many French, Italians or Germans as there were Britons.

Nonetheless, this broader view does not detract from the essential fact that Britain was one of the first nations to enter the modern period of sustained population growth. Across the country this growth was not even; the effects of changes in the basic demographic processes (fertility, mortality and migration) varied from region to region, and between town and country. Growth was accompanied by an accelerating reorganisation of the settlement structure: towns grew, suburbs began to sprawl, new hamlets appeared and old villages expanded. The eighteenth century heralded many of the geographical trends that were to transform the face of Britain in the nineteenth.

## CAUSES OF POPULATION GROWTH

Although the broad patterns of eighteenth century population growth are fairly clear, it is not possible to be very precise either about numbers or causes. The whole realm of population is one of the great statistical lacunae of this period, and for this reason, it has proved a continuous hotbed of academic controversy. The first national census was not taken until 1801, and in this respect Britain lagged behind several European countries, notably those of Scandinavia and some of the German states.[1] The sole part of the country for which there is an earlier count is Scotland, where the ecclesiastical authorities, under Dr Webster, carried out a census for the government in 1755. For England and Wales, the only reasonably reliable earlier estimate is one made by Gregory King in 1695, based on hearth tax returns. Recent reworkings of King's data suggest a population of about five million for 1700.

King's figures and the 1801 census provide the benchmarks; for the intervening years it is necessary to rely principally on the parish registers. A considerable amount of work has been carried out on these registers, in recent years, and by careful manipulation of the numbers of baptisms, marriages and burials recorded, it is possible to make general estimates of fertility and mortality. These estimates can be used to suggest not only patterns of growth, but also probable causes. Nevertheless, the possibility of error becomes particularly great just at the most crucial time, i.e. the latter decades of the eighteenth century. It was then that parish registration becomes unreliable as Anglican organisation was overstretched in the expanding industrial areas, and missed the growing population of dissenters altogether. Not until 1837 was civil registration introduced.

Daniel Defoe, travelling round the country in the 1720s, recognised that England south of the Trent was 'the most populous part of the country, and definitely fuller of great towns, of people, and of trade'. He was broadly correct, as the map of population density for 1700 shows (fig. 2:2). The most densely peopled areas were those around London, and a broad swathe of counties from Devon to Norfolk. But by 1801, this pattern had begun to alter appreciably. The London area was now complemented by the growing industrial counties: the axis of high density was swinging away from the agricultural south, where it had rested over the centuries, to the Midlands, northern England and lowland Scotland. However, virtually every county – with a few Scottish exceptions – had shared in the overall demographic expansion, and densities had increased almost everywhere (fig. 2:3).

The problem of identifying the mechanisms of growth can therefore be viewed at both the national and local levels. At the national level certain factors were operating to produce a general increase in numbers, whilst at the local level, some areas experienced more rapid increases than others. Taking the extremes, the populations of Lancashire and Surrey

probably doubled between 1750 and 1801, whilst those of Devon and
Westmorland grew by less than a fifth. In Scotland, both Cromarty and

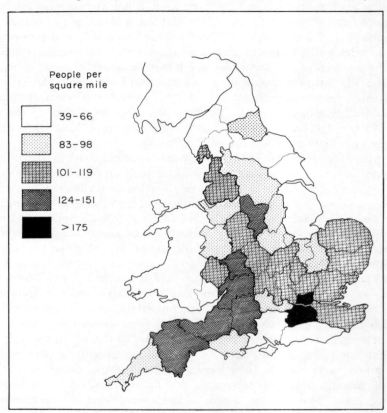

Fig. 2:2   *County Population Density: England and Wales 1700. Source*: Deane
and Cole (1967) p. 103 (population estimates) and Census 1851 (county
areas).

Moray seem to have lost population between 1755 and 1801 (maybe by
as much as 40 per cent in the former case), whereas in Renfrewshire
numbers about tripled. These differing rates simply indicate that the
contributions of fertility and mortality varied through space – as they did
through time, and that migration, at the local scale, was a vital variable.

*Growth: The National Scale*
One of the characteristics of pre-industrial societies is the low level of life
expectancy at birth. Currently it is about 70 years in England; in 1700 it

was about 30. An essential reason for this very low figure was the high level of infant and child mortality. Infant mortality was probably in the region of 150–200 per thousand (i.e. 150–200 infants for every thousand live births died within their first year). Child mortality (i.e. for the ages 1

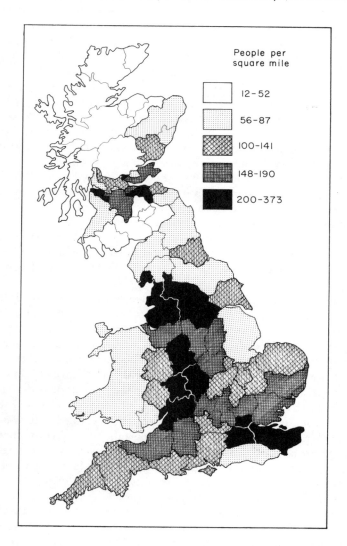

Fig. 2:3  *County Population Density: Britain 1801. Source*: as Fig. 2:2 and Hamilton (1963) – for Scotland.

to 14 years) was of a similar magnitude. Nevertheless, these losses were more than compensated for by relatively high fertility levels; averaged over all women, completed family size was just under five children in the early 1700s. During the century, fertility rates rose slightly, but of more significance to overall population growth was the steady increase in life expectancy, reaching almost 40 years by 1800.

The most frequent cause of death in pre-industrial Britain was disease – not famine, war or anything else. War, it is true, was almost an institution, but armies were small and military casualties not high. They were usually counted in hundreds, not thousands. If armies were wiped out, it was generally by disease. Similarly, famine did not directly claim many lives. The seven-year Scottish famine of the 1690s struck harshly throughout the Highlands, but it was almost the last such occurrence and anyway untypical. Generally poor harvests meant hunger and shortage of food – they did not usually mean no food at all. Grain could be bought from other areas or was often imported, and there was always the hedgerows and rabbit warrens. But again, food shortages and poor diets increased susceptibility to disease. The lean years of the 1720s, when agricultural output probably fell, saw an increase in mortality from epidemics, with life expectancy tumbling temporarily to about 25 years. Yet in other periods when harvests were good, such as the latter half of the seventeenth century, disease raged independently of the level of food supplies.

Pre-industrial Britain was afflicted by two general groups of diseases. Firstly, there were those that were always present in the community: common illnesses such as coughs and colds, measles, mumps and tuberculosis, environmental diseases, such as dysentery and the ague (a malarial condition), and deficiency diseases such as scurvy and rickets. This first group was particularly responsible for the high rates of infant and child mortality. Then, secondly, there were the 'panzer divisions of epidemic diseases': plague, typhus, smallpox, influenza. They struck intermittently, but indiscriminately and frequently savagely. It was the second group that produced the peaks of mortality that were another key characteristic of pre-industrial populations. However, in the eighteenth century, the importance of epidemic disease as a factor in mortality declined, and with it, the peaks of mortality. And there was also a very gradual improvement in the battle against the first group.

Bubonic plague played out its last great ravages in the Great Plague of London in 1665–6, and with a final visit to Nottingham and Newark in 1667, it then departed from Britain. Shortly after it disappeared from the rest of Europe as well, apart from one reappearance in Marseille in 1720–1. The reasons for its departure are unknown. Increasing human resistance seems unlikely – Londoners had lived with continuous small eruptions of plague for 300 years, but such exposure did not prevent periodic intense and fatal epidemics. The Great Fire could not have been the cause, as the plague left the provinces too. If there was a change in the nature of the disease, it is not yet understood.

Undue historical emphasis on the plague has tended to overstate its contribution to high mortality levels. However, the example of its rapid demise does show that epidemic diseases could run their course. Another example is that of syphilis, introduced into England about 1500, raging viciously throughout the sixteenth century, only to calm down considerably in the seventeenth. These cases help in understanding why two more epidemic diseases became less virulent in the eighteenth century. There is widespread evidence of violent attacks of typhus and smallpox throughout the country in the 1720s and 1730s. Both diseases seemed to have declined as fatal agencies thereafter, although both continued to be widespread. Growing natural immunity to smallpox was undoubtedly helped by the spread of inoculation – it may even have been primarily caused by it. Inoculation was widely available and used from the 1760s. Advertisements such as the one here appeared frequently in the provincial press. The Sutton family and their associates claimed to have inoculated no less than 300,000 people by 1776 – and not only privately. In many rural areas and country towns, where infrequent epidemics could be devastating in effect, the parish authorities were keen to sponsor mass inoculations, to save the later cost of supporting families deprived by the disease of their breadwinners. This was a system widely used in other countries too, including Ireland, Sweden, and America.

## INOCULATION

As the Suttonian Method of Inoculation is now universally approved and adopted, this is to inform the Public, That Messrs. Sutton and Read, Surgeons, have taken a House at Hucklecote, near the City of Gloucester, and fitted it up in a genteel Manner for that Purpose, which will be opened for the Reception of Patients, as soon as they can be prepared – The Terms for In-Patients (Tea and Washing excepted) are, six and four Guineas; for Out-Patients according to their Quality and Circumstances – Due Regard will be paid to Objects of Charity.

In Favour of Mr Sutton's Practice, it may be Sufficient to affirm, that, in the Course of these four last years, he has inoculated Twenty Thousand and upwards, without losing one Patient; and that one of his Partners, whom he lately instructed, has, in the

County of Kent, inoculated Five Thousand and upwards with the like Success.

The Public may be assured that the Patients are in general conducted without Inconvenience, Loss of Time, or (if necessary) Avocation from Business; and, what moreover is no less singular than true, this Practice has hardly produced an Instance of Infection.

N.B. Mr Sutton will be at Hucklecote on Tuesday and Wednesday the 19th and 20th of May Inst to treat with Patients who chuse to put themselves under our Care for Inoculation.

*A Typical Advertisement for Smallpox Inoculation.*
*Source*: Jackson's Oxford Journal, 16 May 1767.

Typhus originated amongst rats, like the plague, and once established in humans was transmitted by fleas and lice, both finding a particular welcome in the warm layers of woollen clothing of pre-industrial times. It spread rapidly in overcrowded populations, through jails, armies and the urban poor. Yet it became much less virulent in the second half of the eighteenth century, just as the industrial towns were beginning to grow. Most probably this reflects one of the notable features of the early Industrial Revolution – the rise of the cotton industry. Cheap cotton clothing and bedding came readily available to all (below, p. 104), and unlike heavy woollen materials could be – in fact, had to be – washed and boiled, a simple measure that killed the typhus louse in one of its favourite environments.

There were improvements in hygiene besides this. Cheap soap was another material benefit of the gradual rise in real incomes in the eighteenth century. Its use became common amongst all groups in society. Then a growing awareness of public health issues led many local authorities into active pursuit of 'public nuisances'. Dumping of refuse and night soil was discouraged by heavy fining and attempts were made to cover town drains and open sewers. Another environmental improvement, the reclaiming of fens, marshes and wet clay areas in the tide of agricultural advance, was responsible for the virtual disappearance of the malarial ague. Dysentery remained widespread, but its effects were diminished – as was the incidence of deficiency diseases – by generally improved food supplies and diets.

A cleaner and better fed population was more able to resist both the ever-present and epidemic diseases. But some of the common killers did not decline significantly until later in the nineteenth century. Tuberculosis and scarlet fever are two particular examples. And it was not until then that medical improvements (with the exception of smallpox inoculation and the treatment of syphilis with mercury) played much part in achieving lower mortality levels. Blood letting and quack medicines were the answer to most problems. It is true that there was a considerable expansion of hospital facilities in the eighteenth century, but in 1800 there were still only 50 hospitals in England, only three in Scotland. They performed a limited amount of surgery (the removal of bladder stones and cataract operations, for example), and endeavoured to treat casualty and non-infectious cases. But most refused to accept either young children or those with infectious diseases: the two groups in which mortality rates were highest, but for which the physician and apothecary could do least.

Although declining mortality was in large measure responsible for the gradual increase in the rate of population growth between 1700 and 1800, changes in fertility levels also affected growth. In eighteenth century Britain, as in other parts of Western Europe, the age at first marriage was high, the union being delayed until the prospective partners had saved enough to be independent. In 1700, mean age at first marriage was about 28 for men, a year or two less for women.

Age at first marriage fell slightly in the eighteenth century, but overall by no more than a year or two. Nevertheless, this increased the time over which women were exposed to a high risk of child bearing. The effect was most noticeable in the industrial communities. The decline of living-in arrangements and long-term apprenticeships removed some of the restraints on earlier marriage; more regular and better wages encouraged it. As Adam Smith said, as the wages of labour rise 'this must necessarily encourage in such a manner the marriage and multiplication of labourers'. The industrial villages and towns also attracted many migrants. Migration itself could not, of course, directly affect age-specific fertility, but it could have an indirect effect via an increase in extra-marital relationships. For a long time the church exercised considerable authority in this sphere through the ecclesiastical courts, and as a result, illegitimacy was surprisingly low – under five per cent of all births before 1750. By 1800, it had risen to ten per cent or so. More important was the parallel trend in pre-nuptial conceptions, which rose very considerably. Ten per cent is a reasonable figure for pre-1750, but even in a rural county like Bedfordshire, they had risen to 40 per cent by the 1790s. Weakening church control in rapidly growing communities is a partial explanation, but communities in flux were those in which old norms and standards changed most quickly.

The pattern of differential fertility is well shown by some figures from Nottinghamshire, a county with both agricultural and industrialising villages:

TABLE 2:1   *Differential Fertility in Nottinghamshire Villages*

|  | 1730–9 | 1740–9 | 1750–9 | 1760–9 | 1770–9 | 1780–9 | 1790–9 |
|---|---|---|---|---|---|---|---|
| 62 Agricultural Villages | 3.3 | 3.3 | 3.4 | 3.7 | 3.6 | 3.7 | 3.7 |
| 40 Industrial Villages | 3.9 | 4.4 | 4.8 | 4.5 | 4.8 | 4.7 | 4.8 |

*Note:* 'Fertility' is defined as baptisms recorded divided by marriages recorded.

*Source:* Chambers (1972) p. 64.

### Change: The Local Scale

The national pattern of growth was only the aggregate of local and regional movements. At these scales, change was very variable. Scotland is a good example of this. In the latter half of the eighteenth century, the population of parts of the north actually declined; over most of the Highlands, it grew only slowly. Out-migration and emigration following the break-up of the clan system and the substitution of rents for military service (and later the sheep clearances) were the main reasons. At the peak of the emigrations, between 1768 and 1775, some 20,000 Scots left for America, most of them from the Highlands. Yet on the West Coast and in the Islands, population increase was more rapid. High fertility levels were maintained, and out-migration was kept down, due to the subdivision of crofting holdings and the creation of extra subsistence in fishing and kelp manufacture (below, p. 127). In further contrast, the indus-

TABLE 2:2   *The Growth of Industrial and Agricultural Villages in Nottinghamshire, 1674–1801*

|  | 1674 | % change | 1743 | % change | 1764 | % change | 1801 |
|---|---|---|---|---|---|---|---|
| 62 Agricultural villages | 166 | +12.7 | 187 | 6.4 | 199 | 38.7 | 276 |
| 40 Industrial villages | 230 | +47.8 | 340 | 35.9 | 462 | 96.5 | 908 |

*Source:* Chambers (1957). p. 20.

trialising counties of Renfrew and Lanark in central Scotland experienced some of the greatest population increases in the country, as the result of substantial immigration and high fertility levels.

Agricultural and industrialising areas in general grew at different rates (compare figs. 2:2 and 3). Some more evidence from the Nottinghamshire villages reinforces the point (table 2:2).

The difference was due to more than the variations in fertility levels already noted. Migration was an important factor. It led directly to an increase in total numbers. And, as an age-selective process (those in their teens and twenties being more likely migrants) it altered the age-structure of receiving populations. In this way it could affect the total numbers of marriages, and thus births – a process which would not necessarily change age-specific fertility levels, but which would contribute significantly to rising birth rates in the destination areas.

Migration was particularly important for the growth of the bigger towns. 'Let any person go to Glasgow and its neighbourhood, to Birmingham, to Sheffield, or to Manchester', declared Arthur Young in 1774. Then asking and answering his own question: 'How then have they increased their people? Why, by emigrations from the country'. Migration was the major force in urban demographic expansion. In fact, until about 1750, deaths generally exceeded births in the bigger towns, where the risk and effectiveness of disease was high. Thereafter the situation improved somewhat, until by the last two decades of the century, most big centres were contributing to their own population growth through natural increase. In Manchester, for instance, the excess of baptisms over burials rose from an average of 89 per year in 1765 to 330 in 1783–5, and 674 in 1791. In Middlesex (which included most of London), the improvement was also marked, although a little later. The baptism-burial deficit declined from nearly half a million in 1701–50, to less than 200,000 in 1751–80, and about 20,000 for 1781–1801. In the first three decades of the nineteenth century, estimated natural increase was 132,000. However, despite this improvement, the direct contribution of migration to urban population growth in eighteenth century London was still total, and around 50 per cent or more in the big provincial centres between 1750 and 1800.

It was the rural areas that were the source regions of these migrants, although they did not always move directly to a large town. There is some evidence of a 'stepwise' pattern, from country to small town then large, although many migrants do seem to have gone straight to the bigger centres. On the whole, however, the population of the rural counties continued to grow. Except in a few Scottish counties out-migration did not outstrip natural increase. Agriculture needed a growing workforce. Its new cropping methods and enclosure were labour-intensive, and the extension of the cultivated area required more hands. (see below, chapter three). But it could not absorb the complete growth of numbers in the countryside. The pastoral counties – the upland regions of Scotland,

Wales and the north of England, and the south-west recorded steady net outmigration for most of the century. After 1780, nearly all rural counties had net migration losses. Nevertheless, with the few Scottish exceptions, rural population growth was maintained throughout the century.[2]

## POPULATION MOVEMENT

Mobility had been a fact of life for much of the British population for a very long time, and it seems that for many groups there were few barriers to movement at least as far back as the twelfth and thirteenth centuries. But whilst it is easy to prove mobility, it is much less easy to demonstrate its extent and pattern. The selective evidence available generally refers only to a limited number of places, or to particular social and economic groups. A good example is a detailed survey of the village of Cardington (Beds.), carried out in 1782. In the course of that year, five of the 150 cottage families in the village moved away. Of the children born to existing families who had already reached the age of 15, no less than 64 per cent of the boys and 57 per cent of the girls had left to work elsewhere, either on farms, or as servants. Fully half had gone to villages within six miles of Cardington, and only a quarter had left the county altogether – most of them going to London. Amongst the adult population, only 33 per cent of the men and 27 per cent of the women had been born in the village.

This example is just a single case, but it does not seem to have been untypical. The church marriage registers give a very clear indication of the fluidity of rural life. Most people were not limited to their own villages, but extended their horizons over several parishes around. For a significant minority they went considerably further. The 'betterment' migrants, sent to take up apprenticeships or seeking opportunities in trade and industry, were often in search of vertical as well as horizontal mobility. But many were just 'subsistence' migrants, pushed from overpopulated villages or continuously on the move, travelling for hire at the agricultural fairs, or lured by the apparent dazzle of the towns. The settlement regulations of the Poor Law – which effectively meant that paupers might receive assistance only in their home parish – seem to have had limited effects on migratory movements, certainly far less than some contemporaries believed.[3] The folk traditions of a static, rural society do not therefore portray the life style of the mass of common people. They can perhaps be applied more truthfully to the propertied families, gentry, squires and nobility, who lived out their days, in generations, in Cardingtons across Britain.

Towns drew most of their migrants from within a relatively local radius, although some came considerable distances. In the early eighteenth century, Norwich was attracting apprentices for its cloth trades

TABLE 2:3    *Origins of Cutlery Apprentices in Sheffield, 1700–99*

Distance travelled from home (miles)

|  | 5–10 | 11–15 | 16–20 | 21–30 | 31–40 | 40+ | Total |
|---|---|---|---|---|---|---|---|
| 1700–24 | 47.7% | 26.7% | 7.8% | 11.5% | 2.6% | 3.7% | 348 |
| 1725–49 | 43.2 | 26.2 | 5.4 | 17.2 | 1.7 | 6.3 | 485 |
| 1750–74 | 32.4 | 23.6 | 10.8 | 20.8 | 5.4 | 7.1 | 1064 |
| 1775–99 | 48.7 | 15.3 | 9.2 | 15.4 | 2.9 | 8.0 | 1421 |

*Source:* Buckatzsch (1950) pp. 304–5.

from as far away as north-west England. Some 30 counties featured in the city's migrant field. There was an equivalent number in the case of Bristol. But in both places, the majority of arrivals came from within 20 or 30 miles, just as in Canterbury or Shrewsbury, they came from within 10 or 15 miles. In general, the extent of the migrant field varied with the size of town, and the number of migrants declined rapidly with distance. This is shown very clearly by the origins of cutlery apprentices moving to Sheffield, for which detailed evidence survives (table 2:3). The majority came from adjacent parts of south Yorkshire and Derbyshire, but some had travelled considerably further. In a similar way, London drew most of its migrants from the surrounding counties of Surrey, Kent and Essex, but people from every part of Britain were to be found in its streets (fig. 2:4). News of life and opportunities in London and the towns was readily available to the potential migrant. It came through the post, from the carriers and drovers who plied to and fro, and from the provincial press, itself an innovation of the eighteenth century (see below p. 154). And it came from those who had moved on before.

Permanent migration to a new fixed abode was not the only form of population movement in eighteenth century Britain. Seasonal moves had been characteristic of the pastoral areas for many centuries. In lowland Scotland, villagers moved with their animals to the summer shealings (upland pastures), coming back in time for harvest. The long distance treks of the drovers out of the Welsh and Scottish hills, into Midland England and the Central Valley, were part of the round of rural life. From the Highlands, men and young women travelled south each year in search of summer work in Perth, Argyll and Stirling. Knox, touring the islands in 1787, found that in Mull, 'one half of the young women are perfectly idle, except in harvest time when they go to the Lowlands to shear'.

Many of the men went as well, but to fish for the season in the Clyde or Moray Firth. There was some seasonal mobility in the lowland areas of

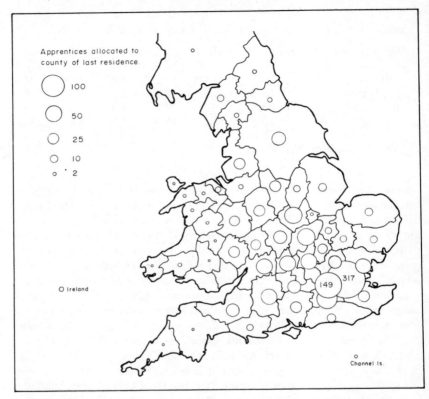

Fig. 2:4   *City of London Freemen: origins of those admitted by apprenticeship in 1690.* Apprentices allocated to county of last residence. *Source*: Glass, in Hollaender and Kellaway (eds.): *Studies in London History* (1969), table 10 p. 387.

England too, particularly amongst labourers shifting across counties with the ripening harvest.

The experience gained in seasonal moves such as these, built upon year by year, transmitted back to neighbours and friends, could lead to more permanent moves. After 1750, for example, many Highlanders uprooted and went to the textile districts of Glasgow and Dundee, areas that they had heard so much of, maybe seen, on their summer journeys south. But for a long time, an element of seasonality remained woven into the routines of industry. The mills of Lancashire and Yorkshire usually paused at harvest time as workers returned 'home' to help on the farms for a week or two. And as late as the First World War the tradition lingered on in the East End, with Londoners packing their bags for a fortnight in the Kentish hop fields.

## THE FABRIC OF SETTLEMENT

With the growth of population and extensive migratory movements, the fabric of settlement inevitably changed. The most obvious indicator of this was the expansion of the towns, in particular London, the provincial ports and the industrial centres (see below, chapter eight). But there were also several forces of change working through the countryside.

Around many of the compact, nucleated villages of England a process of dispersion was taking place. The ones that grew most quickly were the 'open' villages, where ownership of land was split and divided. They lacked the rigid control often exercised by the single powerful landlord. Land for sale in small parcels was usually readily available, and if there was reclaimable waste and common land within the parish as well, squatter settlements began to grow. New cottages started to straggle away from the old village, and new hamlets appeared at road junctions, in time with their own chapels, alehouses, small shops too. Some of these upstart settlements, being favourably located on turnpike routes, eventually usurped the functions of the old centre. Such places can be easily traced today, the church and a few medieval cottages standing alone a mile or two back from a thriving main road village. And it was by this process of dispersal, growth, infilling, that many of the industrialising areas developed. There were few restraints to new settlement on the heaths around the metal working villages of the West Midlands, or in the valleys of the West Riding cloth workers (plate B2).

Another force of settlement dispersion was enclosure, not because it drove small owners off the land, but because of its effect on farm building. In most English pre-enclosure villages, the farmsteads were concentrated in the village centre, farmyards opening up on both sides of the main street (plate A3). It was the most efficient place for them, in the centre of the village's great open-fields. But after enclosure, farmers were anxious to move away, out to sites on their newly ordered farms. New farmhouses were appearing, built of brick or stone, and often named after contemporary events in America, Europe or at home. For example, Arthur Young, travelling over Lincoln Heath in the early 1770s, found 'a large range which formerly was covered in heath, gorse, etc; yielding in fact little or no produce, converted by enclosure to profitable arable farms . . . and a very extensive country all studded with new farmhouses, offices and every appearance of thriving industry' (plates A4 and 5).

In Scotland, however, the nucleated village found in England was not so common – they existed in any number only in the south east in the Lothians and Berwickshire. Elsewhere the people lived in small hamlets, or fermtouns, each surrounded by its communal fields. Few of these fermtouns survive in modern Scotland, although many ruins – called clachans – can be seen in those Highland glens cleared for sheep farming in the second half of the eighteenth and the nineteenth centuries. The rest were swept away in enclosure schemes, and usually replaced by a new planned village, set up by the landlord as a focus for settlement and trade. About 150 planned villages were built in Scotland between 1745 and 1845, some developing a textile trade or fishing as a joint base with agriculture. Several, including Ullapool and Tobermory, were set up by a semi-philanthropic organisation, the British Fisheries Societies (incorporated in 1786).

The arm of the powerful landlord was felt in other ways. Throughout Britain some of the more ambitious emparked large areas, diverting roads and pulling down existing villages to do so. There are many well known examples of the planned, often model settlements erected in their place; Inverary in Argyll, Nuneham Courtenay in Oxfordshire, Milton Abbas in Dorset. But other landlords, preferring the status quo, refused to sell any of their holdings and saw that the settlement laws were rigidly enforced in their parishes. These were the 'closed' villages, many of which, to this day, have changed very little at all.

## POPULATION AND ECONOMY

There was a reciprocal relationship between population and economic movements during the early Industrial Revolution. Economic advance encouraged population growth in a variety of ways (above). A slow rise in real wages allowed better diets whilst innovations in agriculture improved the regularity of food supplies, both important factors in building up resistance to illness. Trade and industry brought new products, cheap mass produced textiles and soap in particular, which enabled people to live in healthier ways. Greater attention to street cleanliness, sewage facilities, and in the bigger places, the provision of piped water supplies, all helped to alleviate the risk of disease and reduce mortality levels. Then rapid population growth in the industrial areas and towns gradually eroded old habits and norms, leading to an earlier age of first marriage with concomitant (but limited) effects on fertility patterns.

Population growth in turn had a wide-ranging impact on economic advance. Rising numbers meant a bigger work force. The agricultural areas (although nearly all experiencing population expansion) released large amounts of labour by out-migration because agriculture could not absorb them all. Universal access to land did not in general exist. With the exception of the Scottish crofting areas, holdings were not usually subdivided to provide for the surviving sons. The younger ones moved away, along with a large proportion of the growing army of country labourers. The end result was the emergence of an urban-industrial proletariat, rather than – as happened in contemporary France and Ireland – a bulging rural peasantry. In Britain, labour moved into those parts of the economy where returns were increasing and regular wages were to be earned – into industry, trade and the service occupations.

But a change of employment did not always mean a change of residence. In many of the poorer agricultural regions the force of growing numbers stimulated the search for alternative or bi-employments. This is a process that can be traced back long before the eighteenth century, in some parts (for example, the Kentish Weald and the dales of Westmorland) to the earlier phases of national population growth. But in the early Industrial Revolution it assumed new significance. Many of the prominent industrial regions of the nineteenth century grew out of a scattering of rural industries; the Lancashire, West Riding and Nottinghamshire textile areas, the south Yorkshire and West Midland metal working districts all developed in this way, in turn drawing in migrants from the better farming areas as their industries prospered.

Rising numbers thus boosted the work force – both in agriculture and, more importantly, in the other sectors of the economy. They also provided a market. There need, of course, be no link between rising numbers and market expansion. A limited rate of market participation, or a real wage level that is static or falling, will do little to boost the size of the market no matter how quickly numbers expand. Both Ireland and France demonstrated in the nineteenth century that rapid economic advance cannot come in a society of self-sufficient peasants. Nor could it come from the demand of wealthy governing elites, whose purchasing power cannot be either sufficiently large or broadly-based to stimulate industrial expansion. Many underdeveloped nations are learning the same lessons today.[4] It came instead in eighteenth-century Britain, a country whose increasing population was nearly all participant in the market economy, where per capita output and income levels were slowly rising. These were the conditions for the development of a broadly-based and growing demand for industrial goods and services. But rising numbers also had to be fed. An increasing amount of food had to leave the farmyard gate for the industrialising villages and towns. And this was the contribution of the agricultural sector in the early Industrial Revolution.

## NOTES

1  The Hapsburg Empire took a census in 1695. National censuses were first taken in Prussia in 1725, Hesse-Darmstadt in 1742, Hesse-Cassel in 1747, Finland and Sweden in 1749 and Norway and Denmark in 1769. Armengaud (1970) gives a brief summary of European demographic agencies and sources.

2  The Scottish exceptions were Banff, Peebles and Roxburgh, but their losses were literally only counted in hundreds between 1755 and 1801, and Cromarty (losing 2,000 of 5,000) and Elgin (3,400 of 30,000). Nevertheless, a county level analysis may well disguise areas of net loss and gain within counties. See, for instance, the discussion on open and closed parishes.

3  Migrants from other parishes were rarely ejected unless they actually became chargeable. Under the 1697 Poor Law Act, many carried a certificate from their home parish (issued by the churchwardens or Overseer of the Poor) declaring that the home parish would accept responsibility for their poor relief and removal back home if this happened.

4  Given the widespread belief amongst development economists that it is only necessary to modernise supply factors (e.g. capital investment, transport, education) in order to achieve growth, the lesson is learnt slowly.

## FURTHER READING

The literature on population change is probably more involved than that of any other aspect of the Industrial Revolution. There has been considerable debate about both numbers and causes, stemming basically from the lack of adequate statistical data before the 1801 Census and the introduction of national registration of vital events in 1837. At present the best summary of eighteenth century population matters is by Ronald Lee, chapter two in *The Economic History of Britain since 1750*, (eds.) R. C. Floud and D. N. McCloskey (forthcoming). The contemporary background to the population problem is dealt with by D. V. Glass in *Numbering the People* (1973) — the subtitle expresses his purpose well ('The eighteenth century population problem and the development of census and vital statistics in Britain').

The key articles on the modern debate on the causes of population growth (as it stood at the end of the 1960s) are contained in a book edited by M. Drake: *Population in Industrialization* (1969). An older but still useful collection was edited by D. V. Glass and D. E. C. Eversley: *Population in History* (1965). A very valuable contribution is J. D. Chambers': *Population, Economy and Society in Pre-Industrial England* (1972). An equally stimulating book, but one that should be handled with some care is Thomas McKeown's *The Modern Rise of Population* (1975). Leslie Clarkson's *Death, Disease and Famine in Pre-Industrial England* (1975) is profitable light reading.

Most of the work in the field is necessarily regional or local in character. A full bibliography of such papers (though now rather out-of-date) is given by Lynda Ovenall in E. A. Wrigley (ed.): *An Introduction to English Historical Demography* (1966). Chambers' research on the Midlands, reported in Glass and Eversley (op. cit.) and his paper 'The Vale of Trent, 1670–1800', *Ec.H.R.* Supplement no. 3 (1957) should be consulted. A. J. Youngson deals with the population problem of the Highlands in his book *After the Forty-Five* (1973). For Scotland as a whole, see Michael Flinn (ed.): *Scottish Population History from the 17th Century to the 1930s* (1978).

A broader perspective is adopted by Andre Armengaud in *Population in Europe, 1700–1914* (1970) and E. A. Wrigley: *Population and History* (1969).

MIGRATION

The published material on this topic is thin. The best summary of sources and general patterns for the period to 1750 is by John Patten: 'Rural-Urban Migration in Pre-Industrial England' *Research Paper 6, School of Geography, Oxford* (1973). See also his article: 'Patterns of migration and movement of labour to three pre-industrial East Anglian Towns', *Jnl. Hist. Geog.* vol. 2 (1976). The two specific studies used in this chapter are by E. J. Buckatzsch: 'Places of Origin of a Group of Immigrants into Sheffield, 1624–1799', *Ec. H. R.* vol. II (1950), and N. L. Tranter: 'Population and Social Structure in a Bedfordshire Parish: The Cardington List of Inhabitants, 1782', *Popn. Studies*, vol. 21 (1967).

SETTLEMENT CHANGE

A bibliography of urban studies will be found at the end of chapter eight. On the rural scene, see the survey by B. K. Roberts: *Rural Settlement in Britain* (1977) and the various volumes in the *Making of the English Landscape* Series, e.g. P. F. Brandon: *The Sussex Landscape* (1974). A collection edited by D. R. Mills: *English Rural Communities* (1973) contains two articles on the dispersion of rural settlement. Changes north of the border are discussed by R. N. Millman: *The Making of the Scottish Landscape* (1975) and T. C. Smout 'The Landowners and the planned village in Scotland, 1770–1830', in *Scotland in the Age of Improvement*, (eds.) N. T. Phillipson and R. Mitchison (1970).

POPULATION AND ECONOMIC GROWTH

There are good discussions of this topic in H. J. Habbakuk: *Population Growth and Economic Development since 1750* (1971) and chapter five of N. L. Tranter: *Population since the Industrial Revolution* (1973). Two essays in E. L. Jones and G. E. Mingay (eds.): *Land, Labour and Capital in the Industrial Revolution* (1967) should be consulted, the first by D. E. C. Eversley on the growth of the home market, the second by P. E. Razzell, is a comparative study of England and Ireland. On population pressure and rural industry, see Joan Thirsk 'Industries in the Countryside', in F. J. Fisher (ed.): *Essays in the Economic and Social History of Tudor and Stuart England* (1961).

# 3 Agricultural Expansion

In 1700 agriculture was the mainstay of British economy and society. And it was still so – albeit to a lesser degree – in 1800. Nevertheless, very great changes took place in this basic sector during the century. Indeed, without expansion and responsiveness in agriculture, the burgeoning national population could not have been properly fed and important sections of industry, such as textile manufacture and the processing trades, would have grown rather more slowly. It was in the eighteenth century that Britain began to reap the benefits of what historians have called the 'agricultural revolution'.

This agricultural revolution was not, as conventional wisdom has assumed, something confined to the 50 years after 1750. It was a rather more gradual process than that, having its roots in the sixteenth and seventeenth centuries, and not reaching its peak until the high farming years of the mid-nineteenth. Neither was it merely a technical revolution, of better ideas, methods and organisation. It was these things, and far more besides: fundamentally, a new scale of production, a revolution in output. Between 1700 and 1870, the population of Britain rose fourfold. The country was more or less self-sufficient in food supplies in 1700 (with the exception of tropical 'groceries'), and was actually a net exporter of wheat until the 1760s. Yet despite this massive population rise, home agriculture was still meeting 80 per cent of home needs in 1870. This represents about a 300 per cent increase in output since 1700, just under 50 per cent of which can be attributed to the eighteenth century, particularly the period after 1750.[1] It was in the eighteenth century that new *methods* – novel crops, better husbandry systems – and new modes of *organisation* – enclosure of the open field and waste, and better farm management – began to spread widely. And it was then that the benefits of these, in terms of a marked and sustained increase in agricultural production, began to accumulate.

Outwardly, using the obvious indicators, eighteenth-century agricultural change does not seem to have been very significant. Two-thirds of the population still lived in the country in 1800. The proportion of the national product attributable to agriculture was still the largest of any sector – about one third. Although this was a fall of some ten per cent since 1700, most of it had occurred in the last two or three decades. The number of people employed in agriculture as a primary occupation grew slightly, to about 1.7 million. But these measures of agriculture's place in the economy understate the degree of change that had taken place within the sector itself. It is the purpose of this chapter to explore the facets of this change, and to assess its importance in the broader context.

## AGRICULTURE IN THE EARLY EIGHTEENTH CENTURY

Pre-industrial Britain, with the exception of the peripheral parts of the upland zone, was not by this time characterised by self-supporting rural communities. The process of production had advanced considerably since the Middle Ages. Agriculture was not only using a range of new methods that had been penetrating slowly in the two preceding centuries, it was also highly market-orientated. It was this latter quality, having its roots in the fairs and markets of Anglo-Saxon times, that distinguishes much of pre-industrial British agriculture from that of the underdeveloped world of the twentieth century.

The market orientation of agriculture was reflected in the number of market towns that were to be found around the country. There were about 800 in England and Wales alone, scattered at intervals of every few miles. So, although the population of the country was only one tenth of its present figure, there were far more market centres than at present, due mainly to the constraints of transport. But these markets were not evenly distributed. The wealthier southern part of England had a rather denser network than elsewhere, except in the downland zones, whereas market areas in the north, in Wales and in Scotland were far more extensive. This pattern reflected not only the varying intensity of agricultural production, but also market specialisation. The cattle markets of the uplands, and the sheep markets of the heath areas maintained considerably wider limits than the corn, dairy and fruit markets of south, south west and eastern England. There were large wheat markets at Ipswich, Farnham, Basingstoke, High Wycombe and Bedford, for example. Ware, Royston, Abingdon and Faringdon had important barley marts. Haddington in East Lothian was one of the biggest Scottish grain centres, but even it was not as large as the market at Dalkeith, outside Edinburgh, which dealt in oats, cattle and sheep. Falkirk was the main centre for Highland cattle sales. Shrewsbury, Wolverhampton and Birmingham had the trade in Welsh cattle, whilst St. Faith's Fair, held outside Norwich, brought many northern drovers and London butchers together. Sheep markets were scattered throughout the country. The annual fair at Weyhill, outside Andover, was the most renowned, whilst 'the largest and most valuable' sheep fair in the north was held at Market Weighton in September when commonly 70–80,000 animals were sold. Some places had a more specialist trade. Norwich had an annual fish fair, Banbury and Northampton were horse markets, Stourbridge Fair, near Cambridge, was famous for its hops and wool, whilst Dorking's line was in poultry.

The corollary of specialist market centres was a degree of specialisation within agriculture itself. The proliferation of markets, and the trade links that were developed between them and the bigger towns, especially London, inevitably encouraged regional diversity. Daniel Defoe, 'that exceptionally keen observer . . . one of the first masters of modern English prose'[2], constantly recorded the specialisation of both regions and markets in his *Tour through the Whole Island of Great Britain*, which he published in the mid-1720s. One of his favourite themes was the effect of the London market on agricultural production. 'This whole kingdom, as well as the people, on the land, and even the sea, in every part of it,' he wrote, 'are employ'd to furnish something, and I may add the very best of everything, to supply the city of London with provisions.' Regions tended to specialise in the production of those items for which they were best suited. Highland Scotland and Wales were committed to raising cattle and sheep, which were driven to the fattening pastures of the Midlands and East Anglia in preparation for the urban markets. The counties within the Thames Basin, along with coastal Kent and Sussex, and East Anglia, were notable granaries. The western regions were predominantly under grass. Then there were the more particular specialities: Norfolk turkeys, cheese in Somerset and Wiltshire, fruit and hops in Kent and Herefordshire, and butter in High Suffolk.

Agriculture over much of early eighteenth century Britain was therefore essentially modern in two respects: it was both market-orientated and regionally specialised. Nevertheless it would be wrong to suggest that it was, by later standards, particularly sophisticated. In terms of agrarian organisation, methods of husbandry and with the amount of land that lay in waste (much of which could have been used for agriculture), it was certainly not so.

*Waste land* in Britain was very extensive in the early eighteenth century. In 1696, Gregory King had estimated that about ten million acres of England and Wales lay in waste – over one-quarter of the total area. 'Waste land' included all 'unimproved' areas that were not used for permanent agriculture or only for extensive grazing. Hence in Scotland, the proportion was far higher – probably over one-half. Large areas of northern England and Wales were waste, even at the end of the century. Cornwall too still had half a million acres in this state in the 1790s. But waste was found in large quantities outside the peripheral and upland parts of the country. The downlands of Hampshire, Wiltshire and East Anglia and parts of the Cotswolds were good for only rough sheep pastures or rabbit warrens. Much of the Fens were still unusable. Despite Vermuyden's drainage schemes of the mid-seventeenth century, they were relapsing into marsh because of flooding due to peat shrinkage. Other fen areas – the Somerset Levels, Holderness, the bogs of Lancashire – were not reclaimed until the latter part of the century.

Even some large areas close to London were unused by agriculture. Much of the Weald was not cleared of woodland until after 1770. Middlesex, Surrey and Berkshire had acres of bracken heath. Writing of the 'Black Desert' of Bagshot Heath, Defoe recommended 'those that despise Scotland, and the north part of England, for being full of wast and barren land, (to) take a view of this part of Surrey . . . a vast tract of Land, some of it within seventeen and eighteen miles of the capital city.' Much of Britain's waste area was brought into agricultural use during the eighteenth century, and even more in the nineteenth. But its relative distribution in 1800 was very similar to that of a century before (fig. 3:1).

The second characteristic of early eighteenth century agriculture that belied its sophistication was its organisation. Much of England's cropped area – possibly as much as one-half – and nearly all of Scotland's, was still worked on the traditional *open-( or common) field* basis. The distinctive feature of this system was that farmers held their land in separated units, scattered through open blocks, or common fields. Certainly enclosure, in England and Wales at any rate, had been progressing slowly for centuries. It had reached a peak with the Tudor wool movement and most open-field parishes by now had some enclosures. Laxton, the famous Nottinghamshire village that still operates its open-fields, was in fact half enclosed as early as 1691.[3]

The regional pattern of remaining open-field was very distinctive: outside Scotland, it was limited mainly to the English clay vales. The rest of England, and Wales, was already predominantly enclosed, or had never been cultivated by any other method (fig. 3:2). Large areas in the Weald, the Chilterns, East Anglia, the south-west, Wales and northern England had been settled in the twelfth and thirteenth centuries, with gradual reclamation by individual farmers of the forest and heath, and had never experienced the communal organisation of the lowland pre-Norman villages. The example of such enclosure direct from the waste evidently encouraged the enclosure of those open-field parishes that had undoubtedly existed in parts of these regions. But it was also these parts of Britain that had plentiful common grazing land in the woods and on

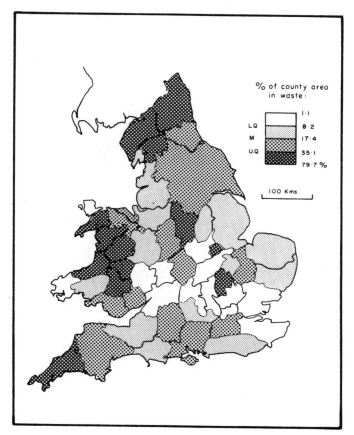

Fig. 3:1  *The Extent of Waste Land in England and Wales, c 1800. Source:* redrawn from Williams (1970) p. 58.

the hills, enabling enclosure to be substituted for open-field at any early date.

The provision of common grazing land – both in the open arable fields, and outside them – was a central feature of both the English and Scottish open-field systems. These systems were significantly different from each other in some respects, but they were not mutually exclusive by any means. The Scottish system was essentially very simple (fig. 3:3). Arable land was divided into the infield and outfield. The infield was the fermtoun's best cropping area, and was usually, but not always, a fairly compact block close to the settlement itself. It accounted for about one fifth of the arable acreage, and was kept in perpetual tillage, sustained by

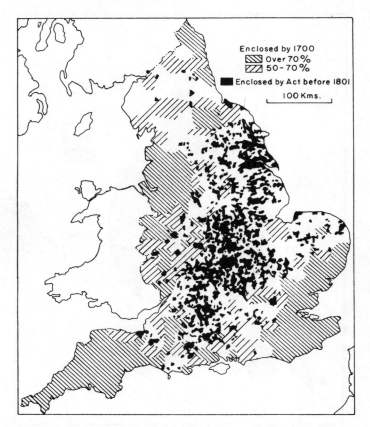

Fig. 3:2   *Open-Fields and Enclosure, 1700–1800. Source*: Redrawn from Fig. 69 in H. C. Darby: *A New Historical Geography of England* (1973) p. 323.

the application (over about one-third of the infield each year) of farm-yard manure. In contrast the outfield was cropped extensively, and often without manuring, on a basis of shifting cultivation. Different patches were sown in succession, and worked for several years until exhausted. Beyond the outfield lay the muir land: rough hill pasture and common. In some parts, summer grazings, or shealings, lying some miles away, were used.

The English open-field system represented a more developed form of the Scottish, but was based on the same interdependence of arable and pasture. Here the equivalent of the infield had evolved into two, three or four common fields, one of which was usually used, in rotation, for com-

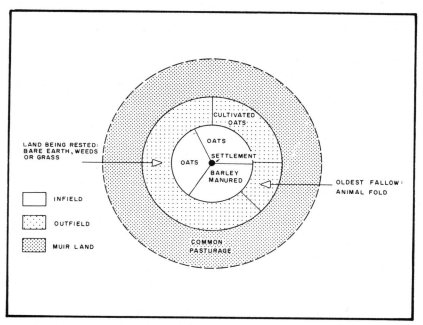

Fig. 3:3 *A Model of the Scottish Infield-Outfield System. Source*: based on Baker and Butlin (1973) p. 551.

mon grazing, having been sown with a grass ley or left fallow. In the three field system, which seems to have been the most common in the Midlands, the other two fields could then be used for a spring and winter sown grain. This was an unnecessary division in Scotland, where all grains were spring sown. Fallowing of the infield also did not occur in Scotland, but in England it provided vital additional pasture to supplement the more limited common and waste that survived in the remaining open-field areas. For the same reason, animals grazed the stubble after the harvest. The English system had evolved, therefore, in response to rather different environmental conditions to those prevailing in Scotland, although where conditions were similar, the systems overlapped. Parts of lowland Scotland, particularly in the Lothians, operated a common field pattern similar to that of England. On the other hand, the use of an outfield system of shifting cultivation had taken place in upland areas south of the Border, and was still used on the Yorkshire and Lincolnshire Wolds, in Derbyshire, and in Norfolk where the reclaimed patches, used for one or two years, were known as 'breaks'.

Common to both the English and Scottish systems – at least, in general terms, was the mode of landholding. Farmers, either as owners or tenants, held land in 'strips', 'riggs' or 'lands'. These strips were on average eight to twelve yards wide, and were separated by a furrow. Strips orientated in the same direction, according to the local relief, were grouped into furlongs, and sets of furlongs into fields. It is this pattern, fossilised under later enclosure, that has produced the characteristic ridge and furrow of the English Midlands. But farmers' strips were scattered through the open fields, their holdings in each being roughly proportional to the size of that field. In Scotland this system was called run-rig. It was described by the Minister of Moulin, in Perthshire – a late enclosed parish, in 1793: '. . . a few farms are still intertwixted together, in the way called run-ridge; that is, the ridges of arable land belong alternately to different tenants, a most incommodious and absurd arrangement'.

A land holding system such as this could produce a pattern of great complexity. A number of commonly agreed rules were necessary to ensure that it functioned reasonably well. Cropping arrangements were essential: usually the fields themselves were cropped in common, but this was not always so. Sowing and harvesting schedules had to be agreed, as did stocking densities for the fallows and leys. But these arrangements were by no means rigid, either between regions or through time. It is this factor which not only contributes to the difficulty of understanding the full complexities of field systems, but also meant that the open-fields were not as unreceptive to new ideas and methods as has often been supposed. A prime example was the increased efficiency of both pastoral and arable farming that had already resulted in some open-fields in southern England from using the sown grasses and legumes – rye-grass, sainfoin and clover – in place of a bare fallow.

Nevertheless, the open-field system of England and Scotland was not the most suitable means of organising eighteenth century agricultural production. It was a legacy of medieval times that persisted because of the problem of providing sufficient grazing for livestock. As soon as this was solved, by the widespread use of the new fodder crops, there was little need to continue with open-field methods. Not only did the lack of consolidation of holdings waste time, it also wasted the arable land lying in ditches or furrows between the strips, it was inimical to improving strains of livestock and it encouraged encroachments with plough and sickle.

The third indicator of the pre-industrial state of early eighteenth-century agriculture was the relatively crude *techniques* used to farm both the open and enclosed fields. Tools, for example, were very simple and remained so for most of the eighteenth century. Iron ploughs did not start to replace the traditional wooden implement until the last couple of decades. Seed drills, invented by Jethro Tull in 1731, were only infrequently seen by 1800. There were no widely used mechanical aids for the harvest which, as a result, was long and arduous, taking at least a month and often six weeks. It provided a seasonal employment peak around which the other activities of the village had to be arranged. In Scotland, the summer grazing of the animal herds on the distant shealings lasted from May until August, when all hands were recalled for the harvest. Not until 1786 was a successful threshing machine introduced, by a Scotsman. It was widely adopted relatively quickly, but successful reaping machines were not introduced until 1812, and diffused rather slowly.

The relatively primitive state of husbandry was revealed in the quality of output. Grain yields, although they varied somewhat, were low — about 20 bushels per acre for wheat and 30 for barley in the early 1700s. These yields did not improve greatly in the eighteenth century — probably only by ten per cent or so. They were only about two-thirds of the average yields obtained by 1900, and only one-third of what the modern farmer would expect. Animal size was similarly on the light side: cattle breeds especially being very small. The Galloways, for instance, weighed only 3–400 lbs. when taken off pasture, Roxburgh cattle when fattened, 6–700 lbs. Today's Highland cross bullock, when sold off the pasture at three to four years old, weighs about 900 lbs, and when fattened, 1200 lbs. Other breeds were similarly diminutive by later standards: the average beast sold at Smithfield in the mid-eighteenth century was not much over 4–500 lbs. in size.[4]

The disadvantages of common grazing undoubtedly had much to do with this: selective breeding of better and bigger strains had to take place under more closely controlled conditions. However, as fundamental a reason was undoubtedly the quality and quantity of feed. This was the consequence of the failure of pre-industrial agriculture to achieve a closer link between animal and crop husbandry. Cattle and sheep frequently died and always lost weight with the lack of fodder in the winter months. In Argyll, no less than one-eighth of the cattle died below the age of two and a half years. Losses were far higher everywhere in severe winters, as at the end of the 1730s. In 1740–1 about one-third of the cattle and horses on Anglesey died for lack of feed. The early eighteenth-century farmer was still extremely dependent on the weather, often to the severe detriment of his stock. This dependence was not lessened until fodder crops – turnips, swedes and grasses – became widely used in arable rotations, so providing a better flow of feed supplies all through the year. Even though they were quite well known in some parts in 1700, their use was far from general.

Agriculture in early eighteenth-century Britain was, therefore, relatively advanced in some respects: particularly in its market orientation and specialisation, but it was still backward in others. Not only were large areas of potential farmland in waste, but agrarian organisation and husbandry practice were still very traditional. It was advance in these latter two areas that was the lynchpin of agricultural progress in the eighteenth century. Certainly, the seeds of advance were already planted, in the widespread existence of enclosure, and in the limited use of new crops and husbandry techniques. But it was an acceleration of these trends, coupled to an immense growth in demand for agricultural products, that brought about the agricultural revolution.


## THE AGRICULTURAL REVOLUTION

The fundamental change in eighteenth-century agriculture was in its scale of production. Overall, output rose by almost a half, with all branches of agricultural activity participating to a greater or lesser degree. Corn output rose from about 15 to 21 million quarters. The number of sheep probably doubled to about 26 millions. Cattle figures were more constant, at about four million, although an increase in the weight of animals make it likely that the supply of beef rose, albeit rather slowly.

These changes in output took place against a background of changing economic and demographic conditions. The marked rise in population from mid-century was reflected in a continuously rising price level (fig. 3:4), itself an encouragement to agriculture as a whole to expand and innovate. The expansion was certainly impressive: meat supplies about kept pace with demand, woollen exports were able to rise by 150 per cent, and corn production, although allowing for a small volume of exports until the 1760s, still provided over 90 per cent of home needs in 1800. Nevertheless, it must again be stressed that advance in agriculture was not simply a post-1750 phenomenon. Much progress was made in the century after the Restoration, and the foundations for expansion, in the spread of new methods and the shift of arable emphasis away from the heavy to the light lands, were laid then.

## Improved Techniques

The most important source of change within agriculture itself lay in improved husbandry techniques: specifically in the introduction of new crops and cropping systems, greater attention to soil fertility, and improved livestock breeding. It was the *new fodder crops* – the leguminous grasses (clover, sainfoin, rye-grass and lucerne) and roots (carrots and potatoes, but especially turnips and later, swedes) that made the greatest mark. Their impact was of paramount importance.

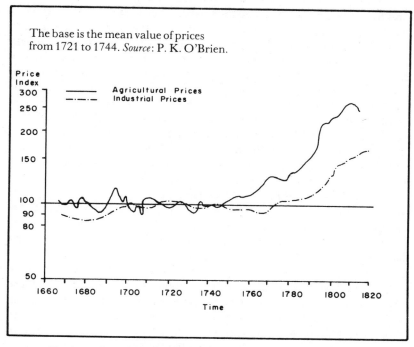

The base is the mean value of prices from 1721 to 1744. *Source*: P. K. O'Brien.

Fig. 3:4    *The Course of Agricultural and Industrial Prices, 1660–1820.*

Firstly, large areas that had lain in waste could now be cultivated. These included not only extensive areas of light soil on the scarplands of England that were previously used only as sheep and rabbit runs, but also the fallows of the cultivated areas that otherwise lay relatively idle, lightly stocked and gathering weeds. Much improved rotations could be adopted, the most famous being that developed on the Norfolk light lands in the late seventeenth century. It had four courses: wheat, turnips, barley and clover, but there were many variants. The nitrogen-fixing properties of the legumes built up the fertility of the light soils sufficiently for the taking of the grain crops, whilst the animal fold on the turnip and clover courses added manure. This leads on to the second point: that the new crops themselves underlay the increase in livestock production in the eighteenth century. The improved supplies of fodder undoubtedly raised the output and quality of meat and dairy produce. For this reason, the fodder crops were adopted, albeit more slowly, on the heavier lands as well, where ley farming, with a leguminous crop course of two or three years inserted in the rotation, gradually became dominant.

The new crops must be credited, therefore, with enabling both arable and livestock production to be increased. They spread widely throughout Britain in the eighteenth century, although they had been known and cultivated in some parts long before this. Turnips were grown as a field crop in Norfolk and Suffolk by the mid-seventeenth century, having been introduced by Dutch immigrants to Norwich as a garden vegetable in about 1565. The leguminous grasses had also been introduced from the intensive Low Countries husbandry, about 1620. They tended to spread more rapidly than the roots, given the ease with which they could be incorporated in the fallow course of existing rotations. They were used on farms throughout the southern half of England by the end of the seventeenth century, and in Wales by 1750, although their adoption was far from general. But a report to the Board of Trade, made in 1702, could state that 'the lands of England have been much improved since 1670 by cinq-foile and other grasses, by which they feed a greater number of sheep than formerly, and the state of the wool is thereby augmented.'

The grasses were taken up more rapidly on the light lands than on the heavy soils. Sainfoin was especially good as a producer of hay on the light soils and spread regardless of whether land in such areas was in open-field or enclosed. The farmers of the limestone uplands of northern Oxfordshire were using sown grasses in their open-fields in the 1670s and 1680s, sometime before the farmers in the enclosed Thames vale. In Worcestershire, these crops were accepted as quickly in open-fields as in enclosed areas. Elsewhere, the heavy clay farmers were generally slow adopters. This was true also for the root crops. Turnips did not thrive in wet clay soils, were more difficult to feed off, and were likely to become diseased. Overall turnips spread more slowly than the grasses. Their introduction required a more fundamental alteration of the cropping rotation, and was largely tied to the opening up of the light soil heaths to arable husbandry as agricultural demand rose in the eighteenth century.

Turnip culture originated in East Anglia. In the early 1720s, Defoe commented that 'this part of England is . . . remarkable for being the first where the feeding and fattening of cattle, both sheep as well as black cattle with turnips, was first practis'd . . . from whence the practice is spread over most of the east and south parts of England'. Nevertheless turnips were not common in Oxfordshire before 1730 and were first used in Worcestershire only about 1700. Not until after 1750 did they become usual on the light lands of the East Riding. Northumberland and Cornish farmers were not using them until the 1770s, and they were not common as a field crop in Wales until the end of the century. Turnips were not especially high in nutritive content, however, and because of this, as well as their vulnerability to bad weather, they were gradually being replaced by the swede, kale and early clover in England by 1800. Nevertheless, turnips introduced a useful flexibility into corn rotations and provided a valuable animal fold.

Scottish farmers, despite their distance from the hearth regions of these new crops, were not left out of this movement. As Scottish landowners came into more frequent contact with England through trading and Parliamentary business after the Union of 1707, so the new methods were accepted there too. The counties of East Lothian and Berwick were most noted for their relatively advanced husbandry, at any rate on the big estates. In the early years of the century, roots and grasses were being used there, and by the 1730s they were well established on the large estates. Clover was used in Perth, and had spread as far as the Hebrides by 1760. Turnips, however, were little used in the western counties of Galloway and Ayrshire until the 1770s, or in the more northern parts of the Highlands until the end of the century; although potatoes, another root crop, had achieved general acceptance amongst the crofters by then. But even in the Lowlands, it was not until the last two decades that tenant farmers, rather than just the big landowners, began to make common use of the new husbandry.

In addition to the widespread acceptance of these new crops, there were other considerable improvements in farming practice. A variety of methods to improve *soil fertility* and structure gained in popularity. One of the cornerstones of the Norfolk husbandry was marling, an age-old practice that was widely adopted in the eighteenth century. 'Marl' was a term applied to a calcareous clay that was quarried, then spread on to sandy and clay soils to neutralise acidity and improve their structure. It was used throughout East Anglia, on the Chilterns and Wealden sands. Liming was general throughout the country, having the same purpose, and by 1800 most villages, and even many farms, had their own lime kilns. Again, it had a long history, being used in many areas by the early seventeenth century. Liming was an essential part of the reclamation process on the moorlands of Devon and Somerset, where the turf was pared and burnt, before ploughing and liming: a process known as 'Devonshiring'.

Marling and liming were complemented by manuring and the action of the leguminous grasses, but on land adjacent to rivers, floating water meadows were an additional means of improving soil fertility. Streams were dammed and diverted across meadows to give a thin flow of water and sediment over the grass. This encouraged a rich early bite, which was especially useful in the spring, just when fodder supplies were running low. Water meadows were a necessary adjunct to the new eighteenth-century light land farming, providing additional pasture. The practice spread from the West Country in the seventeenth century into the West Midlands and the southern downland counties. Water meadows were used elsewhere to a limited extent: for example in Leicester and Northumberland. Around the Humber, estuarine flooding at high tide – known as warping – served the same purpose. The converse of meadow floating – that is, underdraining of the wet clays – did not advance greatly. Although stone-filled drains were in use in East Anglia, effective underdraining did not become a reality in the Midlands and elsewhere until the mid-nineteenth century, with the invention of tile-drains, and the availability of government grants to those farmers who made use of them.

A third important area of husbandry advance in the eighteenth century was in *livestock breeding*, a process greatly aided by the separation of herds after enclosure. Many farmers were involved in improving breeds in the latter part of the century. Robert Bakewell, the most famous, was but one of them. Bakewell's Leicester sheep were used to develop the more popular Border Leicester breed by the Culley brothers in Northumberland, and they were used also by other breeders to improve the quality of the Lincoln and Wensleydale varieties. In Norfolk, the local breed had been almost ousted by John Ellman's Sussex Southdowns by 1800. The Leicesters and Southdowns were not directly competitive, however, being best suited to their own environments – the Leicesters as a rich pasture sheep, and the Southdowns as a fold sheep, feeding off turnips and grasses on the arable.

Bakewell also played a role in cattle breeding, favouring the longhorn animals. In Durham, the Collings brothers raised a new strain of shorthorns, which quickly became popular as milk and beef beasts. By the early nineteenth century, two-thirds of the cattle entering London were Shorthorns or their crosses. Many farmers were involved in improving the Hereford beef breed too, whereas experiments in Scotland (in which Barclay of Urie was prominent) produced the Aberdeen Angus beef cattle. The modern Ayrshire dairy beast dates from about the same time.

The general effect of the spread of these new husbandry techniques was to alter radically the spatial pattern of eighteenth century agriculture. The areas of arable prosperity were shifting away from the heavy clay vales to the lighter chalkland, heath and wold soils. Many of these areas were close to the London market and could profitably expand, a motive that became more general with the overall rise in the price index after 1750 (fig. 3:4). As early as 1700, large parts of Norfolk had been converted from rough pasture to cornland, and in the 1720s, Defoe described a similar trend in Wiltshire where 'many thousand acres of compact ground . . . (are), of late years, turned into arable land and sewed with wheat'. The East Riding Wolds, a great expanse of bare pastoral upland before 1750, had been transformed by sheep and turnip husbandry by the late 1780s, as too had large parts of Northumberland and Lincolnshire. In 1803, the historian of Gloucestershire described the changes there: 'The HILL district includes the Cotswolds . . . Within the last hundred years a total change has taken place on these hills. Furze and some dry and scanty blades of grass were all their produce, but now with few exceptions the downs are converted into arable inclosed fields.' The clay areas, by contrast, switched increasingly to livestock farming, a pattern that was beginning to emerge as early as 1700 (fig. 3:5). Defoe again noticed this trend, writing enthusiastically about the graziers of Leicestershire, and describing the vale of Aylesbury as 'the richest land (with) perhaps the richest graziers in England'.

The expansion of farming on to the lighter soils increased the overall farmed acreage in Britain quite considerably – probably by 25 per cent or so. Nevertheless, the area of waste in England and Wales still exceeded one fifth of the total in 1800. A very real stimulus, both to its further decline, and to the spread of arable husbandry, was the phenomenally high grain price level of the Napoleonic wars from 1793 onwards (fig. 3:4). It was in these years that the cultivated limit, and enclosure, reached their highest level yet on the Pennines and West Country moors, and up the mountainsides of Wales and Scotland. Although by the early nineteenth century there were still 16–17 million acres of pasture and meadow in England and Wales, arable land had increased to between 11 and 12 million acres. The increasing grain acreage was reflected in nearly every county in the government's wartime crop returns of 1801.

*Changing Organisation*

The second important force for change in the agricultural revolution was a structural one – improvements in organisation. These were complementary to the range of new husbandry techniques. Structural change made itself felt in two ways – firstly through the gradual evolution of larger estates and farms, and secondly, through enclosure.

There was no very rapid change in *estate and farm size* in Britain in the eighteenth century, and small units predominated. As late as 1851, 62

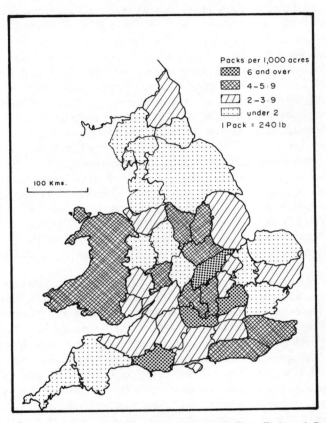

Fig. 3:5   *Wool Production in England and Wales in the Early Eighteenth Century.*
*Source*: J. H. Andrews: Some Statistical Maps of Defoe's England, *Geog. Studies*, vol. 3 (1956). (The original Ms. is dated c1700–12).

per cent of farm occupiers with more than five acres had less than 100. Nevertheless, Britain was not, except in the peripheral parts of the Celtic fringe, a nation of peasant occupiers. With the relative importance of large estates, most farms of over 20 acres were tenanted, and of sufficient size to be viable market units. It was this that constituted a major difference between continental and British agriculture, and gave the latter the edge in market responsiveness and agricultural advance.

Landownership was divided between three different categories. The great landowners, with estates of several thousand acres, gradually increased their share, from about 15–20 per cent of the total area in the late seventeenth century, to 20–25 per cent by the end of the eighteenth. The gentry estates, from the 3–400 acres of the village squire to the 1–2,000 acres of the county families, stayed relatively stable at about half the total. The freeholders, with less than 3–400 acres, declined from one-third to less than one-fifth. The social and economic aspirations of the larger landowners, supported by the money flowing from trade into agriculture, tended to strengthen their position, whilst the smaller owners were weakened by the burden of high wartime taxes at the turn of the eighteenth century, along with poor winters and the prevailing low price level before 1750.

Coupled with this general increase in estate size was a gradual rise in the numbers of large farms. Large farms – which to contemporary commentators meant over 300 acres – were considered to be more efficient and more innovative. Arthur Young, the proselytizing agricultural publicist of the latter part of the century, declared: 'Deduct from agriculture all the practices that have made it flourishing, and you have the management of small farms'. Large farm tenants were generally chosen with very great care by landlords, both with regard to their resources, and their experience and competence. They were therefore more likely to survive and prosper in the long run.

The advantages of gradually increasing estate and farm size were those of greater economic viability, and an efficient large tenantry, although small tenants remained very numerous. But there were important additional gains in this landlord-tenant system. The relationship gave the tenant reasonable stability[5] and access to larger resources. In periods of relative depression, as in the second quarter of the century, many landlords accepted extra costs, by bearing the burden of land tax, foregoing rent, or supplying essential items such as seed. And at all times, most tenancies freed the farmer from the need to provide buildings and maintain hedges and drains. With the landlord providing the permanent capital, the tenant could raise his level of working capital above what it would have been. This was a critical factor in providing a satisfactory context for experimentation, the adoption of new ideas, and for undertaking a more intensive, market-orientated approach.

Landowners and farmers were assisted in their expansionist tendencies by institutional developments outside agriculture. The acceptance of the long-term mortgage from the middle years of the seventeenth century increased landowners' resources, at the relatively low cost of 3–5 per cent interest each year, whilst the spread of country banks in the later eighteenth century enabled farmers to borrow more easily. The gradual rise of a new class of landowners, entering agriculture with their profits from commerce and trade (an increasing trend since the Restoration), greatly enriched the sector. It was this broadening resource base which underlay the second important organisational change: enclosure.

*Enclosure* did more than any one other development to alter the face of the countryside. The medieval open-fields and strips were replaced all over Britain by the modern neat patchwork of regular, hedged fields. But again, it was a very gradual process and certainly not limited to the eighteenth century. And it was not, in itself, of central importance in stimulating increased output and better farming. Rather, it provided a more logical framework for agrarian organisation, and a more reasonable basis for adopting the new husbandry. Enclosure was a prerequisite for successful selective breeding, and with the elimination of common rights in the arable, it assisted in the introduction of new crops and rotations. However, the new techniques had been adopted already in many open-field areas, whilst conversely, enclosure often did not lead to any great improvements in husbandry practice. Young complained about the old three-field rotation of wheat, beans and fallow still being used on newly enclosed land in the Vale of Aylesbury in the late 1760s. Enclosure in the Mendips was followed by exhaustive grain farming in the 1790s, with no regard to soil fertility.

Enclosure had been going on for centuries, either direct from the waste, or enforced on open-field systems. Over half of England and Wales was already enclosed in 1700, with few villages being without some enclosures. There had been an early peak in the movement in Tudor times, when wool prices were riding high. However, the eighteenth and early nineteenth centuries do constitute a watershed in the process, when enclosure by Act, rather than by private agreement or enforcement, became dominant. Parliamentary enclosure was often a more convenient method, particularly when there was some disagreement amongst landowners, and it provided a legal stamp of approval on the new order.

It is probable that about 2.8 million acres of England and Wales were enclosed by Act in the eighteenth century, with as much again in the nineteenth. About one-third of the acreage affected was in waste, in particular the light soils being enclosed for arable husbandry. The rest was in open-field areas. Nevertheless, enclosure by agreement continued apace, although it is impossible to say how much land was affected. In the eighteenth century, 2,032 enclosure Acts were passed in England and Wales, the time series reflecting prevailing conditions (fig. 3:6). The peak of Acts from 1750 through to 1780 coincides with the rapid rise of agricultural prices, at a time when interest rates ruled low, at around three per cent. The later peak, during the Napoleonic wars, reflects the reclamation of the waste and continued open-field enclosure during the very favourable price-income conditions of the war years.

The enclosure Acts established a clearly defined procedure for alloting

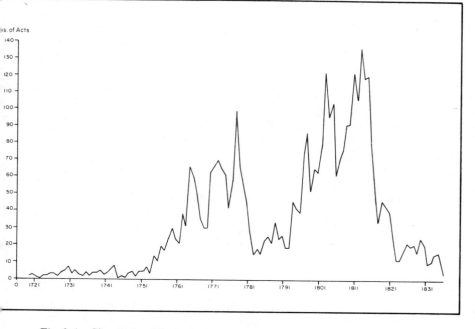

Fig. 3:6 *Time Series of Enclosure Acts, England and Wales: 1719–1835. Source*: SP 1836 VIII pt.2 p. 505.

land between owners. Commissioners were appointed to supervise this, in order to provide compact holdings for each landowner and to fix the line of new roads. Holders of common rights had to be compensated, usually with a small land allowance. Some rights, however, could not be eliminated. Turbaries, where turf and peat could be cut, were sometimes set aside, as were public quarries. The new fields themselves were large and regular in shape, often contrasting markedly with those produced by earlier enclosure. Each one had to be contained, initially usually by railing, with quickset hedging being preferred in the long run, except in the hills where there was plenty of stone to make walls. The new road networks were geometrical too, fitting the field pattern. The roads were generously proportioned, being 30 to 40 feet wide, the centre 12 to 16 feet being metalled. Today it is their exceptionally wide verges, fringed by wall or hedge, beyond which lie large, neat fields, that betray the work of the Georgian enclosure commissioners in the landscape. (plate A4).

In Scotland, the process of enclosure was rather different, although the results, in the lowlands, were very similar. The Scots Parliament passed several general Acts in the seventeenth century to facilitate enclosure. The most important was the *Act anent Lands lying Run-rig* of 1695, which enabled anyone with a significant ownership interest in land to apply to the Sheriff of the county at any time for consolidation of holdings. Most run-rig enclosure, however, was not enforced until the latter part of the eighteenth century (plate A1). Whilst the Lothians and Berwickshire were largely enclosed by 1770, in Ayrshire and Perthshire the process was just beginning. At the same time, the Court of Session, under another Act of 1695, was dividing the commonties, or common lands, upon successful application from proprietors. Nearly half a million acres were dealt with between 1720 and 1850. The result, throughout lowland Scotland, was the present ordered, geometrical appearance of the landscape, offering very little regional variation.

In the Highlands, enclosure often took a different form. Initially the broad Highland straths were enclosed in the same regular fashion as the Lowland areas. But with increasing frequency after the Forty Five, as the old social system broke down, large parts of the Highlands were cleared by the lairds: the clansfolk were turned out, farms amalgamated, and re-leased at higher rents to sheep graziers from the Lowlands. The Dukes of Argyll began clearing their estates in the 1750s, and by 1800, sheep out-numbered cattle by ten to one in Argyllshire. At this date, large parts of the Central Highlands, Perthshire and southern Inverness had already been cleared. In the first half of the nineteenth century, further clear-ances took place throughout the north-west Highlands and Islands. It was the clearances that were chiefly responsible for the emigration of Highlanders to North America, often whole groups within a clan leav-ing on the same ship. In parts of the Western Highlands, the Outer Hebrides and Shetland, however, life in the old crofting townships con-tinued undisturbed. The landscape here was very different: small, strung-out villages dependent on farming and fishing, surrounded by elongated, unfenced holdings, many consolidated into narrow lots, with the common pastures around still shared.

A side effect of enclosure in the Lowlands, and parts of the High-lands, was the planting of trees in amongst the hedgerows and in cop-pices on land that was unsuited for anything else. Progressive landlords, such as the Earl of Haddingtoun in East Lothian, the Earl of

Loudoun in Ayrshire, and the Duke of Atholl, planted large numbers of trees and put up many shelter belts. The Duke alone planted no less than 27 million trees in plantations on his estates. Seeds were brought from London and Holland under the auspices of the new 'Edinburgh Society for the Importing of Seeds of Useful Trees'. Nevertheless, Scotland remained comparatively bare. So too did England and Wales, which with only two million acres of woodland by 1800 was one of the least wooded parts of Europe. A government commission on the state of the woodlands reporting in 1787 concluded that supplies were nearing exhaustion. But by this time, the traditional users of wood: the iron and shipbuilding industries, and the builders, had or were about to change to the more durable materials of the Industrial Revolution: coal, iron and brick. And many of the larger landowners of England and Wales were also planting trees like their Scottish counterparts, both as an investment, and for the adornment of their estates. It was in the late eighteenth century too that the conifer, in particular, the Scots pine and Canadian species of larch and fir, made its first appearance on the heaths of southern England.

*The Diffusion of New Ideas*

An important element in understanding the agricultural revolution is just how these new ideas of technical and organisational change were diffused and accepted. In part it was organisational changes, such as increasing farm size, enclosure and longer leases, that paved the way for improving techniques, although often there was no such link. Sometimes leases were actually used by landlords to ensure a good standard of husbandry, by the inclusion of directive covenants. The Coke leases in Norfolk are especially well known for their insistence, from as early as the 1720s, on the use of rotations, leys and grasses. Directions about marling and liming seem to have been common in leases in the second half of the century. But many leases contained no such provisions about husbandry practices, and in those cases that did it seems that landlords were often merely following the practices of their enlightened – and carefully chosen – tenants. The role of the lease as an instrument of diffusion should not be over-emphasised.

In England, at least, it appears that the larger tenantry and independent farmers were the most important agents of change. It was they who had the resources to experiment, and often the time to travel and read. The Culley brothers, pioneering the new husbandry in Northumberland from 1767, had been sent by their father to train under Bakewell in Leicestershire, and kept up such contacts by travelling widely throughout England and Scotland. They introduced a version of the Norfolk rotation to the north, and in the 1780s sent a man to Dorset to learn the art of constructing water meadows. They did much to improve the standards of Border agriculture by selling the seed of their improved wheat strains, and turnips. By 1800, their turnip seed sales had topped £500 a year. As their reputation grew, more and more farmers hired their Border Leicester breeding tups. And it was in such ways – by travel, personal contact and reputation, that new ideas spread (plate A6).

It is undeniable that some landlords were important innovators too. This was certainly so in Wales and Scotland, where they were the men who could afford to travel and to hire English expertise. The Earl of Haddingtoun introduced the sown grasses to East Lothian in the early years of the century after he had brought some Dorset farmers to Scotland to demonstrate their methods. John Cockburn, another prominent East Lothian landlord, who sat as an MP at Westminster from 1707 until 1741, sent the sons of his tenants into England to learn the new farming practises. It was also in Scotland that the first Agricultural Society was formed, in 1723 – the Society of Improvers in the Knowledge of Agriculture in Scotland, with Cockburn as the leading mover. The Breconshire Society in Wales was founded in 1755, and the Bath Society, which became the famous Bath and West, in 1777. By 1810, there were 70 societies throughout the country (fig. 3:7). Their distribution is rather interesting, showing concentrations in the Scottish lowlands and around the new English industrial towns, just those centres where the rising spirit of scientific empiricism was strongest. The societies encouraged experimentation and the exchange of results, and preached the virtues of bookkeeping and systematic recording. By stimulating personal contact, they were rather more important then the printed literature, such as the Board of Agriculture's *Annals*, which anyway never bettered a circulation of 400.[6]

### Increasing Demand

The third component of the agricultural revolution, and one of great importance, was the increasing demand of an ever expanding market for agricultural products. This arose primarily from the needs of feeding a rapidly growing population, but because of the linkages between agriculture and the rest of the economy, it was also due to expanding industrial and transport requirements. Increasing demand was not, of its own, the whole story: the particular encouragement to expansion came through the benefits of a rising agricultural price level (fig. 3:4), and a price level that was moving ahead more rapidly than that of industry, so turning the terms of trade in the farmer's favour.

The influence of demand on agriculture made itself felt in many ways.

Fig. 3:7   *British Agricultural Societies in 1810. Source*: Letters and Papers of the Bath Society, vol. XII; list reprinted in Hudson (1972).

Its characteristic market-orientation and regional specialisation intensified as demand increased. The spatial structure of agriculture reflected
its adjustment to market forces. At the national level, a certain land-use
zoning was in evidence, and this became more marked as agriculture
itself increased production. Close to the towns, high intensity farming
predominated, whilst farthest from the centres of population, on the
upland fringes, low intensity stock rearing and more self-sufficient agriculture was the rule. In between lay an intermediate zone of varying
intensity and production, according to the quality of the land and communications.

Land use around London was particularly intensive. Market gardens
bordered the Thames to the west of the city on the river gravels. Behind
Westminster and the northern suburbs, and over on the south bank,
were large cattle pastures on which the capital's dairy cows, numbering
some 8,500 by 1800, were kept. Eastward, on the Lea river marshes and
the Isle of Dogs, Smithfield cattle were fattened. Fringing these pastures
was a hay zone, from which cow and horse fodder was supplied. A similar pattern of gardens and pastures was well established around Norwich, and developed in central Lancashire as the towns of Liverpool and
Manchester grew. Here a mixed corn, hay and potato husbandry was
supported on the peats of the recently reclaimed mosses, sustained by
heavy application of industrial waste and town night soil. In Scotland,
the Lothians, adjacent to Edinburgh, had long been recognised as
having the most advanced and intensive farming, and by 1800, the
growth of Glasgow was exerting similar forces in Lanarkshire and Stirling.

Away from the vicinities of towns, agriculture was less intensive,
except where conditions were very favourable. Thus a flourishing fruit
and hop area had been long established around Maidstone in Kent, and
in Herefordshire. Dairying for the London butter and cheese trade became important on the London roads in south Oxfordshire and north
Wiltshire. Market gardening developed on the good soils around Sandy
in Bedfordshire, and in the Vale of Evesham as waggon links to the towns
speeded up as turnpike roads improved. Elsewhere, corn and livestock
husbandry intensified, corn spreading into the lighter lands, with the
clay vales switching to livestock. The margins of the waste were pushed
further back. The Weald, long a backward and remote area despite its
proximity to London, had been largely cleared of wood by 1800 and converted to corn growing. Only in the peripheral parts of the country was
agriculture little affected by growing national demand. Cornwall still
had its half a million acres of waste in 1795 and Pembrokeshire, along
with other counties on the outer edge of Wales, still farmed largely for

subsistence. Much of Scotland, outside the more progressive parts of the Lowlands, only began to stir in the last couple of decades. But even in this upland fringe, the influence of the market was felt. Anglesey, Moray and Nairn became important grain exporters and many hill farmers were committed to rearing stock cattle for lowland fattening.

This agricultural revolution was by no means at an end by 1800: the rate of change intensified considerably in the nineteenth century. Output may have risen by almost 50 per cent between 1700 and 1800, but between 1700 and 1870 it rose by nearly 300 per cent. However it was organisational change and advances in technique, spurred on by a rising price level and market demand in the eighteenth century that laid the necessary foundations for the large scale shifts of the nineteenth.

## AGRICULTURE AND THE ECONOMY

The links between eighteenth-century agriculture and the rest of the economy were wide ranging. However agriculture's contribution to the early Industrial Revolution has to be assessed carefully. The danger of overemphasising its 'achievement' must be avoided, even though its role was obviously extremely important. Certainly the supply of food and raw materials rose substantially, and farmers and landowners invested widely in other sectors of the economy. But the record sheet is not quite so straightforward as this.

The gain from the spread of the new husbandry techniques and organisational change within agriculture was an increasing supply of food and of a wide range of raw materials (wool, leather, tallow, etc.) The supply of food expanded sufficiently to enable Britain to remain more or less independent of overseas suppliers (except, of course, in groceries), despite the rapid growth of population. Corn imports amounted to less than five percent of annual consumption at the end of the eighteenth century. However, the general rise in the level of agricultural prices from the 1750s till the 1820s (fig. 3:4) shows, quite simply, that supply was not increasing at the same rate as demand. If it had, then prices would have remained stable. Rising money wages allowed consumers to maintain, in fact, to slightly increase the quantity and quality of food consumed per capita. But rising food prices only diverted some of the increments in personal incomes away from spending on the products of industry. And as industrial prices rose less quickly than agricultural prices, the terms of trade moved sharply in favour of agriculture.

Agricultural incomes therefore gained from two sources: increasing output, and the rising prices at which it was sold. Whether or not this income gain was of benefit to the economy as a whole depended on how it was spent. Some went on personal expenditure, and the rest into savings or investment. It is convenient to consider the latter first. Probably the larger part of the agricultural surplus was ploughed straight back into agriculture. But landowners and farmers also invested widely outside their farms, notably in improved transport systems such as turnpike roads and canals. Many exploited mineral resources on their estates, the Duke of Bridgwater with his Worsley mines and canal into Manchester being a well-known example. Those owning land on the periphery of towns were responsible for the development of many urban housing schemes, although frequently this was done through middlemen developers. Funds left agriculture in other ways. The land tax was an important source of Government finance. Agricultural savings found their way into the hands of industrialists and traders via financial intermediaries such as banks and bill brokers. This particular linkage was of great importance for British industrialisation after 1750, with the development of a network of country banks and London houses (below, pp. 174–76). Nevertheless, the outflow was compensated in part by the reinvestment of the profits of trade and industry in land. Throughout this period, it was land that held the ultimate key to social status. Many industrialists and merchants bought estates, some of the wealthiest retiring as county landowners – for example, the Arkwrights (from cotton), the Foleys and Knights (from iron). Farmers' sons who had left for apprenticeships in the towns often returned after two or three generations as owners. This inward flow of capital and expertise assisted in the growth of large estates and the spread of more rational methods of farming.

Agriculture was itself a market for industrial goods and services. Not until the nineteenth century did it become a significant market for capital goods, when the demand for iron ploughs, new threshing and winnowing machines, and from the 1850s, for all sorts of harrows, drills and cutters, began to climb. But the personal expenditure of landowners and farmers was undoubtedly of some importance in the eighteenth century in the creation of a middle income demand for consumer goods. However, by no means all the increases in their expenditure went into the products of home industry: as a group, they enjoyed a high propensity to consume imported goods – foreign manufactures, wines, spirits and other luxuries – and to spend on building. Nevertheless, the very size of the agricultural interest, and its rising prosperity, made it a substantial market for industrialists, the service trades and professions.

There are two remaining linkages: labour and raw materials. Enclosure, except in the Highlands, was not responsible for a mass ejection of labour into the towns. The process of enclosure, and the new husbandry techniques, required more labour not less. Without labour saving mechanical innovations until well into the nineteenth century, the number in agricultural employment grew gradually, and between the first census of 1801 and the peak recorded in 1851, expanded from 1.7 to 2.1 million. The burden of enclosure costs did inject considerable fluidity into ownership patterns: the turnover in recently enclosed parishes in Buckinghamshire was of the order of 40 to 50 per cent for the period 1780–1820. But this did not constitute a significant net loss. More important for the economy as a whole was the flow of population out of rural counties as a result of the failure of agriculture to retain anything like the total increment to labour supply that became available with population growth in the countryside. Farming employment simply grew insufficiently fast to absorb the numbers. Unlike large parts of Continental Europe, Britain was not a land of peasant farmers where substantial under-employment might be tolerated. And there were growing opportunities in industry and the towns. For many years, however, those who left to work in other sectors returned to the countryside for the harvest. In the late eighteenth century, the Midland iron trades and the Yorkshire textile firms usually stopped production for several weeks in the summer because of this.

Finally, agriculture provided raw materials for industry. Before the Industrial Revolution, agriculture had very obvious forward linkages to the most important parts of the small industrial sector: the processing trades (food, brewing, leather), and wool textile production. These linkages did not diminish in the eighteenth and nineteenth centuries. But the industrial sector expanded, and broadened its base considerably. The most rapidly growing industries of the Industrial Revolution did not have significant forward linkages from agriculture at all. Cotton, coal and iron became the great basic industries – the nineteenth century staples. They had very little dependence on the products of home agriculture. And in this sense, it is misleading to talk of the 'agricultural origins of industry'.

## NOTES

1 Deane and Cole (1967 p. 78) estimate that the output of home agriculture rose by 43 per cent in the eighteenth century.

2 A quote from G. D. H. Cole's *Persons and Periods* (1938), which contains two perceptive essays on Defoe. The *Tour* itself is particularly useful as an historical source because, to quote its author 'matters of antiquity are not my enquiry, but principally observations on the present state

of things'. (*Tour,* vol. 1 p. 69).

3 The open-field system is preserved at Laxton under the auspices of the Ministry of Agriculture. An informative guide to the village and its farming was written by J. D. Chambers: *Laxton* (H.M.S.O. 1964). There are a few other locations in Britain that also preserve the system (see plate A2).

4 Animal weights are a difficult problem because of the lack of reliable statistics. The evidence assembled by Fussell ('The Size of English Cattle in the Eighteenth Century', *Agric. Hist.* III 1929) indicates a fairly uniform small size. The Scottish examples are drawn from Hamilton (1963). It has been said that only the smaller cattle were driven to Smithfield, being better able than the bigger beasts to take the long journey. Nevertheless, they were fattened for market in Norfolk, the Midlands or on the marshes to the east of London before being sold.

5 This seems to have been so even when land was held without a formal lease, or on annual lease, as was common throughout Scotland and parts of England before the latter half of the century. After 1750, longer leases, for terms of 15, 21 or maybe 30 years, became more usual and these certainly encouraged a wiser, longer-term approach to husbandry and the investment of effort. A major advance in Scotland was the abolition of the 'tacksman' system, under which land was leased by individuals from the laird and then re-leased annually to the farmers. Improving landlords replaced the tacksman with a 19 or 30 year direct lease to the farmer, a process that was popularised by the Commissioners appointed to supervise the Forfeited Estates after the Rebellion of 1745.

6 The Board of Agriculture was set up in 1793, with government support. Arthur Young, the agricultural writer and proselytizer, was its first Secretary. It drew up a series of County Agriculture Reports (in the 1790s and again in the 1810s) which today are a valuable source for students of the period. The Board's *Annals* provided a forum for news of innovations and experiments: the circulation figure of 400 is Young's.

## FURTHER READING

The most recent general book on the agricultural revolution is by J. D. Chambers and G. E. Mingay: *The Agricultural Revolution, 1750–1880* (1966). It is, however, very thin on Scotland, for which Hamilton (1963) and J. E. Handley: *The Agricultural Revolution in Scotland* (1963) should be consulted. But the foremost scholar in the field is undoubtedly E. L. Jones, whose two books *Agriculture and Economic Growth, 1660–1815* (ed., 1967) and *Agriculture and the Industrial Revolution* (1974) provide a very clear statement of the sources of agricultural expansion and its relationship to the economy. P. K. O'Brien's valuable review article 'Agriculture and the Industrial Revolution', *Ec.H.R.* vol. XXX (1977) should be read alongside them. Deane and Cole (1967, chapter two) present some useful statistical reconstructions of eighteenth-century agriculture, whilst Eric Kerridge in *The Agricultural Revolution* (1967) argues idiosyncratically that the term is better applied to developments in the sixteenth and seventeenth centuries.

### AGRICULTURE IN THE EARLY EIGHTEENTH CENTURY

The classic essay on markets and their specialities is Alan Everitt: 'The Marketing of Agricultural Produce', in J. Thirsk (ed.): *The Agrarian History of England and Wales, 1500–1640,* vol. IV (1967). On regional diversity, see Chambers and Mingay, and Daniel Defoe's *Tour*. The authoritative source on open-field systems is A. R. H. Baker and R. A. Butlin (eds.): *Studies of Field Systems of the British Isles* (1973). See also, R. A. Dodgshon: 'The Nature of Infield-Outfield in Scotland', *T.I.B.G.* no. 59 (1973). On the extent of wasteland, see M. Williams: 'The enclosure and reclamation of waste land in England and Wales in the eighteenth and nineteenth centuries', *T.I.B.G.* no. 51 (1970). E. L. Jones: *Seasons and Prices* (1964) demonstrates the dependence of farmers on the weather, as does J. Oliver: 'Problems of Agro-Climatic Relationships in Wales in the Eighteenth Century', in J. A. Taylor (ed.): *Weather and Agriculture* (1967).

### THE AGRICULTURAL REVOLUTION

On the spread of new crops, see Chambers and Mingay; Jones 1967 (the introduction and chapter six); A. H. John: 'The Course of Agricultural Change, 1660–1760', in L. S. Pressnell (ed.): *Studies in the Industrial Revolution* (1960); F. V. Emery: 'The mechanics of innovation: clover cultivation in Wales before 1750', *Jnl. Hist. Geog.* vol. 2 (1976); and the regional references given below.

The standard sources on advance in open-field systems are W. G. Hoskins: 'The Leicestershire Farmer in the Seventeenth Century', *Ag. History* vol. 25 (1951), and M. A. Havinden: 'Agricultural Progress in Open-Field Oxfordshire', *Ag. Hist. Rev.* vol. 9 (1961), reprinted in Jones (1967). See also J. A. Yelling: 'Changes in Crop Production in East Worcestershire, 1540–1867', *Ag. Hist. Rev.* vol. 21 (1973).

An interesting essay on liming is M. A. Havinden: 'Lime as a Means of Agricultural Improvement: the Devon example', in C. W. Chalklin and

M. A. Havinden (eds.): *Rural Change and Urban Growth, 1500–1800* (1974). H. C. Prince: 'Pits and Ponds in Norfolk', *Erdkunde* XVI (1962) deals with marling.

On estate and farm size, see F. M. L. Thompson: 'The Social Distribution of Landed Property in England since the Sixteenth Century', *Ec.H.R.* vol. 19 (1966), and G. E. Mingay: 'The Size of Farms in the Eighteenth Century', *Ec.H.R.* vol. 14 (1962). Mingay also discusses the role of the landlord in his book: *English Landed Society in the Eighteenth Century* (1963), and an essay by B. A. Holderness is valuable in this respect too: 'Landlord's Capital Formation in East Anglia, 1750–1870', *Ec.H.R.* vol. 25 (1972).

J. A. Yelling has recently filled a gap with his book: *Common Field and Enclosure in England, 1450–1850* (1977). Two seminal essays by Donald N. McCloskey should also be consulted: 'The Persistence of English Common Fields' and 'The Economics of Enclosure', both in W. N. Parker and E. L. Jones (eds.): *European Peasants and their Markets* (1975). There are a number of good regional enclosure studies, including: W. G. Hoskins: 'The Reclamation of the Waste in Devon, 1550–1850', *Ec.H.R.*, First Series vol. 13 (1943); M. E. Turner: 'Parliamentary Enclosure and Landownership Change in Buckinghamshire', *Ec. H. R.* vol. 28 (1975); M. Williams: 'The Enclosure and Reclamation of the Mendip Hills, 1770–1870', *Ag. Hist. Rev.* vol. 19 (1971), J. Chapman: 'Parliamentary Enclosure in the Uplands: the case of the North York Moors', *Ag. Hist. Rev.* vol. 24 (1976).

Agricultural societies are the subject of a book by K. Hudson: *Patriotism without Profit* (1972). D. J. Rowe: 'The Culleys, Northumberland farmers, 1767–1813', *Ag. Hist. Rev.* vol. 19 (1971) is a fascinating account of the transfer of ideas within the farming community, whilst R. A. C. Parker: *Coke of Norfolk: a financial and agricultural study, 1707–1842* (1975) deals with the activities of an enlightened landlord.

The state of agriculture around 1800 is discussed by D. Thomas: *Agriculture in Wales in the Napoleonic Wars* (1963); W. E. Minchinton: 'Agricultural Returns and the Government during the Napoleonic Wars', *Ag. Hist. Rev.* vol. 1 (1953), and W. G. East: 'Land Utilization in England at the end of the Eighteenth Century', *Geog. Jnl.* vol. 89 (1937).

REGIONAL STUDIES

Many of these are hidden away as theses on university library shelves. The more worthwhile ones in print include: J. Thirsk: *English Peasant Farming* (1957), on Lincolnshire; A. Harris: *The Rural Landscape of the East Riding of Yorkshire, 1700–1850* (1961); N. Riches: *The Agricultural Revolution in Norfolk*, 2nd edn. (1967); D. B. Grigg: *The Agricultural Revolution in South*

*Lincolnshire* (1966) and A. J. Youngson's book on the Scottish Highlands: *After the Forty-Five* (1973).

PRIMARY SOURCES

The best short guide to these is by D. B. Grigg: 'A Commentary on the Sources Available for the Reconstruction of the Agricultural Geography of England, 1770–1850', *T.I.B.G.* no. 41 (1967). G. E. Mingay: *The Agricultural Revolution* (1977) is a useful edited collection of extracts from primary sources. Many of the Board of Agriculture's *County Reports* were reprinted a few years ago and these are a valuable source of material on agriculture around 1800. Arthur Young's *Tours* and William Marshall's surveys are also readily available.

# 4 The Framework of Industrial Change

> 'People here are not without their Tea, Coffee and Chocolate, especially the first, the use of which is spread to that Degree, that not only Gentry and Wealthy Travellers drink it constantly, but almost every Seamer, Sizer and Winder will have her Tea in a morning. . . . and even a common Washerwoman thinks she has not had a proper Breakfast without Tea and hot buttered White Bread!.'
> (C. Deering: *Nottingham Vetus et Nova*, 1751).

These were some of the comments – not wholly approving – of Nottingham's historian Dr Deering, about life in his home town in the early 1750s. Yet they reflect an observation common amongst contemporary observers and pamphleteers; simply that the everyday things that nowadays are taken for granted, the products of trade and industry, were becoming increasingly usual amongst the 'middling sorts' and poorer people of eighteenth-century Britain. They too were beginning to take them for granted. Trading goods that were 'luxuries' in 1700 – tea, sugar, chocolate, tobacco – were 'decencies' by mid-century. A little later, so too were the products of emerging mass industry: cotton clothing and furnishings, furniture, pottery, soap and hardware. People were beginning to ask for – and were able to pay for – more than just the bare essentials, the necessities of life. And in so doing, they were starting to create a massive home market demand that was to be a most powerful engine of growth in the Industrial Revolution.

## TRADE AND INDUSTRY

This market demand was met by the development firstly of a thriving overseas trade, and secondly, of home-based industry. The two were closely linked. The import trades provided many raw materials for industry, such as high grade iron, cotton and timber, as well as commodities for processing such as coffee, chocolate and sugar. Not all imports were retained for the home market by any means – most coffee was re-exported, for instance – but the demands of processing itself stimulated coal production, metal working and, most importantly, financial and entrepreneurial organisation. Then there were the export trades, an important outlet for industrial production and until 1760, for agriculture too. About one third of total English industrial production was exported throughout the century. In the key export industry, the cloth trade, the proportion was closer to a half. Agricultural exports died away as home demand boomed, but in the peak year of 1750, about seven per cent of total agricultural production, and 20 per cent of exports by value, was accounted for by the one million quarters of grain sent abroad.

Overseas trade had expanded relatively rapidly in the first 80 years of the seventeenth century, largely due to the success of the 'new draperies' – light, colourful cloths – in the markets of the Mediterranean countries, and the passage of the Navigation Acts in the 1650s, which tied trade with the English colonies to English ships and ports. Then European competition, tariff protection and war slowed the pace of growth to about one per cent a year from the mid-1680s to the mid-1740s. But from there-on, foreign trade started to flourish, and expanded at a rate of nearly two per cent a year to the early 1770s, and after the disruption of the American wars, at nearly five per cent a year for the rest of the century. The timing of this upturn in the 1740s is of the greatest significance, because it parallels the upturn in population and agricultural output, providing further evidence of the overall quickening pace of economic change from that time.

The growth of foreign trade is illustrated in figure 4:1. Although the figures must be treated with caution,[1] the general trend is quite clear. Net imports (i.e. those retained for home consumption) plus domestic exports, totalled about £8.5 millions for England and Wales at the turn of the eighteenth century, rising to about £21 millions by the 1770s. Then in a tremendous surge from then on, they had grown to £46 millions for the whole of Great Britain by 1800. Furthermore, this growth rate was reflected in the course of industrial change. Industrial output expanded fourfold in these hundred years.Both trade and industry were growing appreciably faster than other parts of the economy; consequently by 1800 they formed a larger part of the whole than they had a century before. In 1688, Gregory King's figures indicate that about one-third of the national product was derived from industry, mining, trade and transport. By the 1800s, it had risen to 40 per cent.

Again this was the start – the prelude – to the large-scale shifts of the nineteenth century. In 1901, almost two-thirds of the national product was derived from these sources: the end result of massive industrialisation after 1800, based largely on spreading international

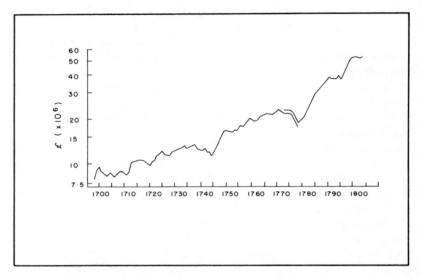

Fig. 4:1  *The Growth of Foreign Trade, 1700–1800* (net imports plus domestic exports: three-yearly moving means). *Source*: redrawn from Deane and Cole (1967) p. 49.

trade linkages. Nevertheless, it was an industrialisation founded in the take-off of the eighteenth century. This was the century that ushered in the steam engine, the factory, mass-produced cottons and woollens, exotic processed imports and coal power. But these were symptoms of industrial expansion and growing wealth: to look for the cause it is necessary to return to the opening concern of this chapter, and analyse the growth of demand – the power of the market.

## THE GROWTH OF DEMAND

The four necessities of everyday life are food, shelter, clothing and fuel. The demand for these was growing in the eighteenth century, simply because numbers were growing. But also an increasing proportion of the population was moving into industry and towns away from the more self-sufficient rural economy. More people were buying their necessities in exchange for money wages, rather than making their clothes at home, producing their own food, or foraging for fuel in the woods, as those in the villages could do. So more people were entering the market: the market was *widening*. However, many people were gradually becoming more wealthy as well: the market was also *deepening*.

Real wages rose in the first part of the century, and although they seem to have been more stable thereafter (but money wages were still rising), disposable incomes continued to increase gradually as there was more, and more regular work available in industry, trade and agriculture. In addition, there was a general growth in the number of middle income earners – those receiving between £50 and £400 a year. About ten per cent of the population came in this category in the late seventeenth century: 15 per cent by 1750, and maybe as high as a quarter by the 1780s. Then there was the built-in demographic habit of late marriage, a ready means of accumulating small savings that could be used for consumer purchases (above, p. 31).

This market deepening had two general effects. Firstly, it enabled people to improve the standard of the necessities they consumed. That this was happening virtually everywhere – with the exception of the Scottish Highlands, which were rapidly overpopulating by the last decades of the century – was frequently remarked upon by commentators. Arthur Young, for instance, wrote of 'this better living (which) consists in the people consuming more food, and of a better sort: eating wheat instead of barley, oats and rye – and drinking a prodigiously greater quantity of beer' – about 35 gallons per head each year, by 1800, in fact. But it applied not only to food, but to better clothing, housing and increasingly in the use of coal rather than wood fuel too. The second effect was simply that people were able to spend something, or more, on items that were not necessities: 'decencies' and 'luxuries' such as sugar, tea, iron pots and pans, trinkets and toys, extra pieces of clothing, house fittings, bedsteads, lamps and books.

It was these two components of demand deepening that were particularly important in stimulating trade and industrial development. It was essentially a middle-class demand, supported by the farmers and gentry in the countryside, and the professional and tradespeople of the towns. But similar habits were spreading, however superficially, to the agricultural and industrial workers that Dr Deering wrote about too. Imitating the ways of one's betters counted for much. 'Thus while the Nobleman will emulate the Grandeur of the Prince', wrote Henry Fielding in 1753, 'the Gentleman will aspire to the proper state of the Nobleman, and the Tradesman steps out from behind his counter into the vacant place of the

Gentleman'.

Expanding demand was reflected in the very rapid growth of sales of many commodities, as can be seen from table 4:1.

TABLE 4:1   *The Growth of Consumption, 1785–1800*

| | |
|---|---|
| Strong beer | + 33.4% |
| Small beer | + 30.6% |
| Tallow candles | + 33.8% |
| Soap | + 41.7% |
| Tobacco | + 58.9% |
| British and Foreign spirits | + 73.9% |
| Tea | + 97.9% |
| Printed fabrics | +141.9% |

Growth of population in England and Wales: +14%

*Source*: Ashton (1955).

It has been tentatively estimated that an average of £10-worth of home-produced industrial goods was consumed by each English family in 1688, about £25-worth in 1750, and £40-worth by 1811. This growth brought about changes in the structure of the market itself. No longer could the seasonal fair, weekly local market or cheap chandlers shop cope with every consumer need. In the towns, specialist shops and itinerant industrial traders became increasingly common. Even in the smaller places, an impressive range of goods was available. Abraham Dent, a grocer in mid-eighteenth-century Kirkby Stephen in Westmorland sold tea, sugar, wine, soap, imported fruit, at least 40 sorts of cloth, flax, a wide variety of paper, magazines and books and patent medicines.[2]

## THE NATURE OF INDUSTRY

The basic structure of demand was directly reflected in the output and nature of industry. It is difficult, in the absence of reliable statistics, to make satisfactory estimates of industrial output. But using the material that is available, Professor Hoffmann compiled an index that gives the proportions of total output by value added attributable to different branches of manufacture. Table 4:2 reproduces his estimates for 1812. The figures are a rough approximation, and no more, of the relative importance of various industries by the end of the eighteenth century.

TABLE 4:2    *Output by Value of Various Industries as a Proportion of Total Industrial Output, 1812*

| | | |
|---|---|---|
| Coal | 6.9% | |
| Iron and Steel | 2.5% ⎫ | 9.2% |
| Iron and Steel goods | 6.7% ⎭ | |
| Copper and copper goods | 1.4% | |
| Ships | 2.1% | |
| Cotton yarn and cloth | 12.2% ⎫ | |
| Wool yarn and cloth | 11.0% ⎪ | 29.0% |
| Linen yarn and cloth | 4.2% ⎬ | |
| Silk yarn and cloth | 1.6% ⎭ | |
| Food and drink | 6.7% | |
| Leather and leather goods | 8.0% | |
| Soap and candles | 1.6% | |
| Building | 9.2% | |
| | 74.2% of the total | |

*Source*: Hoffmann (1955) pp. 18–19.

Certain features immediately stand out in this table. The most apparent is the importance of those industries supplying basic needs – textiles and leather goods (clothing, furnishings, footwear and transport requisites), building (shelter), coal (fuel) and the food and drink trades. As an index of home consumption, the value of textile production is inflated, as a substantial proportion was destined for the overseas trade, whereas the value of coal and food production is depressed, as by no means all food or fuel consumed entered into the market. Iron and steel products, the basis of many consumer items, form a notable component, but it is not as large as might be expected. Although iron and steel were starting to displace wooden machinery, and wood and stone as building materials in big engineering structures (such as factories and bridges), this substitute market had only just begun to open up by 1812. Industrial production in the eighteenth century was tailored largely toward satisfying the most basic needs of the population. And it was not, by later standards, produced by a sophisticated manufacturing structure that required widespread investment in capital goods made of iron and steel. Large-scale fixed-capital industry was emerging in the last quarter of the century, particularly in the quantitively two most important sectors – textiles and the iron industry itself – but it was by no means the dominant form.

Eighteenth century industry was of a rather different nature to the modern type. The concentrations of coal-based manufacturing crowded in cities and valleys that so mark the industrial landscape of Victorian times were not typical of the eighteenth century. Certainly there were regional clusters, particularly in the ports and the provincial textile and metal-working industries. But these clusters were loosely organised, units were usually small-scale, most capital was held in stocks rather than in buildings or machinery and activity was spread around towns and in villages throughout the countryside. Motive power, when it was not animate in origin, was often derived from wood, wind or water. The use of steam power was certainly not general by 1800, even though the steam engine had been available for a hundred years. Most of the regions of Britain that today are considered typically industrial were then very different. The Black Country, for example, could not yet be called by that name. Rather than the crowded, grimy landscape that stands out on either side of today's M6, it was 'a countryside in the course of becoming industrialised, more and more a strung out web of iron-working villages, market towns next door to collieries, heaths and wastes gradually and very slowly being covered by the cottages of nailers and (others) carrying on industrial occupations in rural surroundings'.

Contemporaries marvelled at the signs of the future that were appearing. New steam engines, coal pits, canals and bridges, turnpike roads and big factories such as those built by Arkwright, Boulton and Wedgwood, all claimed attention. But the general record reveals the true nature of most industrial enterprise as being small-scale, dispersed and traditional. Maps, such as those produced by William Yates of Lancashire and Staffordshire show the scattering of water mills, coal pits and forges around farms and villages. (plate B2). Writers like Defoe described such scenes in words. Here is his picture of Halifax in the early 1720s:

'(Their) business is the clothing trade, for the convenience of which the houses are thus scattered and spread upon the sides of the hills . . . . . at every considerable house was a manufactory or work-house, and as they could not do their business without water, the little streams were so parted and guided by gutters or pipes, and by turning and dividing the streams, that none of those houses were without a river . . . . running into or through their work-houses, . . . . the dye-houses, scouring shops and places where they used this water, emitted the water again, ting'd with the drugs of the dying fat, and with the oil, the soap, the tallow . . . . . Then, as every clothier must keep a horse, perhaps two, to fetch and carry for the use of his manufacture; so every manufacturer generally keeps a cow or two, or more, for his family, and this employs the two, or three, or four pieces of enclosed land about his house.' (*Tour*, vol. 2 pp. 193–5)

Interesting and valuable as such observations are, however, a more critical analysis of the nature of, and changes in, industry during the early Industrial Revolution is required. It is necessary to look in more detail at the various inputs to production (the factors of production), and the ways in which they were organised. Such an assessment of the supply side of the industrial equation illustrates how, through the eighteenth century, industry responded to, and gradually changed its response to, increasing market demand.

## CHANGING FACTORS OF PRODUCTION

*Raw Materials:*
The four factors of production that combine together in the manufacturing process are: raw materials, capital, labour and entrepreneurship. The first of these, *raw materials*, is important in two respects, as the source of production material itself, and as the means of power for production.

Throughout the eighteenth century, industrial raw materials were mainly of organic origin: farm products such as wool, flax and leather; timber; wind and water. In 1800, most industrial processes were still worked directly by men, or powered by the waterwheel, windmill or horse-gin. These organic sources of materials and power were dispersed throughout the country, and so, in consequence, were most branches of industrial activity. In towns and villages everywhere there were households, workshops and mills producing small manufactures. However, the use of inorganic raw materials: iron and non-ferrous metal ores, and coal, was increasing rapidly in the last decades of the eighteenth century. These inorganic materials were not widely distributed. They were available only in restricted areas, and were generally expensive to move. Their use was beginning to have a profound effect on the distribution of industry. In Britain, the best ironstones of the time were in the coal measures, so that by 1800, industry was expanding most rapidly on the coalfields, and in those ports with easy access to coal. Indeed, Arthur Young's impression in 1791 was that 'all the activity and industry of this kingdom is fast concentrating where there are coal-pits'.

This impression must not go unqualified. Many of the major industries, in particular the various branches of textiles, were still predominantly reliant on organic raw materials and power sources at the close of the eighteenth century. In Sheffield in 1794, there were five steam-powered cutleries, but 111 water-powered ones. John Aikin, writing about the same time, found that 'there is scarce a stream that will turn a wheel through the north of England that has not a cotton mill upon it'. William Yates' map of Lancashire, published in the 1780s, depicts no less than 330 water mills in that county alone. They were used, according to the map, not only for cotton spinning, but in the woollen trades, for grinding corn and producing paper, and to supply the blast and work the hammers in furnaces and forges.

The use of water power meant that industry could continue to be dispersed in the early stages of the Industrial Revolution. Richard Arkwright, the pioneer of factory production in cotton spinning, moved his firm in 1771 from Nottingham to Cromford, remote in the Derbyshire dales, partly as it had suitable stream-power to drive his water-frame spinning machines.[3] Other factory masters followed him: the Strutts to Belper, also on the Derbyshire Derwent, Oldknow to Mellor, in the Peak beyond Stockport, David Dale to New Lanark, some 25 miles south-west of Glasgow. But water powered mills did not have to be remote, and the majority of textile workshops and new factories were closer to established towns such as Nottingham, Manchester and Leeds. Sir Robert Peel could say that steam power was 'very little in use in the town of Manchester' in 1792, although it was increasing, and this was not only due to the number of small streams around the town, but because many of the small workshops still used hand machinery, or horse gins. In Keighley, a famous woollen textiles town on the other side of the Pennines, there were 30 woollen mills 'upon one little brook' in 1815. So the use of water power also did not mean that industrial sites had to be dispersed. That the cotton and wool textile industries were to be found in concentrations on the coalfields of Central Scotland, Lancashire, the West Riding and Nottinghamshire by 1800, was in part due, paradoxically, to the availability there of many streams suitable for the water wheel.[4] But it was a pattern that was confirmed as more and more textile firms turned to steampower to drive their increasingly large stocks of machinery in the first two or three decades of the nineteenth century.

It was coal, and coal-produced steam that was the quintessence of the Industrial Revolution – one of the supporting pillars of Britain's international industrial dominance in the nineteenth century, Coal, as a source of raw material and power, had become important in several branches of industry during the eighteenth century: in brewing, glass and pottery manufacture, in the processing of imported products such as sugar and chocolate, in salt-making and in mining. The majority of steam engines built in the eighteenth century were for drainage purposes at coalpits and at the deep Cornish tin mines. By 1800, however, coal was of particular importance in two branches of industry, non-ferrous metal smelting, and the iron industry. The former had a long history of the use of coal, in the latter it was very much more recent.

The technique of smelting copper with coal had been discovered in the sixteenth century, and it was introduced in tin smelting shortly after. But in the eighteenth century, the process still required three times the quantity of coal to ore. For this reason, it was cheapest to send the ores from the mining areas in Cornwall and Anglesey to the coalfields of South Wales, Bristol and Lancashire. Small concentrations of copper, lead and tin smelters were to be found around Liverpool and Neath in the early 1700s (there were 12 lead and two copper furnaces in Neath in 1708), whilst Bristol also had brass and bronze works. Cornish smelting, by contrast, was never very successful, because of the cost of importing coal. There was a short lived copper smelter at Hayle in the 1720s, and another was started in 1759, but it was never viable and closed down in 1806.

By the end of the eighteenth century, ironmasters used coal almost exclusively, both as a source of carbon and of heat. But in 1700 they were still completely dependent on charcoal and the water wheel. Pig iron production in this age of charcoal was scattered throughout the countryside, with regional clusterings of furnaces in the Weald, the Forest of Dean, the West Midlands, Nottinghamshire and South Yorkshire, and the Furness area of Lancashire, all wooded areas with ironstone ores. Scotland had a few furnaces in the Higlands, refining ore brought by ship from England. Yet the charcoal iron industry was inherently limited. Because it relied on relatively inelastic supplies of timber, production could not be expanded rapidly without adverse price rises. Nor could ironmasters produce for long beyond the limit of available annual timber growth, except at the cost of future production. No such constraints accompanied the use of coal, however, as coal supplies were effectively unlimited.

Coke was first successfully used in an iron furnace by Abraham Darby at Coalbrookdale, in Shropshire, in 1709. He, significantly, had been a partner in a Bristol brass-works a few years previously. Coke was used continuously to make thin iron castings at Coalbrookdale thereafter, but it was not widely adopted elsewhere until the 1750s, when the nationwide demand for iron began to rise, and with it charcoal prices. Charcoal pig, which until then had been cheaper than coke pig, rapidly became the more expensive. By 1790 there were only 25 charcoal furnaces still working (there had been 61 in 1717), and 90 per cent of the country's pig iron was produced by her 81 coke furnaces. Many of these new ironworks were as isolated as some of the new spinning factories. There was nothing at Merthyr Tydfil in South Wales but a small hamlet when the great Cyfarthfa, Dowlais and Plymouth furnaces were set up in the 1750s and 1760s. John Wilkinson's Bersham furnace, the centre of an extensive iron empire, was in a small village in the hills beyond Wrexham. The pioneer Scottish works at Carron (1759) was in the country north of Falkirk. Coalbrookdale itself was a remote Shropshire valley above the Severn. Most of the other coke works were in established iron-making areas nearer towns and growing industrialising communities – west of Birmingham, north of Nottingham, and south of Sheffield. But any notions of urban-industrial concentrations in the eighteenth-century iron industry are not appropriate.

The shift to coke-smelted pig enabled ironmasters to make an upward shift in the scale of supply to meet demand, just as the cotton spinners were able to do with the adoption of water, and then steam-driven, machinery. The uses for iron rapidly expanded. In part this was due to its adoption as a construction material, replacing timber and stone. Nearly all the rails used on the tramways in the coal-mining districts were iron-plated by the end of the century, lengthening their life-spans considerably. For the same reason, many of the water wheels built after 1750 were iron-clad. Increasingly iron was used to make machinery, instead of wood. Although this process had not gone far by 1800, intricate pieces of steam-driven equipment, such as the cotton spinners' mule, had to be made of iron to withstand vibration. The original steam engines themselves were wooden structures, but it was the use of an accurately bored iron cylinder produced by Wilkinson, that enabled Watt to improve the steam engine so considerably. In building, the process of substitution was just beginning in the 1780s and 1790s. Abraham Darby III built the first iron bridge, over the Severn at Coalbrookdale, in 1779, and his method was taken up by the canal engineers for viaducts in the 1790s (plates D1 and D3). Iron railings were becoming increasingly fashionable in place of stone walls (plate F4). And the first iron framed building was erected by William Strutt at Belper in 1793, a technique that spread rapidly in the construction of big mills, and one that fore-shadowed the great iron engineering edifices of Victorian times. Nevertheless, the main uses of iron in the second half of the eighteenth century were not in construction at all, but in the provision of military supplies during the recurring wars of these years and in a widening range of simple hand tools and consumer goods. The contemporary industrial structure of Sheffield illustrates this very well (table 5:4).

Most iron products, however, were not made of pig or cast iron but of stronger, more malleable wrought iron. This was produced from pig that had been refined in the forge to remove many of the carbon and chemical impurities that give the pig its brittleness. For a long time only charcoal was used in this process, because of the problem of further contamination from impurities in coke. Gradually the coal-fired reverbatory furnace came into use (one in which the flames were reflected off the walls of a dome-like structure, not heating the metal directly), a technique used in glassmaking. But good quality wrought iron made with coke was not possible until Henry Cort patented his puddling process in 1784, which used a method of alternate heating and cooling inside a reverbatory furnace. Cort also devised a rolling mill for the heavy work of beating out the iron, a job previously done slowly using tilting hammers. His rolling mill (versions for light work such as slitting rods had long been in use) could be adapted to produce all sorts of basic products: beams, bars, rails, sheets. Cort's process spread rapidly, he himself demonstrating it around the country, whilst the iron magnate Richard Crawshay promoted it enthusiastically. South Wales became the particular centre of puddling skills. His inventions allowed great economies of scale in the industry, and completed the transition to the use of coal in iron making.

Hence the raw material function in industry was gradually changing, in response to the increased scale of output and the widening range of products demanded by a growing market. It was shifting from man and animal power to water and steam power, and from timber and stone to coal and iron. But, for far longer than convention has admitted, the water wheel, windmill, horse-gin and manually-driven machine persisted. As late as the 1830s, there were 100,000 power looms in the textile industry, but still a quarter of a million working hand loom weavers.

### Capital

In part effect, in part cause, of the gradual shift in the raw material function, *capital* requirements slowly changed as well. But in keeping with the gradual change in the former, there was no dramatic rise in capital investment levels in the early Industrial Revolution. Not until the 1830s and 1840s did the investment ratio (the ratio of fixed capital formation to national income) show a marked rise, as it was not until then that the modern kinds of investment characteristic of an industrial economy (heavy industrial, railway and public utility capital) began to claim a large proportion of the annual additions to the capital stock. Before this, in many branches of industry, the techniques and simple machines that had been used for decades persisted, and increasing output was met by increasing numbers, rather than increasing scale or sophistication of production units. This was a *capital widening* rather than a capital deepening process. The number of hand loom weavers was so high in the

1830s simply because until adequate power looms were introduced in the 1820s, the only way that textile weaving could keep abreast of the increased scale of textile spinning was by expanding the traditional methods. Framework knitting was a manual operation for even longer, until the 1850s. Knitters used a frame based on a sixteenth-century design that cost only £25 or so – the weaver's loom was little more. The water wheel and horse-gin that multiplied as power needs rose were both simple and well-tried pieces of equipment that could be built for around £50. Capital widening was not an investment intensive process.

There were, however, some notable examples of *capital deepening* in the eighteenth century, where the adoption of improved technology involved the intensification of investment in fixed capital stock. The use of steam engines in mining is one such case. Mining was restricted to simple bell-pit or adit operations until the appearance of the steam engine (Savery's 'Miner's Friend' was patented in 1697, Newcomen's engine in 1707) enabled deeper shafts to be opened up. The simple up-and-down motion of the early engines was quite adequate for ventilating the shafts and draining them of water. Mines up to 150 feet deep could be kept open by the Newcomen engine which, although inefficient in its use of fuel compared with Watt's models, long retained its popularity at collieries because of the cheapness of coal at the pit-head (plate C2). Yet even in the 1790s, 16 horsepower improved Newcomen engines could be bought for as little as £200. The increasing output of coal, however, led mine owners to replace packhorse carriage from the pit head with horse-drawn waggonways to the nearest river: an improvement which generated significant scale economies, but involved substantial investment in wooden rails, often iron-clad, and waggons.

The most intensive capital deepening process in the early Industrial Revolution took place in cotton textile spinning, as the result of a chain of disequilibria induced by technological improvements, in a period of rapidly rising demand for cotton goods. The introduction of Kay's flying shuttle in the 1730s had, by the 1750s, due to its wide acceptance by weavers, disturbed the pre-existing balance within the industry. The flying shuttle greatly increased the productivity of the weavers, but the spinners, using their single spindle wheels, were unable to keep pace. Cotton yarn thus rose in price. The pressure was partially alleviated by Hargreave's spinning jenny, which he introduced in 1767 and patented in 1770. The patented model had 16 spindles, but by 1784, some improved versions had 80, greatly increasing the productivity of the spinners. A further problem, however, remained. Spinners could not produce a strong enough warp thread for cotton cloth on a jenny, so that flax warps had to be substituted, so producing a cotton 'mixture'. This problem was solved by Richard Arkwright and his roller spinning machine, or water frame, patented in 1769.

The water frame produced strong, fine yarn, and it vastly speeded up the spinning process. In 1775, Arkwright removed a further technological constraint by patenting a carding engine, a device which could draw out the raw cotton fibres into a continuous sliver ready for the spinning machinery. But both the carding engine and the water frame were too large for domestic or workshop industry. Arkwright and his patentees had to build multi-storey factories in which to house them, of which his Cromford mill (1771) was the archetype. The machines were also too large to be operated by hand, so they were driven by great iron-clad waterwheels, and in some cases by steam engines. For this purpose, mill-owners often preferred the new Boulton and Watt engines, first patented in 1769, but adapted by Watt in the early 1780s for rotary motion. The Watt rotary engine could be directly connected to spinning machinery, and was renowned for its reliability. Rather more common, however, was the use of one of the many improved, and cheaper, versions of the Newcomen engine, to recirculate water from under the water wheel back up above it: a safeguard against the dangers of seasonally low stream flow.

Many of these items were expensive, being substantial pieces of fixed capital. Arkwright's first Cromford mill was insured for £1,500 to cover plant and power unit, and most of the mills built on this model were valued at £3–4,000 in the 1780s and 1790s. David Dale's mill at New Lanark was insured for £4,800 in 1786. Arkwright's machinery itself was not particularly costly, but initially the use of his patents certainly was. One Bakewell firm had to pay him £2,000 for the use of the water frame, £5,000 for the carding engine, with an additional annual premium of £1,000 to cover both. Steam engines were much cheaper, but a 16 horse-power Boulton and Watt model could cost £800 to purchase, and there was still the annual premium to be paid. Samuel Oldknow, the Stockport muslin manufacturer, paid £40 a year on his. The first multi-storey factory to be powered by steam alone, Major Cartwright's Revolution Mill at Retford (1788), was insured for £13,000. Its 30 horsepower steam engine, very large for the time, cost £1,500.

Nevertheless, these figures do not give a realistic picture of the overall capital deepening process in cotton spinning. Large-scale factory mechanisation was by no means typical in the industry by 1800, although it was the pointer of things to come. The Arkwright-type mill was still outnumbered two-to-one by the humbler spinning workshop, a small-scale affair, often occupying a converted house or barn. Arkwright's water-frame was in competition with the jenny, and from the late 1770s, with a new invention, Crompton's mule. Both the jenny and the mule could be fitted into the domestic system, workshop or factory. Samuel Crompton had not patented his mule, and it could be bought very cheaply. Cast-iron mules with 203 spindles were available new in Manchester for £44 in the early 1800s, whilst 144 spindle versions cost just £33. The mule was also capable of producing much finer yarn than even Arkwright's water frame. Consequently it spread quickly, and by 1800, there were 600 mule or jenny workshops in Britain, and only about 300 Arkwright-type mills. However, neither were the latter sort as costly to set up as might appear. Less than one in three of the mills was steampowered in 1800 (even fewer of the muleshops were). New entrants to the industry did not have to erect, or even lease, a whole mill. Robert Owen, who took over New Lanark from Dale and became one of the biggest spinners in the land, started with the lease of a factory in 1789, all of which he sublet, but for one room in which he employed three men. Furthermore, Arkwright lost his patents in 1781, which immediately slashed the cost of installing his machinery elsewhere.

The most cited example of capital deepening in the early Industrial Revolution must therefore be kept firmly in perspective. Large capital sums could be involved, but it was still relatively easy for the small man, be he merchant, engineer or craftsman, to enter the industry, particularly in partnership. In the 1790s most of the smaller mills and workshops of Lancashire were valued at no more than £1–2,000, including their stocks. The Yorkshire woollen mills operated on a similar scale. Ease of entry was one of the main reasons for the vigour of the cotton trade around Manchester and Glasgow. New men were constantly improving pieces of machinery, inventing new processes, adding new product designs. And it was the reason for the vigour of many branches of industrial activity in the late eighteenth century.

There were some other industries in which large sums of fixed capital were sometimes used. The iron industry is the most notable of these. Even in its charcoal stage, the investment in equipment was not inconsiderable: the blast furnace, water wheels to drive bellows and forge hammers, tools and casting moulds. The first coke-based works at Coalbrookdale, started with an investment of £3,500. The large Dowlais works at Merthyr was founded with £4,000 capital in the late 1760s. But it was the reorganisation of iron works into large-scale integrated concerns, with furnaces, forges and manufactories all on the one site, that really increased capital outlays. The Scottish Carron works was the first to be built on this principle, having four coke blast furnaces, a double charcoal forge and a barring mill on the new site near Falkirk, with an improved (but well established) rolling and slitting mill outside Edinburgh. The company was started in 1759 with £12,000 capital, provided by seven partners. This was extended to £50,000 in 1764, and £130,000 in 1773, making Carron by far the most capitalised enterprise in Britain at the time. But it was symptomatic of the rising capital needs in an industry undergoing rapid expansion in the second half of the eighteenth century. These needs were further extended by the gradual introduction of the steam engine into iron making and finishing, as a reliable means of driving bellows, hammers, rolling and nailing mills.

The silk industry operated with large sums of fixed capital. It was the first branch of textile manufacture to adopt spinning machinery, using designs pirated by the Lombe brothers from Italy. Thomas Lombe completed his Derby silk mill in 1721 – it was the first real factory in Britain – and with its great 23 feet diameter water wheel driving machinery on five floors, it was said to represent an investment of £30,000 (plate B3). About ten other silk mills, on a similar scale, were erected in the next 50 years. Some of the water-powered paper mills represented large investments, and a few of the London breweries were very big. Whitbread's plant and machinery was valued at £20,000 in the 1740s, and Truman's at about £30,000 in 1760.

Where did the necessary money for investment in fixed capital come from? After the Bubble Act of 1720, passed in the wake of the collapse of the speculative South Sea Company in the previous year, the company form of enterprise in manufacturing industry was virtually outlawed. Limitation of liability, raising money publicly on the Stock Exchange and transferable shares were all forbidden, except in the unlikely case of their being granted by Royal Charter, Letters Patent or Act of Parliament. It seems that no-one was particularly concerned about this, and Adam Smith voiced the contemporary opinion when he stated that joint-stock enterprise was only proper for public utilities. The only widespread use of this type of business enterprise was for canal companies, each set up by private Act, although the great trading companies (such as the East India and Hudson's Bay Company) that had been incorporated before 1720 continued to operate. The Bubble Act was not repealed until 1825.

Most eighteenth century enterprises were either partnerships or family firms. Richard Arkwright was partnered initially by the wealthiest hosier in Nottingham, and by Jedidiah Strutt. In the 1780s he and David Dale of New Lanark were in partnership for a while. Josiah Wedgwood, the famous potter, was partnered by Thomas Bentley, an established Liverpool merchant, and James Watt joined forces with Matthew Boulton, who operated the Soho Manufactory outside Birmingham. The new ironworks were usually owned by partnerships: those in South Wales, for example, by ironmasters, Bristol and London merchants and capitalists. Established firms could borrow money on bond, a popular means of finance for transport undertakings such as turnpike trusts and river navigations too, and this liberated many small sums from gentry, tradesmen, clergy and widows. A further source was the mortgage, often used by those landowners who developed mines on their estates and small landholders, such as those in the West Riding, engaged in manufacturing activities. But it was ploughed-back profits that provided much of the money for fixed capital. Profits could be extremely high: up to a 100 per cent return to capital for some firms in the early days of cotton spinning, and as high as 30–80 per cent of receipts in coal mining. It seems that there was no overall shortage of capital in eighteenth-century Britain. Interest rates actually fell from about six per cent in 1700 to three and a half per cent by 1750, and fluctuated thereafter, not reaching five per cent until the late 1790s. Fixed capital needs rose slowly, and generally could be accommodated without undue pressure on credit.

Most firms, however, did not hold the major part of their capital in fixed plant, rather it was in *circulating*, or *working capital*. Fixed capital stock expanded in the early Industrial Revolution partly because the proportion of working capital could be reduced, as the production process speeded up. Improving roads and the use of steam engines helped to ease seasonal restraints on production. This enabled stocks to be reduced, as did the maintenance of closer contact with suppliers, and speedier marketing, both dependent on better communications. But even in the more heavily capitalised branches of industry, it was still stocks and credit owing to the firm that made up the largest share of capital. Truman's brewery had total assets of £100,000 in excess of its fixed capital of £30,000, and this structure was not untypical of other branches of industry, including cotton spinning. It is interesting that both Adam Smith, and another great classical economist, David Ricardo, assumed in their models of growth that the only form of capital that mattered was circulating capital.[5]

In financing this part of industrial capital, middlemen such as merchants and dealers within the trade were very important, and in the second half of the eighteenth century, provincial bankers too.[6] The age-old domestic outworking systems in the textile and iron trades were financed by merchant entrepreneurs. Cotton brokers and agents in the ports generally advanced credit to the spinning firms of anything between two and eight months. The spinners themselves advanced stocks on credit to the weavers. Iron and steel factors advanced raw materials on credit to the metal-working firms. The whole financial structure of industry was a complex interaction.

## Labour

In keeping with the modest capital requirements of much of industry, *labour* requirements too were generally not large, although they were slowly altering. Industrial labour was to be found not only in the towns, but also scattered in small pockets through the countryside. Rural industrial activity had developed, often long before 1700, as small farmers struggled to supplement incomes from their holdings, and as villages sought to provide employment for growing populations. Hence industry was often meeting a labour requirement, rather than the other way round: in the ironworking trades of the Midland heaths, in the knitting areas of the East Midlands and Yorkshire dales, in cloth and leather production throughout the country.

Many of these rural industries were controlled from the towns by outworking systems. Outworking originated in late medieval times as merchants began to seek out cheap supplies of country labour to enable them to meet the rising demand for goods (which in the case of woollens, was growing steadily from the fifteenth century with the expansion of English overseas trade.) The merchant supplied the yarn or raw materials on credit to rural cottagers to be spun, woven or whatever. It was distributed by overseers, who later collected the finished product. Often the merchant owned the loom or tools as well. This was how the Wiltshire cloth weaving industry operated, as did the Bradford worsted trade, Lancashire mixtures weaving, and the Scottish linen business. Halifax woollens were produced by independent masters, however, as Defoe's description shows (above, p. 80).

Outworking persisted in many of these areas through the early Industrial Revolution. In 1791, Glasgow cotton merchants were employing 15,000 hand loom weavers. Hayne and Co., the biggest hosiers in Nottingham, had 1,000 knitting frames working up to 16 miles from the town in 1812. One Blackburn spinning firm was putting out to 770 domestic weavers in 1788. Lancashire domestic weaving had been reorganised along more modern lines by then, however. In many areas, weavers' workshops or sheds had been established, usually containing at least 20 looms, but some with as many as 200. Sir Robert Peel, who owned or was a partner in 20 mills by the early 1800s, had 15 of these weaving depots as far apart as Blackburn, Liverpool, Stockport and the Peak. It was a method that enabled him, and other cotton spinners, to keep much closer control over the quality of weaving.

The bigger, centralised labour forces were to be found in the more capitalised branches of industry and those where close supervision of workers was desirable, because of the need to maintain quality, precision, or constant operation of machinery. Matthew Boulton saw the advantages of the factory system as keeping the workpeople 'under our eyes and immediate management . . . . everyday and almost every hour'. Lombe's Derby silk mill had about 300 workers, and Arkwright's first mill in Nottingham employed a similar number. There were 800 workers at his two Cromford mills by 1780. Sir Robert Peel's 20 mills had no less than 15,000 workers in 1803. The biggest cotton printers in the country, Livesey, Hargreaves and Co. of Blackburn, were employing between 700 and 1,000 shortly before they went bankrupt in 1788. Most cotton firms were very much smaller, but these figures were certainly not untypical of the larger ones. A Parliamentary Committee, sitting in 1815–16, was told that Robert Owen had between 1,600 and 1,700 workers at New Lanark, the Strutts at Belper, some 1,500, and McConnel and Kennedy, the biggest spinners in Manchester – 1,020.

The problem of these large workforces, however, was not their size: it was their adaption to the more rigorous, and often alien, work system of factory and mill. Initial labour recruitment seems to have been little problem in the towns, but in the countryside it was a different story. Richard Arkwright soon found that the domestic workers around Cromford had little interest in exchanging their free-will work habits for the discipline of the machinery-controlled mill. He had to advertise in the town newspapers, the *Derby Mercury* and *Nottingham Journal*, and in the end hired most of his workers from Manchester and Nottingham. David Dale sent agents throughout the Highlands to fill the workforce for New Lanark, and many impoverished Highlanders came, attracted by the offer of high wages and cheap housing, from Inverness, Caithness and Argyll. But in both town and country, firms found it hard to retain a stable workforce. The Highlander at a loom was described as 'a deer in the plough'. Mondays and Tuesdays were bad days for attendance, just as they were slack days for domestic workers. Harvest time often claimed a large share of the workforce. Wedgwood had continual trouble with stoppages during the Wakes. But machinery had to be used continuously, and irregular attendance had often to be followed by dismissal or the threat of it. McConnel and Kennedy, an enlightened firm, replaced about 20 spinners a week – a full 100 per cent turnover in a year. These large labour forces were very volatile: amongst both the skilled and unskilled.

Various ways of combating this problem were tried. In the early years of factory employment, many firms used long-term contracts. These were a hangover of pre-industrial bonds. In the Scottish coalfields, miners had long been bound to their pits for life in a kind of feudal serfdom: a system that was not abolished until Acts were passed in 1775 and 1799, under pressure of acute labour shortages. On the north-eastern coalfield, a one year bond was traditional, and widespread there amongst other workers, such as keelmen, salters and fileworkers. Ambrose Crowley bound his men for six months, Arkwright for three, Boulton at Soho for between three and five years, some cotton mills for over five. But such systems were gradually abolished in the face of their failure to stabilise the workforce. A second method, suitable for retaining a core of hands, was the use of unfree labour. The association of factory discipline and workhouse was the particular stigma of the mills, although very rarely did pauper labour account for more than one-third of the roll of a firm. McConnell voiced a widespread opinion when he said that pauper labour is 'more expensive than paid labour . . . and troublesome, inconvenient . . . and objectionable in almost every point of view'. Pauper labour had to be housed, and it had to be retained in situations where inefficient paid labour would often have been dismissed. Nevertheless, it was one way of maintaining a core of labour. Many of the paupers were children, although most child labourers were not paupers: rather they were employed, or bound in ordinary apprenticeships. The proportions of young people in many industries was very high: typically around 40 per cent of cotton mill workers were under 18. At New Lanark, in 1793, 18 per cent of the labour force was nine year old or less. In 1816, 30 per cent of Wedgwood's employees were under 18. In the silk mills, the proportion was up to two-thirds.

The bulk of the adult labour force, however, had to be sought out and retained in ways that have since become conventional: attractions, inducements, bonuses. Wages in the factories were appreciably higher than in domestic trades, and the work was regular. In the mines, wages were a little higher again. Many firms provided their own houses: usually at least a row of cottages, but some built whole model communities, such as Arkwright at Cromford, the Strutts at Belper, Oldknow at Mellor. The acme of this sort of development was Robert Owen's New Lanark (plate B6). Arkwright's village had spacious homes with allotments, a school and chapels for weekend use, and – rather unusual facilities in the factory colonies – an inn and market. Arkwright recognised the former cottage way of life of many of his Cromford workers by providing space enough for them to keep a cow and some pigs each. Many works, however, had their own farm to maintain a supply of fresh food for their employees and fodder for their horses. Ambrose Crowley had a works farm, as did Coalbrookdale, and the Plymouth and Cyfarthfa ironworks. Samuel Oldknow employed a gardener at Mellor to work a three acre plot to grow vegetables, and the Strutts at Belper did this for a time too. Many companies provided their own shops, and these were often used to pay part of the wage packet in kind, a system that achieved notoriety under the term 'truck', and persisted, particularly in mining communities, even after being outlawed by the Truck Act of 1817. Sometimes truck was outright exploitation and simply a source of extra profits but very often it was forced on firms by the shortages of coins in the provinces with which to pay wages. (below, p. 173). Company shops were a service in isolated communities, and could be used advantageously to secure cheap wholesale orders. Some firms also provided medical assistance, by means of a small wage deduction. This was common in the Cornish tin mines, the dockyards and some Welsh ironworks, and Boulton operated such a scheme at Soho. In the coalmining villages Friendly Societies formed by the miners themselves often provided this service, and the weekly subscription was used to support a fund from which payments of five or six shillings a week were paid to sick or unemployed miners.

All firms spent most effort on attempting to retain the small proportion of their workforces that was skilled: it was these men who were paid most, and got the best housing. Cotton mills needed a core of machinery engineers and skilled operatives: New Lanark's machine shop alone employed 87 men. Only about one eighth of Arkwright's Cromford labour force was male: these were the skilled staff, the rest were unskilled assistants and ancillary labour. Nevertheless, industry depended upon its skilled workers and much effort was spent in training them. Even so, skills were perpetually short, trained workers were almost as mobile as the rest, and managers had a continuous job to find them. Boulton and Watt had to train their own engineers, and were usually understaffed at Soho, as well as finding it difficult to secure adequate men to erect their steam engines at their destination. Wedgwood trained his own potters, and had to search continually for good painters around the country. There was a great deal of competition for skills between firms, sometimes amounting to direct poaching. But it was in this way, with the movement of skills between centres and regions, that the essential arts of industry in the early Industrial Revolution were diffused.

The later years of the eighteenth century hence saw the gradual assembly of large-scale workforces in the more capitalised branches of industry, a trend that did eventually supplant the domestic outworking systems, the predominant form of industrial organisation in most trades before the early Industrial Revolution. The essential problem was one of adapting workers to the rigorous regime demanded by the new factories, mills and large mines. Standards of living as a whole undoubtedly rose; what happened to the quality of life is another matter. In some firms, for some workers, it was certainly appalling, but for society as a whole, the shift from the freedom of cottage or craft into a big machine as just a small cog must have had its difficulties and disappointments.

## Entrepreneurship

The remaining factor of production, and of the greatest importance as the scale of operations increased, was *entrepreneurship*. The most successful firms, industries and regions were led by men who saw the potential of a new market, then organised a means of exploiting it, often using innovatory techniques, and could marshall the finance to support both production and selling. Most entrepreneurs were not inventors, but innovators who successfully seized the new opportunities around them.

Richard Arkwright is often applauded as one of the great inventors of the early Industrial Revolution. But his role as an innovator and organiser is much more central to his achievement in the cotton spinning industry. The basic design of his water frame and carding engine had been worked out by others: he improved them so that they became viable pieces of machinery, in fact, vital components in the mass production of cotton yarn for a growing market. He also did not invent the factory. But he used it very successfully as a means of controlling mass production, keeping his fixed capital working 24 hours a day with the introduction of 12-hour shifts. He also went some way towards organising a large scale, modern workforce, with his bonus and welfare schemes, and community building. Nevertheless, one of the reasons why the East Midlands cotton industry, including Arkwright's firm, had succumbed to Lancashire competition by 1800 was because he and others had slipped into a kind of entrepreneurial complacency, and failed to capitalise on later innovations. It was the Lancashire entrepreneurs, many of them small workshop operators, who grasped the opportunity to use the mule, and produce the finer grade yarns that the market was demanding by the 1790s, much finer grades that Arkwright's water frame could manage.

Part of the entrepreneurial function thus lay in organising a suitable means of production. Another facet of this was the training or hiring of skilled operatives. An apprenticeship with Boulton and Watt was the engineer's passport to a job anywhere in Britain, and entrepreneurs elsewhere constantly sought out such men. Coalbrookdale was the training ground of those skilled in coke-iron casting and founding. The Carron Company in Scotland succeeded technically because it hired experienced workers from Coalbrookdale, from the Wealden gunfoundries and even as far away as Sweden right at the outset. The South Wales ironworks recruited widely in the Midlands, Yorkshire, and amongst themselves. In turn, South Wales became the source of those skilled in puddling. Manchester supplied much of the expertise in textile machinery. One reason why the Scottish cotton industry prospered so rapidly in and around Glasgow was because most of the necessary skills were supplied by workers from Lancashire. The copper smelting firms of Swansea, early in the century, learnt by recruiting from Cornwall.

A critical part of the entrepreneurial function lay, however, in seizing a market opportunity. The cotton textile industry was so successful because it satisfied a basic market need, for clothing and furnishings, with a cheap, good quality product. The Lancashire mills flourished by supplying middle-and working-class tastes, whilst the Glasgow mills flourished by building on a local tradition of high quality output, and so serving the upper end of the market. Carron and the new South Wales ironworks were successful as they won the most important cast iron market, that for cannon, and used it as a base on which to build a bridge into the expanding domestic market. Boulton and Watt answered a need for a larger and more reliable source of power with their steam engine. Other firms were successful because they helped to create a new trend or fashion. Abraham Darby III demonstrated that iron could be used as a building material in his famous Ironbridge, and Josiah Wedgwood carefully cultivated a market that rapidly became devoted to his fashionable designs. All firms wishing to remain successfully in the market retained agents to keep them in touch with consumers. Many used outriders and travelling pedlars, whilst the bigger ones had their own representatives, warehouses and even showrooms in the provincial towns and London.

These entrepreneurial functions were often exercised over considerable distances. By 1800, and in some cases, very much earlier, the extent of many firms' spatial relations was very wide. Outworking systems operated over a local or regional sphere of production, although periodic sales were made over greater distances, to London or to one of the big fairs. But the new, large firms often had both large producer areas, and a wide, permanently operative marketing structure. Arkwright, at the peak of his enterprise, had seven mills in Nottingham and Derbyshires, plus one in Manchester, one in Keighley, two in the West Midlands, and interests in Scotland. McConnell and Kennedy, the great Manchester spinners, bought their cotton in Liverpool and London, and used Lancashire weavers to work the coarser yarns, whilst selling the finer grades to Scottish merchants. Wedgwood employed travelling salesmen from his Etruria factory, and maintained permanent showrooms in London, Bristol, Liverpool and Dublin. Boulton and Watt sent Soho engineers to follow up enquiries from potential customers, and kept permanent agents in their main sales regions to instal and maintain their steam engines. Such widespread producing and marketing organisation was made possible by the improvement of communications and the relative ease of travel and information flow in the early Industrial Revolution. But a particularly impressive example of spatial organisation, impressive because it long precedes and fore-shadows the trend, comes from the early 1700s. In 1710 Abraham Crowley was the largest iron-monger in Europe. He had set up ironworks and a warehouse on the Tyne in the late seventeenth century, hiring several of his skilled workers from Liege, in Belgium. He had another warehouse at Bromsgrove which was the hub of an extensive domestic nail-working business. He had five London warehouses, stores at all the naval dockyards, and provincial warehouses at Ware, Walsall, and Wolverhampton. Crowley controlled the whole enterprise by orders sent through the post from his house at Greenwich, on the Thames.

The entrepreneur has been described as fulfilling 'in one person the functions of capitalist, financier, works manager, merchant and salesman'. All these functions had long been present in British society, as had one other: technical skill. But in the early Industrial Revolution, there emerged a type, a class of men (albeit very varied) who could organise the various facets of industrial enterprise to exploit the widening and deepening market of the times.

Watchmaking was an important trade in eighteenth-century England. By 1800, 120,000 watches were being made in London each year. The necessary precision skills had been known and used since Elizabeth's time: it was a craft, and one that depended upon a personal service between customer and craftsman. Matthew Boulton minted the first copper penny in 1797. Two years later his Soho manufactory had made no less than 45 million copper pennies: a feat of mass production for a mass market. The early Industrial Revolution in Britain was a period of transition. The 120,000 beautifully produced, handmade watches were a symbol of her pre-industrial past; the 45 million copper pennies were a symbol of her industrial future.

## NOTES

1 Detailed annual accounts of the quantity and value of imports and exports were kept from 1697 onwards. At first goods were valued at current prices but this practice was abandoned for most goods by 1703. Thereafter trade values for the most part are simply recorded at 'official prices', i.e. circa 1700 market prices. The whole series is therefore almost all at constant prices, which makes it a good volume index

but not a good measure of absolute changes in the value of trade. Over the century as a whole, the use of official prices certainly underestimates the rise in the money value of trade. A further difficulty concerns the effects of smuggling, which is considered to have lowered the value of official imports quite considerably in the 1730s and early 1740s, and again from the mid-1760s until the early 1780s (when Pitt reformed the customs and reduced tariffs).
These problems are discussed lucidly in Deane and Cole (1967) pp. 42–5.

2  Changes in the structure of the retail market are discussed in chapter seven below.

3  This was not the only reason Arkwright moved to Cromford. Chapman suggests that he chose it as he was familiar with the area, having been an itinerant trader there, and because it seemed 'an appropriate destination for the gratification of his social ambition', (i.e. to join landed society). The important point, however, is that the use of water power enabled Arkwright, and others like him, to be flexible in their choice of locations: centralised or remote.

4  There were also important concentrations of wool textile manufacture in two areas well removed from coalfields: around Norwich and in Gloucestershire/Wiltshire. Clothiers here had to rely on hand driven machinery and the water wheel, although steam engines were introduced in the nineteenth century (below, pp. 108–9).

5  Ricardo's *Principles of Political Economy and Taxation* was first published in 1817. In fact, in the third edition (1821), he included a chapter 'Of Machinery' at the end of the book.

6  The role of the bankers is discussed below (pp. 174–5). The banking system was of great importance as a means of channelling funds from surplus areas (generally the agricultural counties of the south and east) to deficit areas (the industrialising regions).

## FURTHER READING

The evidence for the growth of industry in the eighteenth century is best summarised by Deane and Cole, chapter two, and that for overseas trade by W. E. Minchinton, in his Introduction to *The Growth of English Overseas Trade in the 17th and 18th Centuries* (1969).

### THE GROWTH OF DEMAND

This is not a well documented subject, but see 'Patterns of Demand, 1750–1914' by Minchinton, chapter two in C. M. Cipolla (ed.): *The Fontana Economic History of Europe, The Industrial Revolution* (1973); T. S.

Ashton, 'Changes in Standards of Comfort in Eighteenth Century England', in *The Proceedings of The British Academy* vol. XLI (1955); and chapter three, of John Burnett: *A History of the Cost of Living* (1969). Two rather more analytical articles are D. E. C. Eversley, 'The Home Market and Economic Growth in England, 1750–80', in E. L. Jones and G. E. Mingay (eds.): *Land, Labour and Population in the Industrial Revolution* (1967); and E. W. Gilboy, 'Demand as a Factor in the Industrial Revolution', reprinted in R. M. Hartwell (ed.): *The Causes of the Industrial Revolution in England* (1967).

THE NATURE OF INDUSTRY

A useful short summary for the preceding period, to set the scene, is D. C. Coleman: *Industry in Tudor and Stuart England* (1975). On rural industries, see 'Industries in the Countryside by Joan Thirsk, in F. J. Fisher (ed.): *Essays in the Economic History of Tudor and Stuart England* (1961). The Hoffmann estimates are from W. G. Hoffmann: *British Industry 1700–1950* (trans. 1955). A picture of contemporary industrial landscape is best gained by examining some original maps, such as those by William Yates for Staffordshire (1775), or Lancashire (1786), the latter in an edited edition by J. B. Harley (1968).

CHANGING FACTORS OF PRODUCTION

Much of the material for this section can be found in the standard sources on particular industries, referenced at the end of chapter five. A short and useful illustration of most of the points for cotton textiles is S. D. Chapman: *The Cotton Industry in the Industrial Revolution* (1972).

On raw materials, see E. A. Wrigley: 'The Supply of Raw Materials in the Industrial Revolution', *Ec. H. R.* vol. XV (1962), reprinted in Hartwell (1967). On power, see J. R. Harris: 'The Employment of steampower in the eighteenth century', *History* LII (1967), A. E. Musson and E. H. Robinson: 'The early growth of steampower', *Ec. H. R.* vol. XI (1959), and J. Tann: 'The employment of Power in the West of England wool textile industry, 1790–1840', in N. B. Harte and K. G. Ponting (eds): *Textile History and Economic History* (1973) which has some useful material on steam and water power. The transfer from charcoal to coke in the iron industry is discussed by C. K. Hyde: 'The Adoption of Coke-Smelting by the British Iron Industry, 1709–90', in *Explorations in Entrepreneurial History* vol. 10 (1973).

A valuable essay on capital is Phyllis Deane's: 'The Role of Capital in the Industrial Revolution', in *Explorations in Economic History* vol. 10 (1973). The other useful articles on this topic are gathered together in F. Crouzet (ed.): *Capital Formation in the Industrial Revolution* (1972). On sources of finance, see the section on banking in chapter seven below. B. L. Anderson: 'Provincial Aspects of the Financial Revolution of the Eighteenth Century', *Business History* vol. XI (1969) deals with the mortgage as a means of raising credit.

The best source on the adaptation of labour to factory conditions is chapter five of Sidney Pollard's book: *The Genesis of Modern Management* (1965). N. McKendrick's article: 'Josiah Wedgwood and factory discipline', *Hist. Jnl.* vol. 4 (1961), is useful and the following two articles should be consulted: E. P. Thompson: 'Time, Work-Discipline and Industrial Capitalism', *Past and Present* no. 37 (1967), and A. W. Coats: 'Changing Attitudes to Labour in the mid-eighteenth century', *Ec. H. R.* vol. XI (1955). Both are reprinted in *Essays in Social History*, (eds.) M. W. Flinn and T. C. Smout (1974). More detail on particular industries can be found in such books as S. D. Chapman's: *The Early Factory Masters* (1967), about cotton textiles, and Brian Lewis: *Coal Mining in the Eighteenth and Nineteenth Centuries* (1971). Coleman (1975) discusses outworking systems.

Entrepreneurship is also well covered by individual business histories, a list of which is provided at the end of chapter five. But see 'The Entrepreneur in the Industrial Revolution' by Charles Wilson, in *History* vol. 62 (1957), N. McKendrick: 'Josiah Wedgwood: An Eighteenth Century Entrepreneur in Salesmanship and Marketing Techniques', *Ec. H. R.* vol. XII (1960), and E. Robinson: 'Eighteenth Century Commerce and Fashion: Matthew Boulton's Marketing Techniques', *Ec. H. R.* vol. XVI (1963).

A first-rate reference on technological change, a process which concerned all factors of production in industry, is David S. Landes' book: *The Unbound Prometheus* (1969). Two other standard sources are A. E. Musson and Eric Robinson: *Science and Technology in the Industrial Revolution* (1969), and the collection of articles edited by A. E. Musson: *Science, Technology and Economic Growth in the Eighteenth Century* (1972). A useful reference is *A History of Technology. vol. IV: The Industrial Revolution* (1958), (ed.) Charles Singer et. al. It has good straightforward chapters on the steam engine (six), watermills and wheels (seven), and textile machinery (ten).

# 5 The Basic Industries

The industrial picture of the eighteenth century was very different to that of mid- and late-Victorian years, by which time the steam-powered mine and factory, and machinery, ships and railways of iron and steel had led Britain to her peak as the 'workshop of the world'. Yet by 1800, the foundations of the country's later prominence had been laid, and the framework of success, both in individual industries and regions, was plainly evident. Throughout the century, and with increasing speed towards its close, industrial change was taking place on a broad front. In some cases, this meant the expansion, in continuity, of age-old activities, such as Tyneside coal-mining, West Riding woollen manufacture, Lancashire cottons or the linen industry of eastern Scotland. In others, it meant the rapid emergence of new activities, of which the Glasgow cotton industry and South Wales ironmaking were prime examples. But for many it spelt demise, as other products and regions seized the initiative. The early Industrial Revolution saw decline as well as growth, as the ironmasters of the Weald and Forest of Dean, the Company of Framework Knitters in London, or the clothiers of Suffolk, Berkshire and Devon would have testified.

The eighteenth century witnessed, therefore, a realignment of industrial activity. Those firms, industries and regions that best satisfied the basic market needs of the time, and were best equipped to meet the widening and deepening of demand, grew rapidly. To a large extent, the expanding industrial areas were away from the prosperous agricultural ones. This was not coincidental. Industry had developed in many areas of poor or marginal farming, where alternative or complementary means of employment were needed. And those areas with coal and water power often had poor soils and steep, high relief unsuited to agriculture. This was so in much of the Lancashire and West Riding textile areas, on the heaths of the West Midlands, where the metal trades flourished, and in the South Wales iron and coalfield. All these examples, although separate from areas of prosperous farming were by no means remote from them. However, a basic regional 'division of space' was beginning to emerge: between industrialising east Lancashire and the agricultural west, between upland Glamorgan and its vale, between west and east Nottinghamshire, for instance.

The textile industries – cotton, wool and worsted, linen and silk – were the most important group of manufactures. They had been for a very long time (in particular wool), and in 1800, still accounted for the largest share of industrial output, employment and exports. Ironmaking and the metal working trades were growing rapidly. In both these groups there were fundamental regional realignments in the eighteenth century. Then there was mining, especially of coal. This chapter is concerned mainly with these three groups. These were the 'basic' industries, basic in the sense that they were the foundation of the wealth of Britain's industrial sector in the nineteenth century.

### The Cotton Industry

The cotton industry is the most spectacular example of success in the early Industrial Revolution. By 1795, John Aikin could claim that its growth was 'perhaps absolutely unparalleled in the annals of trading nations'. The speed of this expansion is shown in figure 5:1, which graphs retained raw cotton imports (the best available measure of the industry's growth) on a logarithmic scale. Output statistics for the West Riding woollen industry and the Scottish linen industry are also graphed, and a comparison of these three curves indicates that it was cotton that experienced the most rapid growth rate in the eighteenth century. In fact, because the industry gradually increased the efficiency with which it used its raw material, the graph underestimates the rate of change of cotton textiles production.[1] Although cotton did not take off until relatively late, by the 1800s its output was as great as that of the woollen industry (table 4:2), and its exports were worth more.

The techniques of cotton spinning and weaving were brought to England by Flemish refugees, who had settled in Norwich and Manchester by the turn of the seventeenth century. The raw cotton was imported from the Middle East and Cyprus, and by the 1750s, from Brazil too. For a long time it was used only in cloth 'mixtures' with linen, or to a lesser extent, silk. Lancashire, which had had a woollen industry since the fourteenth century, imported Irish flax to make a linen/cotton cloth known as 'fustian'. The finer silk/cotton mixtures were called 'bombazines'. As late as 1772, Manchester's directory listed 76 fustian manufacturers, 49 making checks, 44 making small-ware, nine making woollen cloth and eight making silk/linen cloths, but no pure cotton manufacturers.

The rapid expansion of the industry in the late eighteenth century was therefore built on more than 150 years of experience in working the material. It was experience of great value as market conditions became more

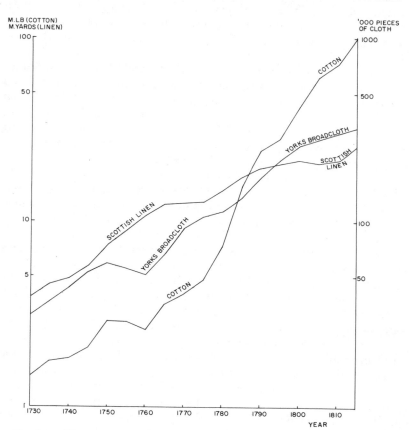

Fig. 5:1  *The Growth of the Textile Industries 1730–1815. Source*: Mitchell and Deane: *An Abstract of British Historical Statistics* (1962). Drawn from data in tables 1, 10 and 18 (Textiles section).

favourable for cotton cloths from early in the century. In 1700, the import of attractive, brightly coloured Indian calicoes was forbidden, and in 1721, wearing them was forbidden as well. Neither ban was very effective, but they did enable home producers gradually to penetrate a wide home market. The cotton boom was the result of the rapid expansion of this market after 1750. However, it was permitted by the technological advances in cotton spinning in the 1770s, and sustained by the elasticity of supply of the raw material from overseas.

These technological breakthroughs in spinning have already been described (above, pp. 86–8) Arkwright's water frame, and the mule, enabled vast quantities of good yarn to be made, and made cheaply. Both machines could spin a cotton warp thread that was strong enough for the weaving loom, so that pure, lightweight cotton cloths, of quality, but low in price, could be produced. They found a great substitute market as cheap woollen cloths were necessarily coarse and heavy, whilst lighter worsteds were very expensive. One despairing woollen merchant was led to cry, in 1782, that 'the ladies think no more of woollens than of an old almanac'! For clothing and furnishings, cotton was ideal. Plain cotton cloth was selling for 2½d a yard in the early nineteenth century, whilst colourful printed designs could be had for 4d a yard. At these prices, even the poorest people could afford to buy their clothing and sheets, so it was a market that was rapidly widening too. Sir Robert Peel, in 1786, said that 'three parts out of four of printed goods are consumed by the lower class of people'. Certainly it was the middle and working classes that provided the bulk of the industry's customers. And probably two-thirds of its output between the 1770s and 1790s was sold within Britain.

Mass home demand, then, was the foundation of the cotton industry's success. But it was by no means only a mass product industry. Continuous improvements to the mule enabled finer and finer yarns to be spun – qualities in excess of counts of 300 were being achieved by 1800, whereas Arkwright at his peak had never managed more than 60, itself an immense stride over the 20s of the jenny. Hence by the 1790s, the upper class end of the market was being won too, with colourful calicoes and fine muslins. Potential overseas consumers also succumbed, and the earlier trading ratio was reversed so solidly that by the 1800s, two-thirds of the industry's output was being sent overseas. But it was the cheaper cloths that remained the basis of the industry's fortunes: an estimate made in 1815 showed that over half the yarn spun was still of no. 40 count or lower.

The whole hectic pace of expansion was sustained, however, by the supply of raw cotton from overseas. After the conclusion of its War of Independence, America became increasingly important in this respect. The introduction of the mechanical cotton gin in the 1790s was a great advance and coupled with the expansion of potential cotton acreage in the south after the Louisiana Purchase in 1803, much increased the elasticity and scale of supply. The USA cotton crop expanded from 2 million pounds to 182 millions between 1791 and 1821.

The three important cotton producing regions were Lancashire, the Peak districts of Derbyshire and Nottingham, and the country around Glasgow. Norwich retained a minor interest in cotton, for use in cloth mixtures, and had 15 cotton firms in 1810. Leeds, too, had a few and there were scattered mills in North Wales and the West Midlands. Each of the three main regions had a foundation of textile expertise: the mixtures business in Lancashire, framework knitting in the East Midlands and linen in Glasgow. But it was entrepreneurial choice and drive that picked out these three regions for cotton, and moulded their subsequent fortunes within the industry. The East Midlands had the first real cotton mills, as it was here that Arkwright chose to set up his vast roller spinning (water frame) machinery, and entered into his partnership with Strutt. Yet within 15 years, in 1784, Lancashire with 41 water driven mills, had as many as Derbyshire (22) and Nottinghamshire (17) combined. And Lancashire had in addition a great number of smaller workshops, using the jenny, and then the mule. The trade around Manchester possessed a vitality of small manufacturers that the remote dale-bound mills of the Peak could not hope to share. It was Manchester that became the centre of exchange of ideas for improvements to machinery, to the finishing trades of bleaching, dyeing and printing, for fashions, and the centre of marketing and credit. Lancashire was well served by its canal network to Liverpool, which after 1795 rapidly overtook London as the main port of entry for raw cotton.

The mills of the East Midlands were scattered, and many were isolated, so they missed these singular advantages. There were far fewer firms than in Lancashire, and they clung obstinately to Arkwright's roller spinning system, when Lancashire and the Scottish industry were long since producing the highly profitable fine yarns that were out of reach of the water frame. By 1816, Arkwright's son had rationalised his empire to include only three mills around Cromford, each producing only relatively coarse yarn. The gradual transfer to steam power in the industry merely accentuated the gap between the Lancashire firms, located on a coalfield, and those of the East Midlands, many of which were distant from one. Forty-two steam engines were at work in the Lancashire mills in 1800, against only 15 in Nottingham and one in Derbyshire.

The Scottish industry, meanwhile, enjoyed a climb to success no less rapid than that of Lancashire. Scotland was importing 150,000 lb. of cotton a year before the American wars. By 1800, this figure had reached five million. There were 39 mills in 1796, mostly within 25 miles of Glasgow, and no less than 120 by 1812. Much of the technology and expertise was borrowed straight from Lancashire. Robert Owen, who succeeded David Dale at New Lanark, came from Manchester. But Glasgow fulfilled a similar role to Manchester as a centre generating economies of agglomeration, and was very well positioned for the direct import of American cotton. The Scottish industry built on the local tradition of fine linen products, and as England had pre-empted the middle- and working-class end of the market south of the Border, concentrated on supplying the upper end, in particular muslins. After 1800, however, the Scottish mills moved down market, into the production of coarser cloths, to meet burgeoning home demand in their own country.

In 1783 the *London Magazine* reported that 'every servant girl has her cotton gown and her cotton stockings'. It was one of the triumphs of the early Industrial Revolution that she had.

## The Woollen Industry

The woollen industry, not unnaturally, was more than a little affected by the rapid growth of cotton. However, the effect was not as bad as the anonymous woollen merchant had feared in 1782. A Parliamentary Committee appointed to examine the state of the industry in 1806 felt that it could 'happily' report that 'it has been gradually increasing in almost all of the various parts of the Kingdom in which it is carried on; in some of them very rapidly'. But this statement tells nothing about very great changes that had taken place during the previous century.

Woollen cloth production was the main industrial occupation of medieval England, to Arthur Young in 1767 'supposed the sacred staple and foundation of all our wealth'. Half of its output was exported, and until the 1750s it accounted for about one-third of total industrial production. At the end of the American war, it still accounted for one-quarter. But during these years it was becoming more localised in production. Traditional cloth areas such as the Taunton–Exeter region and Suffolk declined very markedly, whilst cloth towns of former importance, such as Newbury, Reading, Salisbury and Worcester, lost their trade altogether. It became more and more concentrated in Wiltshire and Gloucestershire (particularly Stroudwater), in and around Norwich, and in the West Riding. Yet even the West Riding, which accounted for most of the industry's increase of output in the last quarter of the century, was expanding its production less quickly than that of cotton (fig. 5:1). The result was that from the 1780s, the relative position of wool textiles declined more rapidly, even though its output grew in absolute terms. By the 1800s, it accounted for about one-tenth of industrial production (table 4:2) as did cotton, and its exports were valued at a quarter of the British total.

The important distinction within the woollen industry was between woollen and worsted cloth. Woollen cloth was made from short fibres, carded in the same way as cotton, and often finished by fulling, to make the weave invisible. Worsteds were made of long wools, which were combed for spinning. They had the advantage of being much lighter than woollen cloth, and more easily adapted to machine working. Long wool sheep breeds were becoming increasingly popular, breeds such as the new Leicester developed by Bakewell and the Culleys, and the Spanish merino, championed at home by George III. But there were important short wool breeds too, the new Southdowns in particular.

Norfolk was the traditional centre of fashionable, light worsted production, a market which the West Riding moved into after 1700, although its cloth never rivalled that of Norfolk in quality. By 1770, three-quarters of the West Riding's output was in worsteds. The west of England was, and to a certain extent still is, the home of high quality, expensive woollen cloths and felts. In the face of increasingly capital-based competition from these regions, and from the cotton industry, the various cloths of other areas (some heavy, others flimsy) lost their markets. The baizes and kerseys of Colchester and Sudbury, Reading and Newbury, and the serges of Taunton and Exeter either went out of fashion or were outpriced. It was the serge industry that suffered the most spectacular decline after 1700, as the Suffolk and Berkshire industries were already small and withering. Serge was made of a woollen weft and a worsted warp, and became very popular in the seventeenth century because it was a relatively light cloth. £500,000-worth was exported from Exeter in 1700. But serge was neither as strong nor hard wearing as the Norwich or West Riding worsteds. By 1740, there was 'a trade but no profit' in Exeter, and by 1800, serge had ceased to be of any importance to the city.

Many differences between the woollen areas were apparent to Defoe as he toured the country in the early 1720s. He found Sudbury in Suffolk, once a great medieval woollens town, 'very populous and very poor'. He estimated that 120,000 people were employed in spinning and weaving in and around Norwich (probably an exaggeration, the figure being about 100,000 in 1800). There 'the inhabitants being all busie at their manufactures dwell in their garrets at their looms, and in their combing shops, twisting mills and other work houses, almost all the works they are employed in being done within doors'. In Wiltshire, he saw the manufacture of 'fine-medley, or mix'd cloths, such as are usually worn in England by the better sort of people, and, also, exported in great quantities'. And he found (giving an excellent description of the outworking system) 'innumerable villages, hamlets and scattered houses, in which, generally speaking, the spinning work of all their manufacture is performed by the poor people; and the master clothiers, who generally live in the greater towns, sending out the wool weekly to their houses, by their servants and horses, and at the same time, bringing back the yarn that they have spun and finished, which is then fitted for the loom'. But in the

West Riding, he made particular note, (above, p. 80) of the independent small master clothiers, of 'the noble scene of industry and application', and of their three channels of consumption. These were the 'true' merchants, buying cloth in Leeds to fulfill specific overseas orders, the London merchants buying to sell in America and Russia, and most significantly, 'the home consumption, their goods being everywhere made use of, for the clothing the ordinary people, who cannot go to the price of the fine medley cloths made in the western counties of England'.

By the 1720s, therefore, the West Riding had the same ingredients that carried Lancashire to success. It was exploiting the mass home and overseas markets with good, cheap cloth, rather than the more limited luxury markets. Its price advantage at the end of the century was such that Norwich and West Country cloth was two to three times as expensive. It had a core of energetic, independent small industrialists, competitive and outward-looking. It had water power and coal, both used later to drive machinery, but also of importance for washing and dyeing the wool, and providing heat for the dyeing and bleaching shops. In 1700, the West Riding produced about 20 per cent of England's wool textiles output, and by 1800, about 60 per cent.

It was in the 1770s that the West Riding began to overhaul Norfolk as the most important wool textiles region in Britain. Its clothiers built on the widening mass demand of a growing population, and the call for soldiers' clothing and blankets in the Seven Years and American Wars. Domestic American demand replaced this after the peace, and by 1800, the United States was buying over half of the West Riding's blanket output. Altogether nearly three-quarters of the region's cloth production was being exported by then. The 1806 Committee estimated that 65,000 people were employed in the industry. Many of these worked as or for small masters, each manufactory taking the cloth through most or all of its production stages. Between 1780 and 1800, however, several hundred small scribbling mills[2], and maybe 30 worsted spinning mills, using the mule, were set up. Many of them were very small, but in the 1790s a few larger factories appeared, four or five in the Leeds district, and some in Huddersfield and Halifax. Most of these used water power. The first Boulton and Watt engine in the industry was bought by Benjamin Gott, of Leeds, in 1792. Eight steam engines were at work in the region's woollen mills by 1800. At this time, coal was selling in Leeds for only seven shillings per ton, whereas in Stroudwater, despite the canal, it cost eighteen to twenty-one shillings.

The Norfolk worsted industry quickly felt the force of West Riding competition. In the absence of any output statistics, it is difficult to know when its absolute growth stopped, but production may have been relatively stable from as early as 1770. Eden, in 1797, claimed that 'the Norwich trade had for some years been in a declining state'. The stagnation of the town's population growth supports this (below, p. 202). Norfolk could not provide sources of power to sustain large-scale machine spinning, and from the early 1800s, started to buy West Riding yarn. In 1810, there were 55 manufacturers in Norwich, 23 engaged in worsted production, 17 in silk and 15 in cotton, a diversity that was reflected in the increasing proportion of quality mixed cloths that was Norwich's reaction to competition. But this area retained its interests predominantly in the upper end of market, which was of course also being invaded by cotton textiles by this time.

West Country production was very much less important than that of either Norfolk or the West Riding. Stroudwater and Trowbridge maintained the manufacture of quality broadcloths, for which the market was also relatively stable. Firms reacted to competition by increasing their efficiency, and between 1795 and 1830, a number of spinning mills were set up. In Stroudwater, there were 23, great stone and brick structures, along four miles of the little River Frome, powered by large water wheels. The Stanley Mill (1813) received 200 horsepower from its wheels, and also has the distinction of being one of the earliest iron-framed factories. In Trowbridge, the river was too small for big wheels, and the woollen firms here were also some of Boulton and Watt's first customers in the woollen textiles industry.

These three regions were the main centres of British wool textiles production in the eighteenth century. However woollen goods were still produced on a small scale in nearly every county. One place that later came to be of some importance for its tweeds was Galashiels, in the Scottish Border. This was a very late development, the town having only 43 looms in 1790, but it was to be the woollen industry's most important centre in Scotland, which it has remained. There were nine mills in Galashiels by 1825. In Wales, there were no particular concentrations, although Montgomery, Merioneth and Denbighshires all had domestic industries of some note. In Merioneth for example, Aikin found in 1797 that 'almost every little farmer makes webs and few cottages in these parts are without a loom'. But the wool textiles mills of Newtown, Llandilloes and Llangollen belong to a later phase, of the 1830s and 1840s.

### Other Textile Industries

There were some other important branches of textile production, in particular linen, the silk industry and East Midlands framework knitting.

*Framework knitting* was a staple domestic industry in west Nottinghamshire, and parts of Leicestershire and Derbyshire. The handworked knitting machine was invented by a local cleric, the Rev. Thomas Lee, in 1589, but the early industry was centred in London, thriving alongside the Spitalfields silk trade. By the 1700s, however, it had begun to migrate away from the restrictive influence of the Company of Framework Knitters, to the cheap labour open villages around Nottingham, Leicester, Loughborough and Belper. These towns remained the chief putting out centres for the domestic industry. Significantly, it was never very extensive in the richer agricultural areas of eastern Nottingham and eastern Leicestershire. In the 1720s, there were about 8,000 frames in Britain, half of them here, and 2,500 in London. By the 1800s, there were over 20,000, with about 85 per cent being found in the East Midlands. Stockings and fine lace were the chief products of the industry, using silk (around Derby), cotton (around Nottingham and Belper), or wool/worsted (in Leicestershire). The basic sixteenth-century frame design was used until the 1860s, when it was finally adapted to steam power motion.

*Silk* production was of some importance, not because it comprised a large proportion of textile output (table 4:2), but because, firstly, it was used as a constituent of the fancier, fashion cloths, and secondly, it was for silk production that the earliest modern factories were erected. Silk working was originally introduced by Flemish weavers in the late sixteenth century, and greatly boosted by the arrival of Huguenot refugees from France in the 1680s. Many of them settled in Spitalfields, in east London, providing the early focus of the industry, but others went to Norwich, Coventry and Cheshire. Lombe had set up his Derby silk mill by 1721, and the town became the centre of the silk stocking outworking trade. In Stockport, there were several silk mills by the end of the century, supplying yarn to the fine cotton manufacturers for their bombazines. In Coventry, the speciality was silk ribbon production. In Norwich, silk was also an important component of the new and improved mixtures that emerged to combat the West Riding worsteds.

Of greater national significance than either the framework knitting or silk industries, however, was the *linen* industry, in both England and Scotland. Flax was grown throughout the country, and few towns were without a flax-dresser and linen-draper. In coastal areas, coarse linen was made for ships' sails, and some towns – in particular Warrington – became important specialist producers of sail-cloth. But in the early part of the century, most home-produced linen was of a coarse quality, whether made for sails or not, so that much of the linen cloth worn by the public was imported from Holland, Germany or France. Over the next century or so, however, the English industry grew to dominate Europe, both in quality and quantity, whilst the expansion of the Scottish industry was hardly less impressive.

The English industry early on received government assistance, with a preferential sales treatment in the colonies, export bounties, and limited prohibition of continental cloths. The import of Russian and German flax was encouraged, however, it being of higher quality than the domestic crop. But the industry's greatest boost came from its role as the partner in the cotton industry, providing a strong linen warp to mix with the cotton weft in fustian cloth, in the period before Arkwright had managed to spin a strong enough cotton substitute. The pace of growth inevitably slowed after this, from the 1780s onwards, but linen remained an important cloth for furnishings, smallwares, thread and fine clothing, as well as for sail and sack cloth. Knaresborough and Darlington were two important centres, the latter described as having a linen industry larger than that 'of any town in England' in the Universal British Directory in 1790. It was in Darlington that a patent for flax-spinning machinery was taken out in 1787. The biggest spinner in the trade, however, was John Marshall, who operated a factory in Leeds that overwhelmed even the factory of the famous wool-textile producer, Benjamin Gott. The firm of Marshalls maintained its pre-eminence from the 1790s up till the 1840s.

The Scottish industry, like the English, was a domestic activity, but it was the major domestic industry in the central lowlands in the first half of the century. It was badly affected by the removal of protective tariffs after the Act of Union in 1707. In 1727, however, a Commission 'for Improving Fisherys and Manufactures in Scotland' was set up, to spend some £20,000 set aside by the Act of Union for this purpose. Nearly half this amount was spent by the Commissioners in the next few years on the linen industry, in a vigorous drive to improve the quality and quantity of its output. Spinners, weavers and bleachers were brought from Holland to teach the Scots better techniques. By 1752, the Commissioners had sponsored the establishment of 24 spinning schools, and several new bleaching fields. The preparation of the fibre had been immeasurably improved by the development of scutching and heckling machines[3] based on continental designs, and the Commissioners encouraged these to be set up in 'lint mills'. There were four lint mills in 1732, and no less than 317 fifty years later, each serving communities of domestic linen workers. The lint mills were the beginnings of the transition away from the domestic system, although it was 1790 before spinning machinery was introduced, and there were only five spinning mills in Dundee – by then the main centre – in 1800. These mills had only 2,000 spindles altogether, a trifling proportion of the total in the Dundee area.

Eastern Scotland – mainly the counties of Fife, Forfar and Perth – had always produced more linen than the west. By the 1780s, and certainly by early in the next century, the east had asserted hegemony with the rise of the cotton trade in the west (table 5:1). The Glasgow area – the counties of Renfrew and Lanark – specialised in the mid-century years in the finer linen fabrics – the cambrics, gauzes and mixtures. Thus, although Lanark produced 2.4 million yards of cloth in 1770, only half that made in Forfar, its value at £193,000 exceeded that of the coarser Forfar cloths (£125,000), quite comfortably. The fine linen fabrics lost out in the competition with the Glasgow fine cottons, however, and as the table shows, the balance of production, by output and value, swung increasingly to the east with its coarser, cheap cloths.

TABLE 5:1    *The Scottish Linen Industry*

Returns of the Stampmaster of Linen Cloth, by selected counties.
Production figures in yards, and by value.

|  | 1727–8 | | 1767–8 | | 1821–2 | |
|---|---|---|---|---|---|---|
|  | yards | £ | yards | £ | yards | £ |
| LANARK | 272,659 | £9968 | 1,994,906 | £172,764 | 22,780 | £1951 |
| RENFREW | 85,527 | £6835 | 674,178 | £66,387 | 25,685 | £3107 |
| FIFE | 361,986 | £30,176 | 1,563,744 | £63,855 | 7,923,388 | £320,146 |
| FORFAR | 595,822 | £14,734 | 4,472,810 | £122,280 | 22,629,544 | £686,858 |
| PERTH | 477,744 | £23,955 | 1,465,133 | £65,606 | 1,605,321 | £80,785 |
| % national total | 82% | 83% | 86% | 82% | 89% | 78% |

*Source:* Board of Trustees Reports, reproduced in Hamilton (1963) pp. 406–9.

The Commissioners did a good job. In their report for 1738, it was said that 'all the Gentlemen of this country, who at your Majesty's most auspicious accession to the Throne, made use of linen brought from Holland, wear now nothing but home-made cloth'. Scots production of linen rose from 2.18 million yards in 1727–8, to 36.27 million in 1821–2. In 1760, when the total consumption of linen cloth in Britain and the colonies was about 80 million yards, the rapidly growing Scots industry contributed 12 million yards (about the same as Ireland), the bigger English industry, about 26 million, with imports supplying the remainder.

### The Iron Industry

No less than the textile industries, the iron industry underwent fundamental changes during the early Industrial Revolution. By 1800, its technical base had completely altered, output had risen substantially, and the industry had become localised in five main areas. But, as in cotton textiles, the changes had come most rapidly in the last two decades of the eighteenth century. The annual output of pig iron in 1717 was about 20,000 tons. In 1788, England and Wales produced 68,000 tons and Scotland 7,000. By 1796, English and Welsh furnaces were making 126,000 tons. A full survey of the industry in 1806 revealed that total output was then 244,000 tons: 149,000 from England, 72,000 from Wales and 23,000 from Scotland (table 5:2). The five regions of South Wales, Shropshire, Staffordshire, Yorkshire and Scotland's Central Valley produced no less than 92 per cent of this total (fig. 5:3). This was a very different picture to that prevailing a hundred years earlier.

TABLE 5:2   *The Iron Industry in 1806* – Output by Region

| Region | Output (tons) |
|---|---|
| Shropshire | 54,966 |
| Staffordshire | 50,002 |
| Yorkshire | 27,646 |
| Derbyshire | 9,074 |
| Northumberland | 2,500 |
| Monmouth | 2,240 |
| Cumberland | 1,995 |
| Lancashire | 780 |
| ENGLAND | 149,203 |
| North Wales | 2,981 |
| South Wales | 68,867 |
| WALES | 71,848 |
| SCOTLAND | 22,840 |
| TOTAL-BRITAIN | 243,891 |

*Source:* BPP 1849, XXII, Appx.: 25–6.

Until the 1750s, iron output rose slowly. It came mainly from areas that had been important producers since medieval times: the Weald, Forest of Dean, the Birmingham Plateau, north Staffordshire, Nottingham and south Yorkshire (fig. 5:2). All these areas had local ironstone supplies, as well as timber to provide charcoal for the furnace and forge. Although Darby first successfully used coke to produce pig in 1709 (and it was in continuous use at Coalbrookdale thereafter), coke smelting spread slowly because, for a long time, coke pig remained more expensive to produce than charcoal pig. Not until the demand for iron began to rise rapidly did the latter lose its price advantage. In 1760 there

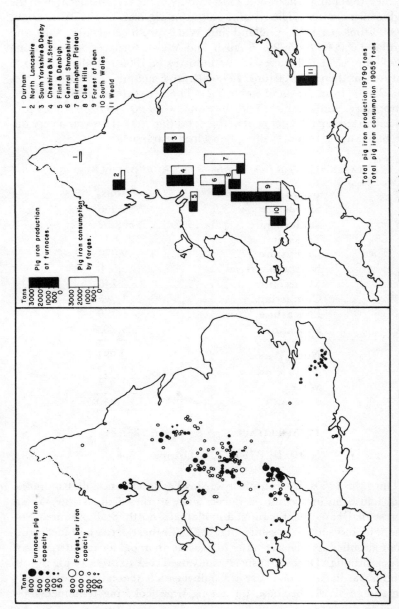

Fig. 5:2 *The Iron Industry in the Early Eighteenth Century*. The map on the left shows iron furnaces and forges in 1717; that on the right shows the regional production and consumption of pig iron in 1717. Source: redrawn from B.L.C. Johnson (1951) p. 168.

were still only 17 coke furnaces in blast in England and Wales, and none at all in Scotland (above, p. 95).

In the early seventeenth century, the Weald was the most important iron producer. In 1574, 51 of the 58 furnaces in Britain were to be found there (table 5:3). The Weald had ironstone, coppice woodland for charcoal burning, it had streams to drive the water wheels that powered the

TABLE 5:3   *Charcoal Iron Furnaces, 1574–1790.* Numbers by Region.

| | 1574 | 1664 | 1717 | 1790 |
|---|---|---|---|---|
| Hampshire | 0 | 2 | 1 | 0 |
| Weald | 51 | 29 | 14 | 3 |
| S. W. England | 4 | 14 | 16 | 11 |
| S. Wales ⎱ Midlands ⎰ | 3 | 10 | 13 | 2 |
| Cheshire, North Wales | 0 | 3 | 5 | 1 |
| Sheffield, North East | 0 | 10 | 9 | 2 |
| North West | 0 | 0 | 3 | 5 |
| Scotland | 0 | 0 | 0 | 0 |
| | 58 | 68 | 61 | 24 |

*Source:* Schubert (1957): 175.

furnace bellows (hammer ponds can still be seen in Ashdown Forest), and it was close to the main markets. These were the naval yards and arsenals on the Thames and Medway and at Portsmouth that took the region's predominant output of gun castings and cannon balls. The Weald was also close to the continent, from which the major early innovation in the industry – the blast furnace itself – had come at the end of the fifteenth century. It was a hundred years or so before the blast furnace spread to other areas. By the mid-seventeenth century, the Forest of Dean had become a prominent iron producer too – in 1717, it had as many furnaces as the Weald, which was suffering an absolute decline. Dean was a great export surplus region, sending its high quality pig up the Severn Valley to the Birmingham forges. Dean pig made good bar and wrought iron for the Midland craftsmen, whereas Wealden pig (known as 'coldshort') was more brittle and less easily worked: it was most suitable for heavy cast products such as anvils and hammers, apart from the important military products.

Both Dean and the Weald declined greatly in relative importance in the eighteenth century. As charcoal iron regions, they lost out to the rapidly growing coke-iron producers. Not only were the coalfields readily accessible to expanding industrial markets, but they could also provide an elastic supply of fuel and Coal Measures ironstone. Demand for pig grew at a rate of 50 per cent per decade from the 1750s till the 1820s, and as the price advantage of charcoal pig disappeared, it was the coalfield areas that assumed prominence as the major iron producers (fig. 5:3). In 1806 there were 162 coke furnaces, but only 11 charcoal ones survived.

Yet the pattern of change is not quite so straightforward as this. Dean did not suffer the marked absolute decline that took place in the Weald. The quality of Dean pig and its value to the Birmingham trades helped sustain the industry there. The Weald was less fortunate. For ordinary cast-iron products Wealden coldshort was outclassed by Dean and the Midland producers. But until the early 1770s, many of its furnaces continued to prosper as ordnance suppliers. For over three centuries, Wealden gunfounders were favoured with all government contracts, and not until the Seven Years War were any awarded elsewhere. Then outside competition, in particular from the new Carron Company in Scotland, began to undermine their position. And in 1775, the Board of Ordnance made the final decision to transfer all its contracts to lower cost producers away from the Weald.

The real beneficiary of this decision was the Carron Company. It had been established by a partnership in 1759, and built as an integrated concern on a large scale, with four blast furnaces, a double forge and a slitting and rolling mill. Between a half and two-thirds of its sales came from the government contracts for cannon and shot, contracts which were executed under the direction of skilled workmen enticed away from the Weald. Until the 1780s, Carron remained the only sizeable Scottish works. The home market north of the Border was too small to support much more capacity, whilst the pig, made from local low-quality ores, was too poor to sell for domestic manufacture outside Scotland. Even in the Napoleonic wars, by which time there were 10 or 12 works operating in Scotland, Carron was the only one that prospered. In 1806, its annual production of over 7,000 tons made up one-third of the Scottish total. So the Carron Company was for long a lone star: not until the 1830s did the Scots iron industry undergo a transformation such as its cotton industry had experienced in the last two decades of the eighteenth century. Neilson's discovery and application of the hot blast in 1828, combined with the use of the rich blackband ores that were found in central Scotland in 1801, enabled the industry to cut its coal use in half and manufacture pig of high quality that found markets as far away as Lancashire and Yorkshire.

Changes in the Welsh industry came considerably sooner. It was built up in south Wales by capital from Bristol and London, its ironmasters coming mostly from the Midlands. Together they brought a large-scale industry into being in the mid-eighteenth century which, as at Carron, was stimulated initially by the demands of the Seven Years War. Before 1750, there were just a few scattered charcoal works here, but 15 years later these had been superseded by a nucleus of new coke-fired furnaces around the village of Merthyr. Merthyr, although desolate and remote, was situated on the northern rim of the coalfield where both coal seams and ironstones outcropped on the surface. The Hirwaun furnace was founded here in 1757, the Dowlais furnace in 1759, the Cyfarthfa and Plymouth furnaces in 1765. Cyfarthfa was set up by Anthony Bacon, a London merchant and MP, who held Ordnance Board contracts until 1782. In 1777, Richard Crawshay entered into partnership with him, taking over the works on Bacon's death in 1786. Crawshay proceeded to make an immense fortune from the business, which derived largely from his impressive output of wrought iron products. Crawshay was the first to take up Cort's puddling process in South Wales and, along with his neighbours the Homfrays at the Pennydarren works, improved it considerably. In 1801, the Dowlais works, led by the Guest family, also began wrought iron production, making the area pre-eminent in this respect in Britain.

By the early years of the nineteenth century there were eight large iron works and several smaller ones scattered across the heads of the valleys. Crawshay's Cyfarthfa, with four furnaces, had the largest output of any in the country – some 9,000 tons of pig in 1806, whilst Blaenavon, also with four furnaces, and Pennydarren with three, were the third and sixth largest, producing 7,800 and 6,800 tons respectively. South Wales made one-third of all British pig (fig. 5:3). In the 1830s, McCulloch described 'the progress of the iron manufacture in South Wales and Monmouthshire (as) rapid beyond all precedent'. Merthyr Tydfil, in 1755 an insignificant village with its lands let on a 99-year lease for only £200 a year, was a booming town of 7,700 people by 1801, connected by canal and turnpike road to Cardiff. In 1831, its population was over 22,000.

The most productive iron-making regions in England in 1806 were Shropshire, Staffordshire and Yorkshire (table 5:2). These were all regions in which the smaller metal trades flourished, but large-scale cast and wrought iron production was also important. The Darby's Coalbrookdale works was in Shropshire, above the Severn, and on the opposite bank was John Wilkinson's Broseley Furnace. Both concerns had works elsewhere, and in 1806 both were producing about 6,700 tons of pig. Wilkinson had built one of the first coke iron furnaces – after Coalbrookdale – at Bradley (Staffs.) in 1756. He started out in armament production, in 1774 patenting a device for boring cannon from solid castings, enabling lighter, more accurate weapons to be made. But armaments were only a small part of his later output, which covered a very wide range.

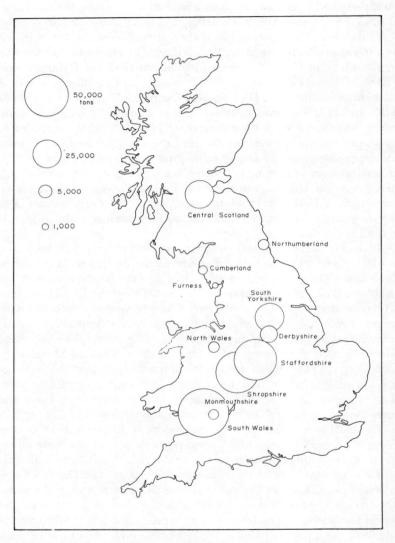

Fig. 5:3    *The Iron Industry in 1806* – output of pig iron by region. *Source*: table 5:2.

In 1788, MacPherson recorded that 'it is worthy of observation that orders were sent from Paris to Mr. Wilkinson, a gentleman of great eminence in the iron manufacture, for iron pipes to the extent of no less than forty miles, to be used in supplying that capital with water'. It is a revealing comment, pinpointing an important use for iron products, and reflecting the iron industry's break into the export markets.[4] Wilkinson also invented a cylinder boring lathe, a machine that proved to be one of the keys to the success of the Boulton and Watt partnership. With it he was able to produce the highly accurate cylinders that were so central to Watt's improvements in the efficiency of the steam engine.

The metal trades of the town of Birmingham had a long history, and by the end of the eighteenth century, were both diverse and numerous. The town's directory for 1777 listed no less than 129 button-makers, 56 toymakers, 52 platers, 46 brass founders, 39 buckle-makers, 36 gunmakers and 21 ironmongers (table 7:1). Sheffield, in Yorkshire, was also an important provincial manufacturing centre. Despite its relative isolation in the Pennine foothills, it had developed as a lively steelworking community. It was a local man, Benjamin Huntsman, who in the 1740s discovered the principle of crucible refining for making quality steel so sealing Sheffield's supremacy as the centre of the steel trade. The steel was made from Russian and Swedish bar iron, imported up the navigable river system via the port of Hull. Steel workers, cutlers, tool makers and founders had their works scattered in and above the steep valleys around the town. The Sheffield directory of 1797 shows just how complex its industrial structure had become (table 5:4).

Sheffield steel was sold and used outside southern Yorkshire. Its factors marketed steel across the Pennines to tradesmen in south Lancashire and north Cheshire, a long-established metal working region. Warrington was well-known for its files and tools, Prescot for watch parts, Leigh for nails and Ashton-in-Makerfield for locks and hinges. The firm of Peter Stubs of Warrington was one of the most renowned in the area. Originally an innkeeper and filemaker, Stubs employed domestic outworkers, supplying them with raw materials and tools, and collecting the finished files every week or fortnight. He exchanged many of his files for more steel from the factors. It was a system very similar to that operated by the Sheffield cutlers, the Derbyshire nailers and Abraham Crowley from his Newcastle and Bromsgrove works. In 1802 Stubs centralised his business in a new set of workshops and warehouses, and began to make a wider range of tools, such as chisels, pliers, vices and watchmakers' instruments, which he sold not only to the factors, but also through his own contacts as far south as Birmingham, Bristol and London, and as far north as Newcastle and Glasgow. He also exported,

TABLE 5:4    *The Metal Trades of Sheffield in 1797*

| | |
|---|---|
| Steel converters and refiners | −16 |
| | |
| Merchants and factors | −52 |
| Nail factors | −3 |
| | |
| Pocket knife cutlers | −36 |
| Pen and Pocket knife cutlers | −98 (153) |
| Table knife makers | −81 |
| Haft pressers | −9 |
| Forkmakers | −15 (20) |
| Fine scissor makers | −38 |
| Common scissor makers | −20 (19) |
| Razor makers | −33 (11) |
| | |
| Filemakers | −40 (10) |
| Awl blade makers | −4 |
| Edge tool makers | −12 |
| Joiners' tool makers | −4 |
| Saw makers | −14 |
| Sickle makers | −25 |
| Shear makers | −9 |
| Scythe, hay and straw knife makers | −26 |
| Lancet and Phleme makers | −13 |
| Surgeon's instrument makers | −2 |
| | |
| Bellows makers | −2 |
| Button makers (5 metal, 7 horn, 3 plated, 1 other) | −16 |
| Case makers | −8 |
| Comb makers | −5 |
| Inkstand makers | −7 |
| Snuffer makers | −3 |
| Silver and plated goods manufacturers | −22 |
| Founders | −12 |
| Anvil makers | −4 |
| Fender makers | −5 |

Numbers in brackets refer to firms marked 'in the neighbourhood' in the Directory.

*Source:* Sheffield Directory (1797).

via Liverpool, to the United States – a link indicative of the growing importance of the American market for the British iron industry. And Stubs himself was but one example of the many small metal-working firms that represented the finer end of the transformation of the iron industry in the late eighteenth century. It was a qualitative as well as a quantitative transformation.

### The Coal Industry

'The mineral riches of Great Britain, if not superior, are at least equal to those of any other country. We cannot, it is true, boast of mines of gold or silver, but we possess that which is of still more importance to a manufacturing nation, an all but inexhaustible supply of the most excellent coal'. So wrote McCulloch in 1837, and time has certainly not proved him wrong.

Coal output rose sharply in the eighteenth century, from about two and a half million tons in 1700, to over ten million tons in 1800. However, it had been growing throughout the seventeenth century too, as coal replaced charcoal in a range of activities (brewing, salt and sugar refining, brick, tile and pottery manufacture, soap, glass, nailmaking and the non-ferrous trades). Until 1770, when the national output was about six million tons, the eighteenth century pattern was a mere continuation of the earlier trend. It was a general increase in coal usage in the last part of the century, and the creation, through the new canal system, of a means of moving it long distances that underlay the great expansion of the coal industry from 1770 onwards.

In 1700, coal was mined in several areas in Britain (fig. 5:4). Most of Scotland's coal came from the counties around the Firth of Forth, where it was used in glass and limeworks, distilleries and saltpans. Scotland was producing about half a million tons a year, some 150,000 tons of which was sent to the saltpans. But most of the mines were small, as they were in England. In both countries, less than a dozen workers was the norm. This was true of the Midlands, Lancashire and Yorkshire, although there were a few large pits employing over 60 or 70 workers there. Around Bristol, an important coal market, there were only 123 colliery workers, including carriers, in more than 70 pits at Kingswood in 1684. In 1778, the 90 working pits of the Forest of Dean were producing no more than 20 tons per week on average. In the 1790s, the mines of the Rhondda, to become so famous after 1850, were mostly just small drift workings, each with five or six men at the most.

The largest mines were to be found in by far the most important coalfield, in the English north-east. Coal-mining was the preoccupation of many landowners in Northumberland and Durham, rather than a secondary activity as was the case elsewhere. The average number of workers per pit was about 40 in the 1760s and many pits were several hundred feet deep. Over threequarters of the output of the field was shipped coast-

Fig. 5:4 *The Eighteenth-Century Coal Industry* – illustrating the location of coalfields and the main routes of the coal trade.

wise, a very large amount going to London, the rest being channelled up navigable rivers into the agricultural counties of eastern England. Over 800,000 tons was shipped in 1690, some two million tons each year by 1800. The north-east was Britain's first intensive coalfield, because the fuel could be dispatched easily to a large market. But large-scale mining created problems, particularly with drainage. Steam engines used as pumps had to be employed in the deeper shaft mines to pump up underground water. The Newcomen engine was popular for this purpose, as its high coal consumption was not of primary concern, although a number of bigger collieries (not only in the north-east, but in the Midlands too) bought Boulton and Watt engines after 1775, these being generally far more reliable. The improved efficiency of all steam engines following the adoption of Wilkinson's new iron-bored cylinders enabled deeper shafts to be operated. In the 1790s, a number of collieries also began to use steam winding gear, to replace the old horse-gin.

The increasing depth of shafts was generally greater than the increase in area worked underground, as a colliery operator's chief costs were those of underground transport and the maintenance of tunnels. It was often cheaper to sink a new shaft, rather than extend the use of the old one. Increasing demand for coal was therefore satisfied by more and deeper workings. In the north-east, this meant that collieries spread further away from the river Tyne and Wear, and moved into the deep, concealed coalfield towards the coast, well to the east of Newcastle. In 1794, there was a 774 feet deep shaft in operation at Hebburn, whilst in the north-west coalfield in Cumberland, a shaft at Whitehaven had reached a depth of 993 feet in 1800. The transport of coal from the heads of these increasingly dispersed pits was by horse waggonways, known as Newcastle roads in the north-east, where they ran down into the Tyne and Wear valleys. Waggonways were widely used in the Severn Valley too (in both these areas, they had first been built in the early seventeenth century) and were introduced into the Welsh valleys in the late eighteenth century to connect with the new coal canals there.

It was the construction of canals on a nationwide scale that enabled the coal industry to meet growing market demand after 1760. Of the 165 canal schemes sanctioned by Parliament between 1758 and 1801, no less than 90 were primarily intended by their promoters for the movement of coal. Land carriage of coal was undeniably expensive, its cost often doubling or trebling with every 15 or 20 miles moved from the pithead. Land carriage was also seasonal, particularly on the non-turnpiked crossroads, so restricting winter sales. But canals enabled large, regular shipments of coal to be sent long distances for as little as $\frac{1}{4}$d per ton/mile. Many colliery owners invested in canal schemes, and the pattern of development of eighteenth century coalfields, not surprisingly, reflected the pattern of waterway improvement.

The use of all coalfields was extended. The Yorkshire field had long been worked around Wakefield, near the navigable River Calder, and southwards into Nottinghamshire alongside the River Trent. The central part of this field was not opened up until an extensive turnpike road network had been promoted by Yorkshire merchants in the 1740s, and the River Don had been improved beyond Rotherham by Acts passed in 1733 and 1751. The rich Barnsley Nine Foot seam was not intensively exploited until the Barnsley Canal and the Dearne and Dove Canals were opened in the 1790s. The start of extensive large-scale mining in south Wales came with the opening of four great canals into the valleys between 1794 and 1799, at a cost of £420,000. In central Scotland, the rapid growth of Glasgow led to the promotion of the Monklands Canal (1793) into the Lanarkshire coalfield, just as it had earlier encouraged the establishment of the turnpike to Edinburgh along the same route. The link between new transport arteries and coalfield development was clearly reflected in Lancashire too. The biggest collieries before 1750 were the Prescot Hall and Whiston mines, both beside an early turnpike road into Liverpool. Prescot Hall was raising about 21,000 tons of coal a year by 1750. The opening of the canalized Sankey Brook in 1757 boosted the flow of coal southwards from around St. Helens to the Cheshire saltfield, and output along the canal had risen from under 5,000 to about 80,000 tons per annum by the end of the century. The northern part of this field was opened up with the improvement of the River Douglas in the 1740s. The growing demands of Manchester were met with the opening of Britain's first true canal, the Duke of Bridgewater's, in 1761.

The construction of canals enabled market demand to be met and by cutting transport costs, also extended that market. Rising demand came partly from domestic needs, with London's imports of sea-cole alone growing from 500,000 chaldrons a year in the 1750s, to over 800,000 in the 1790s. It also came from the increasing use of steampower (there were probably about 1,200 steam engines in Britain by 1800), and from the expansion of coal-using industries. Foremost amongst these was the booming iron industry, but there were many others, from non-ferrous smelting, soap and salt working to pottery manufacture, sugar refining and brewing. However, the growth of the coal industry up to 1800 must not be exaggerated. Coal production rose fourfold in the eighteenth century. It rose twentyfold in the nineteenth. It was after 1800 that the revolutionary expansion of the coal industry occurred, although the upturn had started in the mid-eighteenth. George Stephenson's suggestion that the Chancellor of England should sit on a sack of coals rather than a woolsack was singularly pertinent for his time, but it would have been far less appropriate in the earlier years of the Industrial Revolution.

### Other Industries

This chapter has considered the basic industries of the eighteenth century: textiles, the iron trades and coal mining, industries that accounted for the bulk of the industrial expansion of the period. But there were many other important branches of manufacturing taking part in the growth of the early Industrial Revolution. Some of these, such as construction and food processing were large numerically, whilst others such as chemicals or shipbuilding were small, but had a significance way beyond their size. Some were widespread, operating throughout Britain to serve local markets, others were more localised, particularly in the ports and on the coalfields.

Every town in Britain had its masons, carpenters, joiners, bricklayers, glaziers and plumbers: men, who although they often had a dual occupation in another craft, were the *construction* 'industry' of the eighteenth century. There was no need for large-scale organisation until the days of canal building, and this affected a limited number of workers. Most towns also had their own *clothing crafts*, such as tailors, hatters and shoemakers, the latter being especially numerous, as the lists in urban directories show (table 7:1). So too were the tanners, who prepared the raw material, although the nature of their work meant that they were usually banished to the outskirts of settlement. The biggest concentration of tanneries was in Southwark and Rotherhithe, on the south bank of the Thames, using the hides of animals sold for meat at Smithfield market. Overall, the *leather* industry was very large (table 4:2), providing materials for a wide range of products. These included the straps which acted as a crude suspension system for coaches and carriages before the days of the metal elliptical spring, and the drive belts which were used to harness the power of steam engines to machinery.

Millers and maltsters were to be found in most towns too, and many innkeepers made their own beer. However, the *food* 'industry' was beginning to show signs of modernising into bigger units. Several of the London breweries were large-scale concerns supplying not only the metropolitan market, but sending their best beer-porter – into the provinces too. By 1815, the 11 leading London brewers were producing two million barrels a year, or one-fifth of the nation's output. Imported foodstuffs were processed at the ports of London, Liverpool, Bristol and Glasgow for wider distribution. Bristol had 15 or 16 sugar houses at work in the eighteenth century and alongside them a distilling industry, producing spirits for export and sale at home. There were cocoa and coffee works in the city too, and some tobacco was processed. Glasgow, however, was the main centre of the latter trade.

Another industry that was localised in the bigger ports, although it was widely carried on all round the coasts, was *shipbuilding*. The Naval Dockyards, on the Thames at Rotherhithe and Greenwich, on the Medway, and at Portsmouth, were in fact the largest employers in early eighteenth-century Britain, with up to 800 workers each. On the Thames, in particular, a host of ancillary activities had developed, ranging from Abraham Crowley's ordnance and wares depots to ropeworks. Merchant shipbuilding was an important activity in all the big ports. Between 1787 and 1800, Bristol yards produced 176 vessels with a total tonnage of 22,644 tons. Most were small, but a few were quite large, some being over 400 tons. London yards, in the same period, produced 576 ships, with a total tonnage six times that of Bristol's. The main English shipbuilding ports are shown in table 5:5. In nearly all ports, however, a few shipwrights, a ropemaker and some sail-cloth makers were to be found, building coastal vessels, fishing boats, hoys or colliers.

TABLE 5:5    *Ships Built At the Major Shipbuilding Centres, 1787–99*

|  | Number | Tonnage |
|---|---|---|
| London | 576 | 129,557 |
| Newcastle | 419 | 92,794 |
| Hull | 458 | 57,746 |
| Sunderland | 318 | 56,420 |
| Whitby | 234 | 54,704 |
| Liverpool | 322 | 48,955 |

*Source:* Jackson (1972) p. 184.

A number of other branches of industry were localised, on the coalfields. One of these was *glassmaking*, which supplied the growing demand for window glass in the seventeenth and eighteenth centuries, as well as flint glass for tableware. Coal was the critical locationary factor, as glass was made in a reverberatory furnace that used a great deal: for this reason, glassmaking was concentrated in the north-east, on the Thames (where good sea-cole was readily available), and at subsidiary centres such as Bristol and Stourbridge. The necessary sand and alkali were often transported over great distances. Norfolk sand was used in Newcastle, which was producing more window glass than all the other centres put together by 1800. There were then 11 glassworks in Bristol,

A1  The countryside around Haddington, East Lothian, on Roy's map of
Scotland (1747–55). This was one of the more progressive Scottish farming regions. The map shows a landscape in transition, with enclosures amongst the
open fields. Haddington itself was a great corn market. (*The British Library*)

A2    Open-fields at Braunton, north Devon. These are still worked, but on an allotment basis. Open-fields also survive on the Isle of Portland (Dorset), at Soham (Cambs.) and Laxton (Notts.). (*Museum of English Rural Life, Reading*)

A3    Laxton (Notts.) – an open-field village much as it was. Laxton retains three big common fields, although some of its land is enclosed. The farmsteads are all found in the village itself, giving easy access to each one's scattered holdings. (*Radio Times Hulton Picture Library*)

A4   An area of Parliamentary enclosure in Derbyshire, enclosed under an award of 1779. Note the large rectilinear fields, stone walls and enclosure road with wide verges. (*Author*)

A5   The independent farmstead typical of enclosure: built in the centre of the farm rather than in the village. This view is a few hundred metres from the one above. The house is dated 1784, indicating fairly quick implementation of the award. (*Author*)

A6 Agricultural diffusion: breeders commonly let their rams out for the season at a fee, and this was an important means by which improvements were diffused. The animals are Bakewell's New Leicesters; the scene is the annual hiring session on his Dishley estate (1809). (*Museum of English*

B1 Coalbrookdale: 'Morning View' by William Williams (1777). It emphasises the works' isolated location, like much industry of this period. (*Clive House Museum, Shrewsbury*)

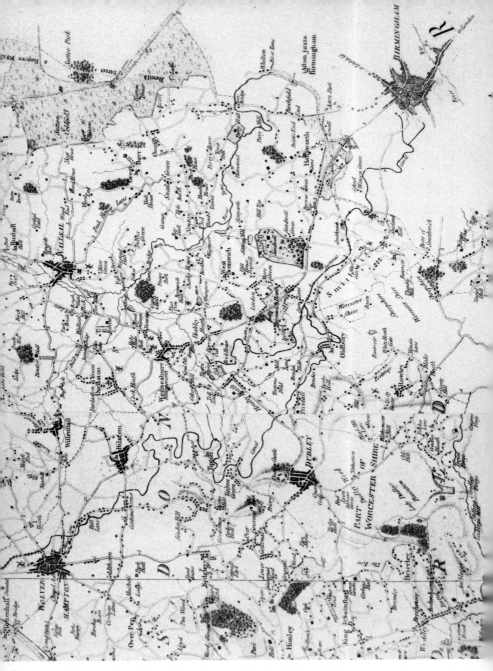

B2   Part of William Yates' map of Staffordshire (1775), showing the area that became the Black Country, but then only 'a countryside in the course of becoming industrialised'. Note the Birmingham Canal weaving through the landscape, the coalpits and forges around Wednesbury and east of Stourbridge, and the Soho Manufactory north-west of Birmingham. (*The British Library*)

B3　Lombe's silk mill at Derby, an engraving dated 1798. This great structure, the first real factory in Britain, was completed in 1721, and powered by a water wheel 23 feet in diameter. (*Derbyshire County Library*)

B4　Pottery kilns beside the Trent and Mersey Canal in Stoke-on-Trent. The area had long had many small-scale pottery concerns, but it rose to national prominence with the fortunes of men like Wedgwood, Spode and Minton – men who symbolised the spirit of entrepreneurship of the Early Industrial Revolution. (*Royal Commission on Historical Monuments, England*)

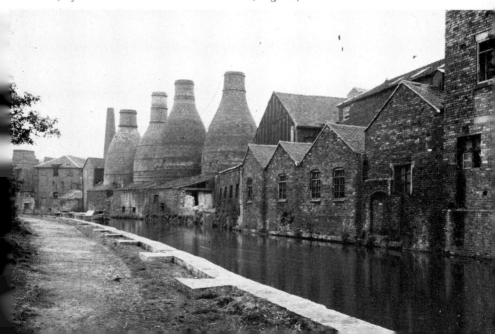

B5 An eighteenth-century weaver's cottage, near Huddersfield, Yorks. The living quarters were downstairs, the workshop above. The long window threw plenty of light on the loom. (*Radio Times Hulton Picture Library*)

B6 Part of the factory colony of New Lanark – workers' houses built by Robert Owen after he took over the mill in 1799. (*Scottish Tourist Board*)

C1 A late seventeenth-century post-mill at Nutley in the Sussex Weald. Windmills were a good substitute for water power (Plate B3), and were widely used in the arable areas of southern and eastern England, and as 'marshmills' for drainage purposes on the Fens. (*Author*)

C2 Beighton's engraving of a Newcomen steam engine (1717). Its size emphasises that steam engines were certainly not bought 'off the shelf'. The manufacturer supplied the mechanical parts; they were assembled, and the superstructure built, in situ. This is a simple lifting engine, as they all were until Watt patented his development of rotative motion in 1781. (*The Science Museum*)

D1 Pontcysyllte Aqueduct, regarded as one of the great achievements of canal engineering. It carries the Ellesmere Canal over the River Dee in a cast iron trough 12 feet wide and 1000 feet long. Built by Telford, and finished in 1805. (*British Waterways Board*)

D2 Bingley Five Rise Locks (1777), one of several flights carrying the Leeds and Liverpool Canal over the Pennines. The canal was started in 1770 and the two ends were completed by 1777; however, the trans-Pennine section was not built until 1790 – 1815. (*British Waterways Board*)

D3  The world's first cast-iron bridge, designed by Abraham Darby III and still spanning the Severn gorge below Coalbrookdale. Originally no bolts were used in its construction, the 378 tons of metal being held together by interlocking joints and wedges. The Severn itself was an important trade artery. (*The Science Museum*)

D4 A long-distance stage waggon: a slow but reliable means of transport for small goods and passengers who could not afford the stage coach. The cumbersome broad wheels were required by law, the intention being to minimise rutting of the road surface. (*The Science Museum*)

D5 A tollhouse, built by the Ipstones Turnpike Trust in Staffordshire. Its windows face both ways along the road; the toll schedule was above the door and the gate immediately adjacent to it. (*Author*)

E1 Smithfield market, London – an aquatint of 1811. It dealt in the sale of sheep (in the pens) and cattle. There are a few pigs in the foreground. (*Museum of English Rural Life, Reading*)

E2  A country market. Corn and cattle are on sale – the gentleman in the black coat could well be a city factor. A corner was reserved for women, selling fruit, vegetables and dairy products. (*Museum of English Rural Life, Reading*)

E3  Milsom Street, Bath – built in the 1770s and eighties. A few bow windows survive. Eighteenth-century Bath had a wide range of fixed shops to meet the needs of its wealthy clientele. (*Royal Commission on Historical Monuments, England*)

F1    Battle, Sussex – a market town with a main street of seventeenth-and eight-eenth-century houses, inns and shops. Several have new Georgian fronts. (*Author*)

F2    Scarborough in 1791, showing the old town and its important fishing fleet. But Scarborough was also a spa, and became the first seaside resort (note the bathing machines) – hence the growth of the new town further round the bay. (*Crescent Museums, Scarborough*)

F3    Late eighteenth-century artisan housing, Newtown (Powys). This terrace was far more generously planned than the courts and cellars of the bigger towns. (*Dr. P. J. Perry*)

F4    Edinburgh New Town – Moray Place, built in the 1820s as one of the new developments adjacent to Craig's original plan. Note the iron railings, gas lamps and granite setts: all indicative of a high status area in the early nineteenth century. (*Scottish Tourist Board*)

making window glass for the west, and for export to Ireland and America, as well as bottles, in which beer, cider, spirits, wine and Hotwell spring water were sold. The most significant development in the glass industry in the early Industrial Revolution, however, was the opening of the great Ravenshead glassworks at St. Helens in Lancashire in the 1770s. This works was built by a company, the British Cast Plate Glass Manufacturers, which was one of the few examples of an industrial enterprise that received incorporation, by Act of Parliament, in this period: the Act was passed in 1773. Ravenshead introduced the manufacture of plate glass into Britain, used for mirrors and coach windows as it was thicker, stronger and clearer than ordinary window glass. The company employed French expertise from the renowned plate glass works of St. Gobain, in Picardy, and was later taken over by Pilkington Brothers, a name still famous in the trade.

Glassmaking, as many other branches of manufacture, relied on a product of the small, but vitally important *chemical* industry. Potash or soda was required to mix with sand to produce the glass silicate. Potash was prepared in tiny quantities from wood ash, and Britain's supplies were generally imported. Soda was made in the ports from the ashes of plants: either from the saltwort, which grew in Spain and the Canaries, and yielded a soda rich substance called barilla, or from kelp, brought from Ireland or the coastal villages of the Scottish Highlands, where its collection was an important secondary employment. Both these alkalis were used in other branches of the chemical industry. Potash, combined with tallow or other animal fats, was used in the manufacture of soft soap, which was needed by the woollen industry for scouring (removing the grease from the wool), and for fulling. Soda was a necessary ingredient of ordinary household soaps. There were soapworks in Liverpool and Bristol, the latter producing a hard white soap considered by contemporaries to be superior to any. But the greatest concentration was in London on the south bank of the Thames. Potash was also used there to soften leather in the tanneries, and in the manufacture of gunpowder. Another local trade using the animal wastes of the metropolitan market was the glue industry. The complex of activities stretching eastward from Southwark along the river was an excellent example of interlinkages and economies to be gained from locational concentration.

Another important branch of the chemical industry was that which developed with the textile finishing trades. Potash was used in the bleaching and cleaning of cloth, but of greater importance in this respect was dilute sulphuric acid, and a derivative of the process when it was combined with salt – chlorine. The main acidworks in Britain was at Prestonpans, on the Scottish coalfield not far from Edinburgh, an enterprise established by John Roebuck and Samuel Garbett, who had started in the business in Birmingham in 1746. The old method of gradual bleaching in the sun, the cloth being stretched out over a 'tenter' and doused periodically in sour milk, was too slow to cope with the tremendous increase in textile output by the 1770s. Bleaching agents were thus a vital development, a major economy of scale. Pure chlorine, however, was not ideal, being too corrosive (below, p. 22). A great advance was Charles Tennant's invention of bleaching powder, patented in 1797 and 1799, the result of absorbing chlorine in slaked lime. Tennant created a Glasgow firm that was to become the biggest chemical producer in the world in the 1830s and 1840s. A final branch of the chemical industry was the age-old refining of salt, a widespread activity on the coalfields of the Firth of Forth, Tyneside and Lancashire.

One of the most localised activities of the early Industrial Revolution was *non-ferrous metal smelting*, which was found mainly in South Wales. By 1800, the area between Kidwelly and Port Talbot, centred on Swansea and the Neath Valley, had 90 per cent of the country's *copper* smelting capacity. Copper was used in making brass and bronze, and in its metallic form in coinage (Matthew Boulton's pennies, for example), buttons, utensils, guns, brewing vats, rollers for textile machinery, and for sheathing boat hulls. The 'Copper King' of the late eighteenth century was a north Welshman, Thomas Williams, a former country solicitor, who controlled two Anglesey copper mines, owned smelters in Swansea and south Lancashire as well as works in north Wales and the Thames Valley, and warehouses in London, Birmingham and Liverpool. Before the output of his Anglesey mines began to decline in the late 1790s, he managed for a few years assets worth about £1 million, making him probably the biggest entrepreneur in Britain at the time. There were copper and brass works in Bristol and Liverpool too. It was in Bristol that Abraham Darby had been a partner in a brassworks at the turn of the century, and the Baptist Mills works there was still turning out wire, ornaments for the Guinea trade, copper pans for sugar making and sheets for sheathing ships many years later.

Another product that was used almost as widely as copper was *tinplate*, the manufacture of which expanded very rapidly in England and Wales after 1750. Tin had long been used to protect iron products from rusting, and demand was rapidly growing for these: kettles, pots, pans, food boxes, lantern frames. Tinplate was first produced by the sheet method – rolled iron sheets coated with tin before being made into utensils – at Pontypool in south Wales in the late seventeenth century. New works were later established at other iron forges in the west Midlands and south Wales, gradually migrating to achieve total concentration in the

Swansea region by the late nineteenth century.

A final case, and a famous concentration of manufacturing activity, was the 'Staffordshire Potteries around Burslem, and the neighbouring villages, which have of late been carried out with such amazing success', according to Arthur Young in 1771. *Pottery* was a long established speciality of the area, but it rose to international fame with 'the inventive genius of Mr. Wedgwood', in Young's words. Wedgwood, of course, was only one of many, although he was the most renowned at home and abroad. The Potteries were a prime example of entrepreneurial drive in industry, and the advantages of locational economies. The area had basic skills and specialities which were developed by Wedgwood, Spode, Minton and the other potters, in a spirit of competition and rivalry: a spirit that achieved mass-produced, quality products that captured a very wide market. These were the same principles that were creating the nuclei of great concentrations of industry in the west Midlands, Yorkshire, in the north-east, around Manchester and Liverpool, in south Wales, in Bristol, Glasgow and London. The industrial face of Britain in 1800 had all the clues to the international success of its Victorian heyday.

## NOTES

1 In fact, figure 5:1 probably also underestimates the growth rate of the West Riding woollen industry, as it excludes worsteds – which by the 1770s accounted for three-quarters of the region's output. There are no production series for worsteds available, but their production was probably growing more quickly than that of broadcloths. Given the productivity problem with the cotton figures, however, the relative difference in growth rates depicted still holds.
2 Scribbling mills housed the preparatory machinery: scribbling, carding and slubbing machines which prepared the raw wool for the jenny. They were introduced from the Lancashire cotton industry and spread quickly from the late 1770s. It was common for the larger clothiers to buy these machines and set them up in their own existing fulling mills, to be driven by water power. The smaller clothiers thus brought their wool to these mills for the preparatory processes and returned later to have their cloth fulled.
3 Scutching machines separated the fibre from the woody part of the flax stalk, whilst heckling machines, equipped with a steel-toothed comb, teased out the flax fibres.
4 Before the last quarter of the eighteenth century, when the export trade in finished iron products got under way, the iron trade was

mainly in imports, particularly of high quality Swedish and Russian bar iron. The improvement in home produced pig, however, cut the volume of Swedish bar imports from c50,000 tons p.a. in the late eighteenth century to only 15,000 by 1815.

## FURTHER READING

COTTON

The best source on the market for cotton goods and the organisation of the trade is M. M. Edwards: *The Growth of the British Cotton Trade, 1780–1815* (1967). On the industry in general see S. D. Chapman: *The Cotton Industry in the Industrial Revolution* (1972), and *The Early Factory Masters* (1967). On the Scottish industry, see Anthony Slaven: *The West Coast of Scotland, 1760–1960* (1975), or one of the regional texts. The early history of the industry is the subject of the classic by A. P. Wadsworth and J. de L. Mann: *The Cotton Trade and Industrial Lancashire, 1600–1780* (1931). On particular firms see G. Unwin: *Samuel Oldknow and the Arkwrights* (1924), or R. S. Fitton and A. P. Wadsworth: *The Strutts and the Arkwrights* (1964), or the more recent book by C. H. Lee: *A Cotton Enterprise, 1795–1840: a history of McConnel and Kennedy, fine cotton spinners* (1972).

WOOL

The woollen industry is not so well served by up-to-date texts, but see the brief but wide ranging: *The Wool Textile Industry in Great Britain*, (ed.) J. Geraint Jenkins (1972). The standard article on the growth of the industry is by P. Deane: 'The Output of the British Woollen Industry in the Eighteenth Century', *J. Ec. Hist.* vol. XVII (1957). A good recent collection of essays on all aspects of the industry is that edited by N. B. Harte and K. G. Ponting: *Textile History and Economic History: Essays in Honour of Miss J. de L. Mann* (1973). Miss Mann's own *The Cloth Industry in the West of England 1840–1880* (1971) is a detailed study of one of the important woollen regions. There is as yet no general work to replace H. Heaton's *The Yorkshire Woollen and Worsted Industries* (1920), but R. G. Wilson's book: *Gentleman Merchants: the Merchant Community in Leeds, 1760–1830* (1971) examines an important part of this regional economy. The date of the decline of the Norwich industry has long been the subject of debate. See J. K. Edwards: 'The decline of the Norwich textile industry', in *Yorkshire Bull. of Econ. and Soc. Research* vol. XVI (1964), which argues that absolute decline did not take place until the nineteenth century, and M. F. Lloyd-Pritchard: 'The Decline of Norwich', *Ec. H. R.* vol. 3

(1951), which considers that the first half of the eighteenth century was the critical period.

## IRON

Two good general books: H. R. Schubert: *A History of the British Iron and Steel Industry from c450B.C. to A.D.1775* (1957), and Alan Birch: *The Economic History of the British Iron and Steel Industry, 1784–1879* (1967). However, important research has been done on the iron industry in the last few years, and no general account should be read without reference to the following articles: C. K. Hyde: 'The Adoption of Coke Smelting by the British Iron Industry, 1709–90', *Expl. in Ent. History* vol. 10 (1973), G. Hammersley: 'The Charcoal Iron Industry and its Fuel, 1540–1750', *Ec. H.R.* vol. XXVI (1973), H. C. Tomlinson: 'Wealden Gunfounding: An Analysis of its Demise in the Eighteenth Century', *Ec. H.R.* vol. XXIX (1976) and Philip Riden: 'The Output of the British Iron Industry before 1870', *Ec. H.R.* vol. XXX (1977). Two earlier articles by B. L. C. Johnson are useful: 'The Foley Partnerships: the Iron Industry at the End of the Charcoal Era', *Ec. H.R.* vol. IV (1952) and 'The Charcoal Iron Industry in the early Eighteenth Century', *Geog. Jnl.* 117 (1951).

There are several business histories of variable quality. The better ones include: M. W. Flinn: *Men of Iron: The Crowleys in the Early Iron Industry* (1962), R. H. Campbell: *The Carron Company* (1961), A. Raistrick: *Dynasty of Iron Founders: The Darbys and Coalbrookdale* (1953), and a valuable edited collection of documents, M. Elsas: *Iron in the Making, Dowlais Iron Company Letters, 1782–1860* (1960).

There is less readily available material on the small iron trades, much of the information in this section having been derived directly from local trade directories. However, see T. S. Ashton: *An 18th Century Industrialist: Peter Stubs of Warrington, 1756–1806* (1939), W. H. B. Court: *The Rise of Midland Industries, 1600–1838* (1953), E. Robinson: 'Eighteenth Century commerce and fashion: Matthew Boulton's marketing techniques', *Ec. H.R.* vol. XVI (1963), and M. B. Rowlands: *Masters and Men in the West Midlands Metal Trades before the Industrial Revolution* (1975).

## COAL

The standard source is still T. S. Ashton and J. Sykes: *The Coal Industry in the 18th Century*, 2nd edn. (1964). A good summary is Brian Lewis': *Coal Mining in the Eighteenth and Nineteenth Centuries* (1971). A valuable regional study, which also outlines the problems of historical research very well, is John Langton: 'Coal Output in S.W. Lancashire, 1590–1799' *Ec. H.R.* vol. XXV (1972).

OTHER INDUSTRIES

On the non-ferrous metal industries see H. Hamilton: *The English Brass and Copper Industries to 1800*, 2nd edn. (1967), J. R. Harris: *The Copper King: A Biography of Thomas Williams of Llaniden* (1964), an essay by R. O. Roberts, 'The Development and Decline of Non-Ferrous Metal Smelting Industries in South Wales', in W. E. Minchinton (ed.): *Industrial South Wales, 1750–1914* (1969), and W. E. Minchinton: *The British Tin-plate Industry: a history* (1957).

Studies of other industries include: L. Weatherhill: *The Pottery Trade and North Staffordshire, 1660–1760* (1971), and N. McKendrick: 'Josiah Wedgwood: An Eighteenth Century Entrepreneur in Salesmanship and Marketing Techniques', *Ec. H.R.* vol. XII (1960); P. Mathias: *The Brewing Industry in England 1700–1830* (1959); D. C. Coleman: *The British Paper Industry, 1495–1860* (1958) and A. G. Thompson: *The Paper Industry in Scotland, 1590–1861* (1975); T. C. Barker: *Pilkington Brothers and the Glass Industry* (1960).

REGIONAL STUDIES

Many of the references above are regionally oriented, but on specific regions see: Anthony Slaven: *The West Coast of Scotland, 1760–1960* (1975), W. E. Minchinton (ed.): *Industrial South Wales, 1750–1914* (1969), and A. H. John: *The Economic Development of South Wales 1750–1850: an essay* (1950); J. Rowe: *Cornwall in the Age of the Industrial Revolution* (1953); J. D. Chambers: 'The Vale of Trent, 1670–1800: a regional study of economic change', *Ec. H.R.* Supplement no. 3, (1957); and Barrie Trinder: *The Industrial Revolution in Shropshire* (1973).

There are a few accessible contemporary studies, for example John Aikin: *A Description of the Country from Thirty to Forty Miles round Manchester*, (1795, repr. 1968), *Svedenstierna's Tour of Great Britain, 1802–3* (trans. 1973), and Defoe's *Tour*.

# 6 Internal Trade and Communications

'Bid Harbours open, public ways extend, Bid Temples, worthier of the God, ascend, Bid the broad Arch the dang'rous Flood contain, The Mole projected break the roaring Main; Back to his bounds their subject sea command, And roll obedient Rivers thro' the Land; These Honours, Peace to Happy Britain brings, These are Imperial Works and worthy Kings'.

*Alexander Pope* (1731).

With the development of industry and agriculture, and the growth and redistribution of population in the eighteenth century, came a steady expansion of internal trade. And with this expansion of trade, there was constant improvement and innovation in the transport system and in transport services. To contemporaries, it was this, as much as anything, that represented progress: Alexander Pope spoke for many as he upheld the symbols of new harbours, extending roads and navigable rivers. But they were, of course, far more than mere symbols. They were the means by which essential flows of goods, people and information were maintained through the economy, and with which the march of the early Industrial Revolution could be carried throughout Britain.

## THE GROWTH OF INTERNAL TRADE

In the seventeenth century, the coal trade was described as 'one of the greatest home trades in the Commonwealth of England' (fig. 5:4). Although some coal was distributed overland by river and road from the interior fields, its basic artery was the seawise shipment of coal from the Tyne and Wear, down the east coast to London. Smaller flows of Newcastle coal went to many other major and minor ports – even beaches – as far west as Exeter: in particular, Hull, King's Lynn, Yarmouth, Ipswich and Southampton. From the quayside the coal was distributed by sledge and waggon to the townsfolk, whilst much was sent inland through the system of navigable rivers to towns and counties some way from the coast.

The coal trade illustrates several general points about patterns of internal trade in the seventeenth and eighteenth centuries. The north-east was peculiarly suited to the mass export of coal, having easily worked seams close to the coast, from which the material could be shipped to the major markets. The region had an obvious *comparative advantage* over others in the production of coal: it is this principle which underlies the exchange of products (i.e. trade) between regions. Secondly, the quantities involved in this coal trade were considerable, and growing all the time. In the 1700s, London was importing some 800,000 to one million tons of coal a year. By the 1750s, this had risen to between 1.2 and 1.5 million tons, and by the 1790s, to between 2.4 and 2.6 million tons. Thirdly, the organisation of the coal trade was complex. It covered long distances and used several modes of transport. Coal was transferred from the mines by middlemen, called fitters, who took it in waggons to the staithes, or loading wharves, and there paid keelmen to take it out into the river in 20-ton keels to the waiting colliers. The coal was then bought from the fitters by the ships' captains who, after a journey of some 350 miles down the coast to London (this could take several weeks in winter), resold to the coal factors in the capital. It was the job of the factors to find buyers: some of the coal went to wholesalers in the city, the rest was sold for shipping inland up the Thames or its tributaries, or by road into Surrey and Middlesex, or for further passage to the small north Kent or, south coast ports. Coal being unloaded at Abingdon wharf in Berkshire had travelled 450 miles, over a period of some weeks, and had passed through the hands of four or five middlemen since clearing the mine on Tyne or Wearside.

Most regions had or were developing comparative advantages in the production of something, if not from resource endowments (as in the north-eastern coalfield, or Cornish tin-mining area), then based on long experience in a particular trade, or entrepreneurial drive, labour skills, or lower labour costs. Once the process of specialisation was begun, the trading of goods with other regions consolidated that specialisation: hence the growth and concentration of the cotton industry in Lancashire, the East Midlands and around Glasgow, or of woollen cloth manufacture in Norwich, the West Riding and the west of England, the pottery trade in north Staffordshire, and metal working in south Staffordshire and south Yorkshire. But comparative advantage applied equally well in agriculture, with even the remote upland fringes raising cattle and participating in trade. Farmers followed the course of husbandry for which their situation (soils, climate, distance from market, experience) was best suited. Regional specialisation was one of the notable characteristics of eighteenth-century agriculture, and few farms were completely divorced from the market (above, pp. 44–5).

Daniel Defoe described the great trade between the provinces and London; it was one of the central themes of his *Tour*: 'the neighbourhood of London . . . sucks the vitals of trade in this island to itself,' he wrote, in characteristically colourful style. Goods came into the capital by all modes of transport, and in great quantities. The ports of East Anglia and the south-east sent corn, as did those in the Humber and Borders. Kings Lynn alone shipped 62,410 quarters to London in 1735 (as well as over 10,000 quarters to Newcastle in exchange for coal). More corn came overland by waggon and barge from Hertfordshire, Bedfordshire and Buckingham, and the counties in the Thames basin. Regular waggon loads of butter were sent from Oxfordshire, as well as shiploads from Suffolk and Yorkshire, a total of 12,000 tons a year in the 1730s. By 1750, 2,500 tons of cheese were reaching London from the west of England and the Midlands, as well as quantities of fresh market garden produce from Bedfordshire and the Medway ports. Meat walked itself to market, driven overland from the Scottish Highlands, the Borders and North Country and Wales, to fattening pastures in the Midlands, East Anglia and Essex. In 1700, half a million sheep and 75,000 cattle were sent on to be sold at Smithfield market. In 1800, the amounts had grown to no less than 750,000 and 100,000 respectively. Then from Norfolk and Suffolk came droves of turkeys, often 300 to a thousand in a drove according to Defoe, who met them coming in the opposite direction. Usually they walked, but sometimes they were carried, along with chickens, in four-storeyed carts, or 'new-fashion'd voitures' drawn by pairs of horses.

London was the centre of a great system of trade within Britain, by far and away the largest centre of population and most important port, it drew traffic to itself in great and increasing volume. But it was not the only centre. Every part of Britain had its own focus of trade: Bristol in the west, Birmingham and Nottingham in the Midlands, Norwich, Kings Lynn and Hull in the east, Liverpool and Carlisle in the north-west, York and Newcastle in the north, Edinburgh, Glasgow and Aberdeen in Scotland. Around these larger centres of trade was a mass of sub-regional and local market towns, each at the midst of its own increasing circle of commerce, acting as a central place for the surrounding communities and countryside. Often these smaller markets were mere stepping stones in the regional or national pattern of trade. London factors frequently intervened to buy corn, cloth or manufactures for the capital or foreign trades.

The flows of traffic between regions, from firm or farm to market, from country to town, were often considerable. In 1698, carriers on the River Lea brought 3,750 tons of malt from Ware into London, whilst in 1766 1,100 loads of timber left Godalming wharf, on the Wey, for the Thames. The gatekeeper of the Birdlip Hill Turnpike Trust in Gloucestershire, which looked after a stretch of the main London to South Wales road, recorded no less than 16,000 sheep, 14,000 cattle, 21,000 single horses and 24,000 animals in draught between June 1767 and June 1768. Outside Bristol, in one week alone in June 1765, 259 coaches, 491 waggons, 722 carts, 206 drays (or sledges) with 11,759 horses, travelled past Lawford's gate on the Midland road. Yet away from the main arteries, traffic flows were often very light, with peaks on fair or market days only. The Hastings road in mid-Sussex had a through traffic of little more than 50 carriages and waggons, and 200 to 300 single horses each month in the late 1760s.

## TRANSPORT SERVICES

This growing volume of internal trade was conveyed by a sophisticated network of transport services. But these were very varied in form, because the demand for transport itself was not homogenous. The ships that plied the coasts, and the river and canal barges were primarily the means of moving bulk, non-perishable goods cheaply. Where no water transport was available, packhorse trains or waggons fulfilled this role. But road transport services were better suited to short distance trade, or the speedy long distance transfer of small or perishable goods, whereas horse, coach or stage waggon were the usual means of passenger transport and of conveying information (plates D3 and 4).

The *road transport* system had reached a considerable stage of development. In 1637 John Taylor, innkeeper, poet and pamphleteer, published his *Carriers Cosmographie*, which listed nearly 200 towns, as far apart as Barnstaple, Monmouth, Leeds and Denbigh, that had direct carriers' services into London or Southwark. Most of these were packhorse carriers, it seems, only a handful of waggon and coach services being mentioned. Other centres had equally comprehensive networks of carriers for their size and function. In the 1670s, Oxford people had weekly carrier services to such places as Northampton, Warwick, Worcester and Winchester, and monthly links to distant counties such as Devon, Derbyshire, Shropshire and Lancashire. A list of carriers dated 1699 from Kendal, the economic centre of Cumbria and a town of 5,000 people, shows that it had packtrain services to Newcastle, Liverpool, Manchester, Leeds, Hull, Norwich and London, (the last service being operated by two partnerships, one of four men with 60 horses, one of two men with 24), as well as several neighbouring towns.

Wheeled traffic was common in southern England, especially in and near London by 1700, and usual throughout the Midlands by mid-century. By 1800, it was the normal means of communication for carriers in most parts, although packhorse trains were still common in Wales, Scotland, the Pennine Hills, and the south-west. In fact, the first coach between Edinburgh and Glasgow did not run until 1749, and it was the mid-1770s before a regular coach from Chester began to operate through north Wales to Holyhead. In the 1780s, the Chester Guide advertised waggon and coach services to a number of English towns, yet only pack-horse services to those of north Wales. Newcastle-upon-Tyne was a bust-ling regional centre of 35,000 people by this time, and its Directory advertised extensive connections to towns all over the north of England and into Scotland as far as Glasgow, as well as to London. Several of these services ran two or three times each week, but all were at least weekly (fig. 6:1). London itself had no less than 180 coach services to pro-vincial towns in 1705, and 342 by 1836.

Apart from the roads, however, the *water carriage* system, of navigable waterways and the sea, itself 'a river around Britain', played a vital role. For the transfer of non-perishable bulk goods, water transport was con-siderably cheaper per ton/mile than land carriage, certainly no more than half, and often very much less. A packhorse could carry between two and three hundredweights, a waggon needing several horses was limited by law to a load of 30 hundredweights in summer in 1662 (raised to three tons in 1741, and six tons in 1765), whereas one horse could haul up to 50 tons on a well constructed river or canal towpath. The *river basins* of Britain were, therefore, extremely important arteries of trade in the eighteenth century, in particular those that traversed the major agricul-tural and industrial regions: the Severn, the Humber, (fed by the York-shire Ouse, Aire, Calder and the Trent), the Cambridgeshire Ouse and the Thames. The Severn was unusual as it was the only great river that could be navigated without flashes or locks. It carried coal downstream from the Shropshire mines, with Droitwich salt, and corn, fruit and cheese from its tributaries the Avon and the Teme. Upstream went barges of Dean pig for the Staffordshire metal workers, timber, brass and bronze goods and groceries from Bristol. The boats on the Severn were between 20 and 80 tons in size, usually open barges. These West Country barges were also used on the Thames, but in the upper reaches beyond Oxford, the goods frequently had to be unloaded into 'lightening' boats because of the risk of grounding in gravel shoals. River barges invariably had sails, but also needed another form of assistance: sometimes horses,

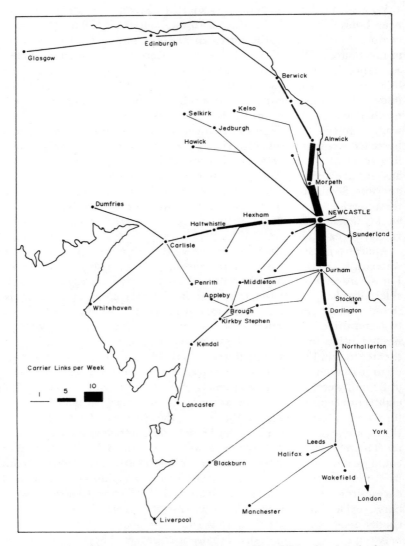

Fig. 6:1 *The Carrier Network of Newcastle-upon-Tyne, 1778* – showing the frequency of carrier links between Newcastle and its hinterland. *Source*: Newcastle Directory (1778).

but often ordinary manpower. The 'halers', as they were called, worked in groups of up to 60 on the Thames. The canals of the late eighteenth century, however, had properly constructed towpaths for the use of horses.

The *coastwise trade* was extensive all round the shores of Britain, on account of the length of coastline in relation to land area. And the coastal trade was of far greater volume than overseas trade – as late as 1841, the tonnage of coastal shipping entering ports was three times that of shipping from overseas destinations. The coastal trade was concentrated on the eastern shores. Of a total of 97,000 tons of English coastal shipping in 1709, nearly 50,000 tons belonged to the ports of Scarborough, Whitby, Newcastle, Yarmouth and Kings Lynn, variously engaged in the fishing, corn and coal trades. The colliers were the biggest boats, at 300 or 400 tons, several times larger than most. The decked-in hoys that sailed from the north Kent ports of Margate, Faversham and Whitstable, laden with corn for Bear Key in London were fast, shallow-bottomed vessels of 60 to 120 tons a piece. They worked to advertised schedules, and frequently carried passengers too. Before the railways reached Thanet in the 1840s, the hoy, and later, steamboats, performed the regular passenger services to the new seaside resorts.

The great advantage of water transport was its cheapness. Timber brought out of the Weald to the coast cost about one shilling per ton/mile to transport by road in the 1670s, whilst iron cost between 5d and 7d. Yet timber could be shipped from the Forest of Dean, via Bristol, to Chatham for as little as ½d to 1d per ton/mile, and pig iron cost no more than ¾d per ton/mile to ship from Rye to London in 1673. Nevertheless, the water transport system by no means overshadowed the land transport system, even for bulk goods. The two were closely interdependent. The cost advantage of water transport was often reduced by the longer distances that had to be traversed by river or canal. Many areas were too far from a navigable waterway or the sea to make use of them. There again, water transport had certain disadvantages. It was often very slow and frequently disrupted. Little trade took place on the rough North Sea in winter, and the colliers did not sail between December and February. In times of war, when it was difficult to organise effective convoys, valuable goods such as groceries were diverted overland. Fish from the east and south coast ports was sent by packhorse train to London, so that it was saleable when it arrived at Billingsgate. In 1709, Hastings fishermen were sending 320 packhorses to London each day laden with fish. The journey took 12 to 15 hours, but by sea it took at least 48. Delays often occurred on river navigations because of seasonally low water, or enforced waits for millers to open their weirs. An extensive programme of road improvements was undertaken in the West Riding in the 1740s, sponsored by local manufacturers, because of high lock dues on the Aire and Calder, as well as delays from low water, heavy frosts and flooding in different seasons. The trade in butter from Wiltshire and Oxfordshire was lost by the Thames carriers as the goods could not be got to market fresh enough by river. Even in 1809, it took three and a half days to navigate from Oxford to London, and six days to return – a journey that could be accomplished in eight hours by road.

On the whole, therefore, the water and road transport systems were complementary. Water transport, where it was accessible, coped best with long distance transfer of bulky and non-perishable goods. Road transport both acted as a feeder and distributor for the water-based system, and was important in its own right for the transfer of small goods, perishables, passengers and information. But the cost of the speed and flexibility which the road carriers offered was a level of transport charges considerably higher than those of the water carriers.

## INNOVATION IN TRANSPORT SYSTEMS

The growth of internal trade led inevitably to pressure on the existing transport systems. Road and water systems that were essentially medieval in conception and design could not for long maintain the transfer of expanding volumes of traffic without improvement. Thus a succession of innovations characterise the history of both transport networks and services from the mid-seventeenth century onwards.

Before the advent of the turnpike trusts, *road repair* was the responsibility of each parish, a common law obligation of some antiquity. This obligation had been formalised under the famous Tudor 'statute labour' Acts of 1555, 1562 and 1586, requiring parishes to elect two unpaid Highway Surveyors every year to supervise road repair. All parishioners were to work for six days annually on the roads, or – if they occupied land valued at £50 a year or owned a draft of horses – to send a cart and man instead. The Scottish Parliament instigated a similar system in the seventeenth century, but there the Justices of the Peace were responsible for supervising the annual repair operation. However, the system never worked well, especially on the main roads where there was heavy through traffic originating from outside the parish. And the parish responsibility extended to the repair of the surface alone, not to the reconstruction or improvement of roads that was so greatly needed as flows of traffic increased.

The inadequacies of this statute labour system were recognised by

Parliament in a long series of *ad hoc* measures. In the mid seventeenth century, Justices were periodically given permission to levy road rates on parishes for a limited term, a measure that was made permanent by an Act of 1691. Marylebone parish, then on the outskirts of London, was just one of many that had to make extensive use of this Act, levying 13 rates between 1705 and 1723 to help in the repair of the Edgware and Great West Roads, thereby taxing local people more and more heavily as through traffic grew. So Parliament then attempted to restrict the types of traffic thought to be particularly harmful to road surfaces. This is why weight limits were imposed on waggon loads, accompanied by restrictions on the number of horses that waggons or coaches could use, and the type of wheel construction permitted.[1] But not only were such measures hard to enforce: in the face of growing internal trade, they were self defeating. Only a means of road repair that had adequate financial backing, which meant charging users themselves, and one that was adapted to meet future traffic needs, rather than simply patching up an inadequate medieval system, could cope with the eighteenth-century expansion of trade.

This was provided by the turnpike trusts, which were established individually by Acts of Parliament to take care of specific sections of highway. They were empowered to levy tolls on road users (according to prescribed schedules), and to borrow money on the security of the tolls, for the maintenance and improvement of their roads. Turnpike Acts were readily granted from the mid 1690s, as parishes petitioned Westminster, often with evidence of considerable extra contributions to road repair over preceding years. By 1750, there were 143 trusts in existence, repairing 3,400 miles of road. Although they were local bodies, often controlling only 20 miles of road or so, they had combined to form a coherent network of improving roads. Lines of turnpike road radiated from London, particularly to the north and west, and into the Midlands. There was an extensive network of trusts in the industrialising and rich agricultural counties of the West Midlands, as well as several links over the Pennines between the growing economies of Lancashire and Yorkshire, and some important coal routes further north. The line of trusts on the Great North Road was almost unbroken to the Scottish Border.

After 1750, with the nationwide expansion of agriculture and industry, and the growth of population and towns, the turnpike road system spread with increasing rapidity (fig. 6:5). There were over 500 trusts and nearly 15,000 miles of turnpike road in England and Wales by 1770, and nearly 1,000 trusts and 22,000 miles at the peak of the system in 1836. The network was intense, and extensive, spreading into the far corners of England and Wales and as far north as the Highland line in Scotland (fig. 6:2). Some of the later trusts were considerably larger than the early ones, and many of those in Wales and Scotland controlled networks covering a whole county, which were usually split into 'divisions' for management purposes. Even so, the average size of new trusts created in the 1750s and 1760s was only about 30 miles, although many grew by adding extra mileage granted by Parliament when the 21 year term of their Acts was renewed.

Turnpike trusts – they were not companies – were promoted in Parliament by local landowners and farmers, who wished to cut the cost of highway repair to themselves and facilitate the marketing of their produce, and by industrialists and entrepreneurs who sought to minimize regional transport difficulties. The merchants of Leeds and Wakefield were the moving spirit behind the turnpiking of West Riding routes in the 1740s, and joined with tradesmen and merchants in the Lancashire towns to get the trans-Pennine roads turnpiked. In the Midlands, coalpit owners were frequent promoters of trusts. Abraham Darby III and John Wilkinson were both active Trustees in Shropshire, and Josiah Wedgwood took an eager interest in turnpike schemes around the Potteries. On most trusts, however, it was local farmers, tradesmen and clergy, Justices of the Peace and landowners who served as Trustees, often only a dozen or so running the affairs of the trust at monthly meetings, controlling their paid Surveyor and labourers, and entering into contracts for road repair.

These turnpike trusts brought about very tangible improvements to the country's main roads. An Oxford writer in 1767 thought that 'there is no one circumstance, which will contribute to characterise the present Age to Posterity so much as the Improvements, which have been made in our Publick Roads'. Most trusts not only maintained the surfaces of their roads, but widened them, cleared side ditches and built new drains and bridges. In the latter years of the century, trusts began to re-lay their roads on properly drained foundations, and to lessen gradients and straighten stretches, improvements which became widespread with the work of Robert McAdam and Thomas Telford after 1800. Undoubtedly some turnpike roads remained in a poor condition, but praise, not condemnation, was general. British roads were the admiration of foreigners, and Arthur Young, the inveterate agricultural traveller, found three-quarters of the 1,000 miles of turnpike road in his Northern Tour in 1771 ranging between 'pretty good' and 'excellent'.

The real evidence of the impact of the turnpike trusts, however, was the gradual modernisation of transport services and the effects on travel patterns that they permitted. As turnpike roads spread, so too did wheeled traffic, and as surfaces improved, loads carried increased and

Fig. 6:2 *The Turnpike Road Network of England and Wales, 1770. Source*: Pawson (1977) p. 151.

the number of horses used fell. Stage coach services, which were generally seasonal during the first few decades of the century, running on imprecise summer schedules alone, were working to exact year-round timetables by 1770, speeding on roads that were smooth enough not only for daytime but night-time travel as well. Travel times shrank, and the towns of Britain moved closer together (fig. 6:3) as mails, stage coaches

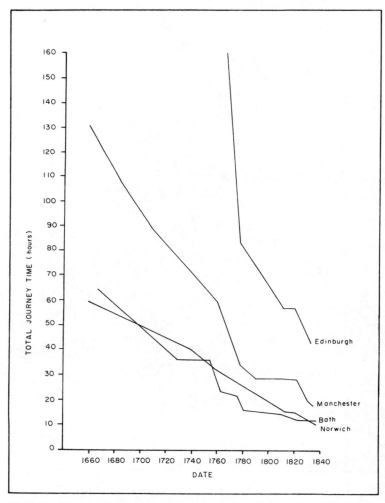

Fig. 6:3 *Time-Space Convergence Curves, 1660–1840* – the curves show the decline in total journey time between the four towns and London, using the fastest available coaches. *Source*: Pawson (1977) p. 288.

and waggons speeded up. And there was no great increase in transport charges: the increasing efficiency of carriers, combined with competition between them, kept charges to a rather lower rate of increase than prices as a whole.

All this was achieved without significant state intervention. Parliament's most important role was its design and sanction of each turnpike Act. But the trusts themselves almost without exception, were locally controlled bodies, deriving their income solely from the tolls and money borrowed locally on the security of those tolls. The only major area of public spending before 1800 was in the Scottish Highlands, where an extensive programme of road building was undertaken after the Jacobite rebellions of 1715 and 1745. General Wade constructed 250 miles of military roads and 40 bridges between 1726 and 1737, and after 1745, a further 800 miles of road and 1,000 bridges were added, crisscrossing the Central Highlands as far north as Inverness. However, these were roads for troops, not trade, and gradually fell into disrepair in the latter years of the century. After a report by Thomas Telford in 1803, the Commission for Highland Roads was established to bring the Highland route network up to coaching standards. The cost of £500,000 was divided equally between the government and local landowners. Telford was later employed to improve the Shrewsbury to Holyhead road as well. It was the main link to Ireland (joined to Britain by the Act of Union in 1801) and Parliament spent over £750,000 on this project between 1815 and the 1830s. Smaller amounts of taxpayers' money were spent on improving the Carlisle to Glasgow and Portpatrick routes and the Great North Road between Morpeth and Edinburgh at the same time.

The state took a similarly limited role in the improvement of inland waterways and the creation of the new canal network. Every scheme had to be approved, to protect the interests of the various parties affected: landowners, farmers, millers, fishermen as well as carriers, but the promotion and finance in each case was again a local effort. England's *rivers* were chiefly maintained by Commissions of Sewers, large bodies of Trustees who were primarily concerned with flood prevention and drainage. They could compel landowners to clear their part of the river, or levy a rate for maintenance purposes. However, the needs of regular navigation required improvements such as new cuts, dredging, the regulation of weirs and the construction of locks, all things which lay beyond the powers of the Commissions of Sewers. Such improvements had to be carried out by separate bodies or individuals, under powers granted, sometimes by Letters Patent of the King, but more usually by Parliamentary Act.

The earliest example of such a grant was to the Corporation of London to improve the River Lea, in 1424 and again in 1571. Letters Patent were given for improvements to the Warwickshire Avon, the Soar, Lark and Tone in the early seventeenth century. After the Restoration, Acts were passed for the Stour, Wye, Medway, Great Ouse and a number of other rivers. Between 1697 and 1700, just when the first turnpike schemes were being approved by Parliament, there were new Acts for the Colne, Tone, the Aire and Calder, the Trent, Bristol Avon and the Dee. Then, from 1719 to 1721, there was a speculative burst of activity with new Acts for the Derwent, Douglas, Great Ouse, Idle, Kennet, Weaver, Mersey and Irwell. These schemes were implemented in a variety of ways. In a few cases, a Commission with rating powers was established, as for the Thames (under a succession of Acts of 1606, 1624, 1695 and 1751), the Wye and the Lug, working in a similar way to the Commissions of Sewers. Many of the earlier schemes were implemented by individuals, who were granted toll rights in return (the Tone, Warwickshire Avon, Welland, Great Ouse, for instance). Some were carried out by partnerships (e.g. Wey, Medway and the Kennet), and one or two, like the Weaver, by trusts, empowered to borrow money on the credit of the tolls. A few later schemes, such as the Don, Dee and Douglas, were carried out by a form of company, with a limited number of marketable shares, a development which foreshadowed that of the canals.

Improvements such as these were at best piecemeal when seen from a national perspective. Often they were not too successful locally either. Despite the grant of powers to Bath Corporation in 1619 for improving the Somerset Avon, nothing was done until the eighteenth century. The deficiencies of the Aire and Calder Navigation have already been highlighted: by the 1740s the system was in a poor state of repair, yet high tolls were still being charged. Navigation on the Thames was never very satisfactory either, difficulties with the shoals and millers' weirs persisted despite the efforts of the Commission. Moreover, even with all the river improvement Acts passed before 1750, many parts were still remote from navigable water, in particular the growing industrial areas of Birmingham and south Staffordshire, north Staffordshire and the south Wales valleys. It was the need for cheaper bulk transport in such areas, and the market for coal in the new factories, workshops and towns, that spurred the construction of canals.

The cradle of the *canal* age was south-west Lancashire, a region stimulated by the growth of both Liverpool and Manchester. Liverpool's salt trade to Ireland and Europe was dependent upon cheap transport from the salt fields in northern Cheshire, and coal from the mines on the other bank of the Mersey. The River Weaver out of Cheshire had been improved by 1733; the Sankey Brook Navigation from the coalfield around St. Helen's – involving several major new cuts – was completed between 1754 and 1757. Four years after this, in 1761, the Duke of Bridgewater's famous canal, from his mines at Worsley into Manchester, was opened. Being a completely new route, and using aqueducts and tunnels, it showed just what engineers could achieve. The fall in the price of coal in Manchester, from 7d to 3½d a hundredweight, then showed what canals themselves could achieve. In the next 70 years, over 3,000 miles of improved river and canal navigation were completed in Britain, adding to the 1,000 already in existence. But it was not a uniform growth. The first great upturn in construction came in the 1760s and early 1770s. It slowed with the relative depression in trade in the 1770s, and the difficulty of raising finance during the American wars. The second great upturn came with the rapid expansion of the economy in the late 1780s and 1790s, tailing off after 1800 when most of the more viable routes had already been completed. Over £2 million was invested in canal construction before 1780, and over £15 million between 1780 and 1815 (fig. 6:4).

Several important routes were completed in the first phase of canal building, and several more were started, only to remain partially constructed whilst awaiting the more favourable climate of the late 1780s. In 1766, both the Trent and Mersey (or Grand Trunk) and the Staffordshire and Worcestershire Canals were authorised. James Brindley, the brilliant Staffordshire millwright who had taken charge of the Duke of Bridgewater's operations, engineered both canals. The Grand Trunk provided a 93-mile cut between the Trent at Wilden Ferry and the Mersey, so linking east and west. Completed in 1777, it skirted the Potteries (Wedgwood was its Treasurer), and ended their isolation from cheap water transport. The potters had previously had to rely on packhorses to bring ball clay and flint anything up to 40 miles from wharves on the Severn, Weaver or Trent. The Staffordshire and Worcestershire joined the Grand Trunk south of the Potteries, and connected with the Severn south of Bewdley, at a point where the new town of Stourport mushroomed. It was finished in 1772, the same year as Brindley's Birmingham Canal, which joined that town to the Staffordshire and Worcestershire via Wolverhampton. By 1776, Birmingham had two more such links, the Stourbridge and Dudley Canals. Between them, these four projects brought cheap water carriage into south Staffordshire and the Birmingham Plateau, another area isolated from good river navigations.

Several other important routes were started at this time. Midland coalowners promoted the Coventry and Oxford Canals, started in 1768 and 1769 respectively. But the construction of both was held up for a considerable time due to financial difficulties in the late 1770s and early 1780s, and they did not provide a direct link between the Thames and Grand Trunk until 1790. Work started on the mammoth Leeds and Liverpool Canal in 1770, but was suspended in 1777. It did not resume until 1790 but when it was finished in 1815, it provided – at the aston-

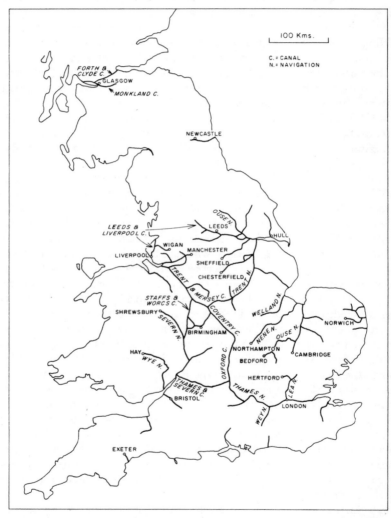

Fig. 6:4    *The Canal Network in Britain, 1789. Source*: compiled from Hadfield (1969).

ishing cost of £1.2 million – a 127 mile cut from Wigan, through Burnley and Skipton to Leeds. In Scotland, the Forth and Clyde Canal was begun in 1768. It was designed to give Glasgow easy access to the agricultural counties in the east, and via the North Sea, to the industrial markets of northern Europe. But it was not finished till 1790. The Monkland Canal, started in 1770, eventually brought coal from the Lanarkshire field into Glasgow, but took an equally long period to complete.

The second generation of canal construction therefore saw the completion of many important routes started some time before. It also contained a large number of new schemes. The Birmingham and Fazeley Canal was finished in 1790, linking with the Coventry Canal, and giving Birmingham – 'the Kremlin of canals' – direct canal routes to the north and south. The ironmasters of the Severn Gorge area were the driving force behind the Shropshire Canal (1788–92). Richard Arkwright was active in the promotion and finance of the Cromford Canal (1789–95), which linked his mills via the Erewash Canal to the Trent. Fifty-one new canal companies were established during the 'Canal Mania' between 1791 and 1796, including several more in the Birmingham area, and four in south Wales. These were the Monmouthshire, Glamorgan, Neath and Swansea (1790–9) which, with the Brecknock and Abergavenny, and the Aberdare, both finished by 1812, were vital to the expansion of the south Wales coal and iron industry. The most conspicuous project of these years, however, was the Grand Junction Canal, a direct link of 93 miles between the head of the Oxford Canal and London. Built at the cost of £1.8 million, and finished in 1815, it enabled northern and Midland shippers to avoid both the narrow Oxford canal and the inefficient Thames navigation.

Many of these canals were extremely successful, not only as transport links, but as investments too. In the 1830s, the Grand Trunk, Oxford, Coventry, Erewash and Forth and Clyde canals, and the Loughborough and Mersey and Irwell Navigations all paid dividends of over 25 per cent, whilst their share prices stood at six or seven times their nominal value.[2] Nevertheless, a number of projects were also very unsuccessful. One earlier example is the Thames and Severn Canal, built between 1783 and 1793, to link the Thames at Lechlade to the Stroudwater Canal. Continuous problems with water retention in the Cotswold summit level, and the refusal of the Thames Commissioners to make real improvements to the river above Oxford, restrained its viability. It was effectively superseded by the Kennet and Avon (1794–1810), which joined the river Kennet (a navigable tributary of the lower Thames) at Newbury to the Avon at Bath. Many more struggling concerns emerged in the aftermath of the Canal Mania, a lot of them in agricultural areas as speculative schemes quite unjustified by potential traffic.

The canal system of eighteenth-century Britain was significant in several ways. Firstly, it provided a greatly improved means of transporting bulk goods, in particular coal, at a time when the pressures of economic growth were rising to unprecedented levels. Secondly, it was a massive exercise in harnessing private initiative and finance. Canal companies were the only joint-stock enterprises to be widely sanctioned in the early Industrial Revolution. It was a form of organisation that was necessary to cope with the first large-scale and relatively rapid investment of social overhead capital in Britain. The whole canal system was built with minimal state assistance, and is ample proof that capital was not in short supply in the eighteenth century. A very wide range of people invested in canals, and certainly not just landowners, but industrialists, tradesmen, farmers, clergy, professional men and women living near the line of each scheme. It was the canals, rather than the railways, that introduced the better-off to the marketable share, and the chance to invest savings and earn dividends.[3]

Thirdly, the canal system was a response to local and regional needs. It was not co-ordinated according to any general plan. The disadvantages of this are readily apparent. Most of the earlier schemes were built as 'narrow canals', able to take only long boats, measuring about 72 feet by 7, which could carry no more than 25 or 30 tons. Many of the later canals, such as the Grand Junction or the Leeds and Liverpool were 'broad canals', of considerably higher capacity. A central plan might well have ensured the earlier completion of some interregional routes such as the Leeds and Liverpool, and Grand Junction. The only important element of central control, as with the turnpike system, lay in the original grant of powers by parliamentary Act. Under the terms of the Bubble Act of 1720, only Parliament could authorise the establishment of joint-stock companies. It was also the only way in which compulsory purchase powers for land could be obtained.

Fourthly, the building of the canal system was the school for the creation of a profession of civil engineers and surveyors: men such as Brindley, Smeaton, Rennie and Telford were the most famous amongst many who had to come to grips with the problems of tunnels, locks, summit levels and aqueducts. Brindley's mile-and-a-half long Harecastle tunnel on the Grand Trunk Canal was the first such ever built outside the mines. Telford completed the massive Caledonian Canal in 1822, and designed the Chirk and the 1,000 foot long Pontcysyllte Aqueducts on the Ellesmere Canal (1805) – merely the most conspicuous of his many achievements (plate D1). Rennie built the Crinan, Kennet and Avon, Rochdale and Lancaster Canals, and made an even greater reputation in the construction of bridges and docks. He built Waterloo, Southwark and London bridges. Smeaton worked in the Calder Navigation and the Forth and Clyde Canal, advised on port improvement at Dundee, Peterhead, Banff and Aberdeen, and had lasting influence through his society for engineers, the Smeatonians – the forerunner of the Society of Civil Engineers – founded in London in 1771. The creation of the canal system was the first real opportunity that men had to grapple with large scale civil engineering problems: experience that stood them in excellent stead for the construction of the solid infrastructure of the Industrial Revolution: docks, harbours, railways, factories and warehouses.

Innovations in *coastal transport* were less remarkable, but nevertheless, important during the eighteenth century. The real advance in shipping design, the steamship, did not become common until well into the nineteenth century. Although William Symington successfully experimented with a steamship at Dalswinton in Dumfriesshire in 1788, it was 1812 before regular commercial services began. This was a passenger run on the Clyde, in which nine steamboats were engaged by 1814. Similar services followed between Newcastle and Shields, and London and Gravesend. By 1821, there were 188 steamships, aggregating 20,028 tons, in service in the coastwise trade around Britain, although overall steam tonnage did not exceed sailing tonnage until 1866. Of greater significance as a technical innovation in the late eighteenth century, was the copper sheathing of ships' bottoms, which protected them from damage by barnacles, weed and worms.

Harbour facilities on the other hand, underwent continuous improvement from the 1690s as coastal and overseas trade increased. The country's first wet dock was completed at Rotherhithe on the Thames in 1700, the second at Liverpool in 1709, and the third at Bristol in 1717. Harbour commissions were established to build or improve harbours at Bridlington in 1697 and Whitby in 1701, both important fishing ports and harbours of refuge for the collier fleets, and at Whitehaven (1708), Sunderland (1717) and Maryport (1747), all coal ports. New harbours were opened on the south coast at Newhaven and Littlehampton in the 1730s, and in the 1760s at Shoreham. Ramsgate harbour was built as a port of refuge under an Act of 1749, costing nearly £600,000 between then and 1816, yet proving its worth by sheltering 39,444 vessels between 1780 and 1830. In Scotland, harbour improvements were made at Leith (in the 1750s, a wet dock being added in the 1790s), at Ayr, Greenock, Banff and Aberdeen, where a 1,200 feet long breakwater was constructed. The real spate of port improvements came however in the years after 1790 and was closely linked to the growth of foreign trade. Liverpool, which had built 20 acres of wet docks between 1743 and 1788, had 47 acres by 1821. Bristol, after several false starts, completed a floating harbour of 80 acres on the River Avon in 1809. Considerable improvements were made to the River Clyde, to harbour facilities in Glasgow, and at Port Glasgow, its outport. London's port had remained basically unaltered through the eighteenth century, despite a threefold increase in trade. However, after the Committee of West Indies Merchants had threatened to transfer their trade elsewhere in 1793, the City Corporation finally took notice of long-voiced criticisms. The London Docks were completed in 1803, the West and East India Docks in 1806, the Surrey and East Country Docks in 1807, and the Commercial Docks in 1815, adding a total of 175 acres of new dock space.

## TRANSPORT AND ECONOMY

The major improvements in Britain's transport systems can be characterised as a series of innovation waves from the mid-seventeenth century onwards (fig. 6:5). As responses to the pressures of economic expansion, they proceeded hand-in-hand with it. The turnpike boom accompanied the upturn of the mid-century years, spilling into the first generation of canal construction, and then both slowed until the rapid take-off of the late 1780s, after which canal investment and port improvement rose to new heights. Yet the waves of river, road and canal innovation all came to an abrupt halt with the emergence of the steam railway in the 1820s and 1830s.

The most tangible effect of these transport innovations, and the improved transport services that accompanied them, was the provision of better carriage for goods and passengers. Faster, more reliable, less seasonal transport induced a series of economies of scale in production and widened the choice of goods and services available to consumers. The need to hold a high proportion of assets in stock lessened as markets could be reached more easily, and more regularly. The resources saved could be channelled into fixed capital investment and the extension of the market (above, p. 90). The provision of cheaper transport opened up whole new areas to industrialists, tradesmen and farmers. The effect on the carriage and availability of a commodity like coal was especially noticeable, but right across the range of manufactures, the effect of cheaper transport was to diminish local self-sufficiency, and encourage regional specialisation. Mass product industries, such as cotton textiles and the metal trades, relied on and flourished by being able to penetrate a wide market from a limited number of producer areas.

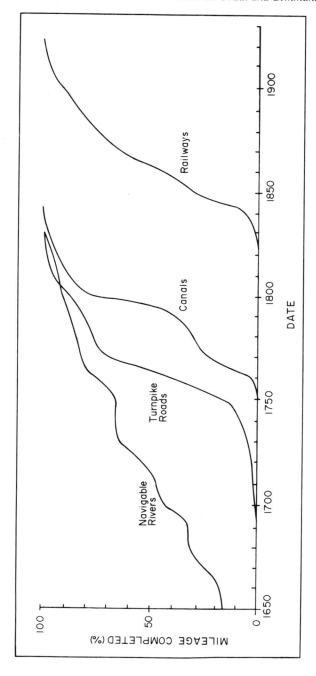

Fig. 6:5 *The Diffusion of Transport Innovations in Britain, 1650–1920 – show-ing mileage completed. Source: Pawson (1977) p. 13.*

The effect of better passenger transport cannot be directly compared with that for goods, as passenger transport itself was often a consumer rather than a producer good. However, the modes of passenger transport were critically important in as much as they were often the vehicle of transfer of flows of *information*. Speedier and more reliable information flow was a central characteristic of the Industrial Revolution: indeed, it was essential for it. It was through the postal system that firms kept in touch with their suppliers, buyers and customers. The mail was the only effective means by which the new, large firms of the eighteenth century could coordinate their various parts: Abraham Crowley showed the way (above, p. 97), but Wedgwood, Boulton, Arkwright, Wilkinson, all depended on the letter-post as did the smaller manufacturer and trades-man, the merchant and farmer. For the farmers and gentry in the countryside, the carrier was their means of keeping in touch with the ser-vices of towns, for essential goods, money transfers and the like. The nation's shopkeepers relied on the post and carrier for their links to the wholesalers.

The postal system, originally only for Royal dispatches, had become a public service by the first half of the seventeenth century. The Post Office Act of 1660 laid down rates and routes: the latter being limited to the main roads until Ralph Allen began the systematic expansion of cross-post services during his term as Postmaster General in the 1720s. Until the 1780s, however, the post was carried on horseback; its speed was sup-posed to be six miles per hour. The first mail coach ran between London and Bath in 1784, and within a few years, most postal routes were oper-ated by coaches introduced by John Palmer, then Postmaster General, who as manager of a Bath theatre, had originally suggested the idea. Its soundness was demonstrated by the continuous increase in speed of the mail coaches, which were running at eight mph by 1811, and ten mph by 1836, and carrying not only letters, but small parcels, money, and pass-engers.

Another important element in the information system was the devel-opment of the provincial press. There were never very many newspapers in print at any one time in the eighteenth century – 28 in English towns in 1758, but the circulation of each one was extremely wide (fig. 6:6). Papers printed in one town were delivered by coach, post or carrier to many others, where agents distributed them to townsfolk and through the countryside. Newspapers were a symptom of progress, their wide cir-culation being a measure of the extent of basic education, but they were also a vehicle of progress. The pages of the provincial press were half filled with national news from London, Parliament and continental dis-patches, but they contained as well some of the basic instruments of the modern economy: market information, advertisements, sales notices. From the prices in his newspaper, the farmer might decide where and when to sell his produce; the entrepreneur advertised the advantages of his new product; canal companies offered their share issues for sale; turnpike trusts publicised the letting of repair contracts or the hiring of labourers.

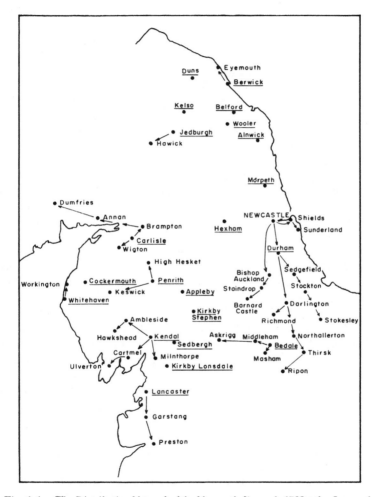

Fig. 6:6   *The Distribution Network of the Newcastle Journal, 1739* – the Journal had distribution agents (usually Postmasters) in the towns underlined on the map. Most agents also distributed to surrounding places, by the arrowed routes. *Source*: drawn from information in Wiles (1965).

The regional effect of improving transport and communication was plain. Rapidly developing regions were those with good or improving transport services. Birmingham occupied a central position in the turnpike network and the canal system. Coal mining developed throughout southern Lancashire with the opening of new navigations, and the textile industry with improving roads. The livelihood of the north-eastern coalfield depended upon its collier links to London, and the extension of waggonways from mine to waterside. Such examples can be multiplied: they can also be found in agricultural regions. The most developed farming areas close to London were the Home Counties of Hertfordshire and Bedford with regular waggon services and the Lea Navigation to the capital, and the coastal parts of East Anglia and north Kent, with good shipping services into the Thames. A rich area of market gardening had developed between Canterbury, Faversham and Maidstone along the Great Dover Road and close to the Medway ports. More remote areas were less favoured, whether geographically close to, or distant from major centres of population. Counties such as Cornwall and Pembrokeshire did not really awaken to outside agricultural markets until the coming of the railway. But north west Middlesex and the Weald, right on London's doorstep, also remained backward and undeveloped for most of the eighteenth century. That part of Middlesex was by-passed by the main turnpike roads, and although the Weald had through turnpike routes as early as the 1750s, it remained notorious for bad roads. Not until the 1790s did commercial wheat growing widely begin to replace local farming and Wealden forest, and that was under the stimulus of high wartime prices.

The effect of improving transport on towns was also marked (below, pp. 2–3). Small markets declined in the face of competition from the larger ones. Agricultural trade became concentrated in fewer centres: the ones with better prices, a wider range of buyers, better facilities. Many small rural towns had stagnant or declining populations by the end of the eighteenth century, yet the bigger ones were growing rapidly. The cities were expanding outwards, and the beginnings of ribbon development and the suburban village were apparent as home and workplace became increasingly separate for those who could afford it. The urban landscape was beginning to take on a standardised air. The neat stuccoed front of the Georgian house was replacing the traditional variety of the vernacular, one result of the pervasive spread of ideas and styles with better communications. And many townspeople who at the start of the century had never, or rarely, seen a wheeled vehicle, were setting their time pieces by the arrival of the daily coach at its end.

NOTES

1 The restriction of weights began in 1621 when James I issued a procla-
mation that four-wheeled waggons were to carry no more than one
ton; in 1654 Cromwell first sought to limit the number of horses used –
to four; the Broad Wheels Act of 1755 was the first to rule on the
widths of wheels. The regulations were altered many times, culminating in impressively long lists in the General Turnpike and High-
ways Acts of 1773. They were not abandoned till 1835.

2 Many canals were extremely profitable before the 1830s of course.
Many of the industrial canals were paying between five and ten per
cent within a few years of starting operations. Others were complete
financial failures. See J. R. Ward: *The Finance of Canal Building* (1974),
Appx. 1 for details.

3 Canal shares were of large denomination (often a minimum of £100)
which limited the range of investors. It was not usual for all the money
to be paid up at once. The universal share – fully paid up and of small
unit value – comes in the later nineteenth century.

FURTHER READING

The two best general descriptive works are H. J. Dyos and D. H. Aldcroft: *British Transport* (1969), and P. S. Bagwell: *The Transport Revolution
from 1770* (1974). For a more analytical account, placing transport in its
context of growing trade and economic advance, see Eric Pawson: *Transport and Economy: The Turnpike Roads of Eighteenth Century Britain* (1977).

INTERNAL TRADE
A much neglected topic, but see John Chartres: *Internal Trade in the Sixteenth and Seventeenth Centuries* (1977), and for a summary of eighteenth
century patterns, Pawson (1977), chapter two. Little has been written
specifically on the waterborne trade since T. S. Willan's *River Navigation
in England, 1600–1750* (1936) and *The English Coasting Trade, 1600–1750*
(1938). On agricultural trade see Alan Everitt's chapter 'The Marketing
of Agricultural Produce' in J. Thirsk (ed.): *The Agrarian History of England
and Wales, 1500–1640* (1967) which ranges beyond those dates and Daniel
Defoe's *Tour*. A valuable regional reference, about the West Riding, is R.
G. Wilson: 'Transport Dues as Indices of Economic Growth', *Ec.H.R.*
vol. XIX (1966).
    On London's centrality in the system of trade see E. A. Wrigley: 'A
Simple Model of London's Importance in Changing English Society and

Economy, 1650–1750', in *Past and Present* no. 37 (1967), and F. J. Fisher: 'The Development of the London Food Market, 1540–1640', *Ec.H.R.* First Series, vol. V (1935) – although dealing with an earlier period it demonstrates the point well. A useful article on the external relations of a provincial city is: W. E. Minchinton: 'Bristol – Metropolis of the West in the Eighteenth Century', *Trans. Royal Hist. Soc.*, Fifth Series no. 4 (1954).

TRANSPORT SERVICES

The standard sources on river and coastal services are T. S. Willan's two books (1936 and 1938). Dennis Baker describes the hoy trade in: 'The Marketing of Corn in the first half of the Eighteenth Century: North East Kent', *Ag. H.R.* vol. 18 (1970). On canal carrying, see Harry Hanson: *The Canal Boatmen, 1750–1914* (1975), E. C. R. Hadfield's: *British Canals*, 4th edn. (1969), and an article by G. L. Turnbull: 'Pickford's and the canal carrying trade, 1750–1850', *Transport History* 6 (1973). Most of the material in this section on road transport services is from Pawson (1977). A regional illustration is provided by M. J. Freeman: 'The Stage-Coach system of South Hampshire, 1775–1851', *Jnl. Hist. Geog.* vol. 1 (1975). On the droving trade see K. J. Bonser: *The Drovers* (1970), and A. R. B. Haldane: *The Drove Roads of Scotland* (1952).

INNOVATION IN TRANSPORT SYSTEMS

The parish system of road repair, and the spread and operation of turnpike trusts is discussed in Pawson (1977), which also contains a bibliography of local turnpike studies.

The improvement of rivers for navigation is discussed fully by T. S. Willan (1936). There is still no study of the role of canal development in the Industrial Revolution. E. C. R. Hadfield: *British Canals*, 4th edn. (1969) is the standard narrative account, complemented by his several regional volumes. There are a number of studies of individual canals, e.g. H. G. W. Household: *The Thames and Severn Canal* (1969). The definitive work on canal investment is J. R. Ward: *The Finance of Canal Building in Eighteenth Century England* (1974).

On ports and the development of dock facilities, see D. Swann: 'The Pace and Progress of Port Investment in England, 1660–1830', in *Yorks. Bulletin of Econ. and Soc. Research*, vol. XII (1960). Hamilton (1963) deals with Scotland, as does Bruce Lenman: *From Esk to Tweed* (1975). There is a good summary of London dock expansion in Dyos and Aldcroft (1969). A few other ports have received separate treatment: W. E. Minchinton: 'The Port of Bristol in the Eighteenth Century', reprinted in Patrick McGrath (ed.): *Bristol in the Eighteenth Century* (1972), Gordon Jackson: *Hull in the Eighteenth Century* (1972), Paul Clemens: 'The Rise of

Liverpool, 1665–1750', *Ec.H.R.* vol. **XXIX** (1976).

There are a number of references on eighteenth-century engineers: W. H. Chaloner: *People and Industries* (1963) – containing short articles on the Duke of Bridgewater, Telford and MacAdam; L. T. C. Rolt: *Thomas Telford* (1958), D. Swann: 'The Engineers of English Port Improvements, 1660–1830', *Transport History* vol. 1 (1968) and S. W. Skempton: 'The Engineers of English River Navigations, 1620–1780', *Trans. Newcomen Soc.* **XXIX** (1953).

TRANSPORT AND ECONOMY

The general issues in this section are discussed in Pawson (1977), with reference to the improving road system. There are two good books on the provincial press of the period: G. A. Cranfield: *The Development of the Provincial Newspaper, 1700–60* (1962), and R. M. Wiles: *Freshest Advices* (1965).

# 7 The Service Sector

A very numerous group of economic and social activities that lay outside the producer sectors of agriculture and industry, although intimately associated with them, was that of the service trades. As a group the 'services' covered a wide range of occupations that are not easily defined, but because of their importance in everyday life, and in the progress of the Industrial Revolution, they rank as a basic sector alongside agriculture and industry. In 1801 about one third of the work force was engaged in, and possibly as much as 40 per cent of the national income was contributed by, the services.

## THE GROWTH OF THE SERVICE SECTOR

Some services, in particular the old professional triad of law, medicine and the Church, the business activities of transport and distribution, and domestic service, had a long history. However, none were particularly numerous (or in most cases, cheap) before the economic expansion of the eighteenth century. The mass of people in pre-industrial Britain rarely had cause, opportunity or means to use a service regularly, except that of the Church. Most service needs were self provided. Shopkeepers were not necessary for villagers who grew their own food and made their own clothes. Simple goods could be bought from pedlars, periodic fairs or by personal arrangement with local craftsmen. Rudimentary home education and medicine often sufficed. Even in the towns, many households were almost self sufficient from their kitchen gardens, with milk being bought direct from the urban dairy. Otherwise, the weekly market, general purpose shops (grocers or chandlers) and the inn met most people's needs. Only in the biggest towns did a wide range of professional and specialist basic services exist.

As the nature and scale of economy and society changed through the eighteenth century, this situation gradually altered. Services became more numerous, accessible and specialised. Not only could growing centres of population everywhere support a wider range of services, but expanding industries and agriculture needed, and a nation increasing in wealth demanded, a higher standard of more specialist services. The operations of any of the bigger firms of the period illustrate this. Josiah Wedgwood employed potters, painters, packers and a host of other workers directly concerned with production at Etruria. But he also had to have clerks to process orders, keep accounts, make up wage rolls and negotiate transport rates, salesmen to travel the country and warehousemen and retail staff in his London, Bristol, Liverpool and Dublin showrooms. He relied upon independent road and water carriers and the postal services, protected his plant and stocks with insurance, and financed part of his activities with the help of bankers.

The process of division of labour within the growing economy encouraged many services that had formerly been carried out within the framework of existing enterprises to develop as separate entities. Specialisation was fostered by the increase in scale and regularity of business operations: more information and transport services were required and better finance and insurance arrangements needed to underwrite growing fixed and circulating capital stocks. The increasing complexity of business activity raised the demand for the professional skills of lawyers, accountants, engineers and surveyors, as well as making the provision of basic education vital: men had to be able to read and write to deal with instructions, plans and accounts. As towns grew, a range of new services, such as crime prevention, public health, street maintenance and institutional entertainment, came into existence. And as personal living standards rose, demand for professional services formerly used only sparingly, for entertainment and culture, and for domestic service, all widened.

The eighteenth century therefore witnessed the growth of age-old services and the development of many new ones. This expansion was very much an urban phenomenon as most service activities, by their very nature, had to be located in towns. In the national capitals of London and Edinburgh, and regional centres such as Bristol and York, service occupations predominated amongst those listed in town directories by the third quarter of the century. Even in industrial towns such as Manchester and Glasgow, those engaged in services were as numerous as industrial workers (table 7:1). And in the smaller country towns as well a range of basic and professional services could be found (table 7:2).

The meaningful division of activities within the service sector is a difficult task. In any scheme, many occupations can be placed in more than one category, and there is the problem of those that involve both manufacturing and service functions. In this chapter the services have been

TABLE 7:1    *Occupational Structures of Three Large Towns in the 1770s.*

EDINBURGH, 1774

| | | | |
|---|---|---|---|
| 217 | Merchants | 52 | Tailors |
| 188 | Advocates | 46 | Barbers |
| 171 | Writers | 45 | Smiths |
| 169 | Grocers | 45 | Stablers |
| 141 | Clerks to H.M. Signet | 45 | Milliners |
| 110 | Vintners | 39 | Physicians |
| 94 | Lords and Advocates Clerks | 35 | Clergy |
| 86 | Baxters | 33 | Surgeons |
| 80 | Shipmasters | 30 | Bankers |
| 79· | Shoemakers | 24 | Painters |
| 64 | Wrights | 21 | Booksellers |
| 61 | Brewers | 21 | Jewellers/Goldsmiths |
| 56 | Schoolmasters | | |

*Source:* Williamson's Directory of Edinburgh (1774).

BIRMINGHAM, 1777

| | | | |
|---|---|---|---|
| 248 | Innkeepers | 46 | Brass Founders |
| 129 | Buttonmakers | 39 | Shopkeepers |
| 99 | Shoemakers | 39 | Bucklemasters |
| 77 | Merchants | 36 | Gunmakers |
| 74 | Tailors | 35 | Jewellers |
| 64 | Bakers | 26 | Maltsters |
| 56 | Toymakers | 24 | Drapers |
| 52 | Platers | 23 | Gardeners |
| 49 | Butchers | 21 | Plumbers/Glaziers |
| 48 | Carpenters | 21 | Ironmongers |
| 46 | Barbers | | |

*Source:* Edward P. Duggan: 'Industrialization and the Development of Urban Business Communities', *Local Historian* vol. 11 (1975).

MANCHESTER, 1772

| | |
|---|---|
| 140 | Innkeepers |
| 75 | Fustian manufacturers |
| 58 | Warehousemen |
| 49 | Check manufacturers |
| 46 | Hucksters |
| 44 | Smallware manufacturers |
| 27 | Shoemakers |
| 26 | Barbers |
| 25 | Tailors |
| 24 | Grocers |
| 24 | Clergy |
| 23 | Carpenters/Joiners |

| | |
|---|---|
| 23 | Hatters |
| 23 | Fustian cutters |
| 21 | Lawyers |
| 17 | Yarn merchants |
| 15 | Linen drapers |
| 15 | Butchers |
| 14 | Fustian dyers |
| 14 | Corn factors |
| 13 | Fustian callenderers |
| 13 | Toy/Hardware shops |
| 12 | Bakers |
| 11 | Cabinet makers |
| 11 | Gardeners |

*Source:* Manchester Directory (1772).

TABLE 7:2   *The Major Occupations in Three Small Towns in the 1790s*

These listings are from the *Universal British Directory* (1793). All occupations with three or more representatives recorded are included.

*Bewdley, Worcestershire*

| | |
|---|---|
| 7 | Lawyers |
| 7 | Mercers |
| 5 | Physicians |
| 5 | Grocers |

| | |
|---|---|
| 3 | Clergy |
| 3 | Merchants |
| 3 | Innkeepers |
| 3 | Maltsters |

*Appleby, Westmoreland*

| | |
|---|---|
| 11 | Innkeepers |
| 7 | Joiners/Carpenters |
| 6 | Grocers |
| 4 | Shoemakers |
| 4 | Schoolmasters |

| | |
|---|---|
| 3 | Lawyers |
| 3 | Physicians |
| 3 | Spirit Merchants |
| 3 | Weavers |
| 3 | Tailors |

*Cardigan, West Wales*

| | |
|---|---|
| 13 | Innkeepers |
| 8 | Shoemakers |
| 7 | Shopkeepers |
| 5 | Attorneys |
| 5 | Joiner/Carpenters |
| 5 | Tailors |

| | |
|---|---|
| 5 | Shipwrights/Ropers |
| 4 | Clergy |
| 3 | Surgeons |
| 3 | Merchants |
| 3 | Butchers |
| 3 | Hatters |

divided into 'tertiary', 'quaternary' and 'personal' categories. Tertiary services, essentially manual tasks or the lower order of administrative skills (e.g. the distributive trades and transport) became very numerous. Quaternary services – the higher orders of professional occupations (such as banking and the law) – were never especially numerous but assumed an importance far in excess of their size. The personal services – such as the Church, medicine and domestics – met primarily the social needs of the population, rather than the economic requirements of business.

## THE TERTIARY SERVICES

### Distribution

In 1688 Gregory King estimated that there were 2,000 'eminent merchants and traders', 8,000 'lesser merchants and traders' and 50,000 'shopkeepers and tradesmen' in England. They were the core of a system of wholesaling and retailing that was a vital adjunct of production and overseas trade, the necessary link between producers and consumers. And as agricultural and industrial output expanded, and became more specialised and localised, efficient and permanent forms of distribution became essential.

In the early eighteenth century, however, the whole character of distribution was very different to what it is today. Retailing and wholesaling functions were, by and large, not yet concentrated in fixed shops and warehouses, but were performed by low-cost forms of organisation appropriate for the needs of the time. Most internal trade was carried out at periodic, but regular, fairs and markets, and by itinerant dealers. Fixed forms of organisation only became more common as communications improved, as production increased, and as the market became more affluent. By no means all the retail tradesmen listed in the directories (tables 7:1, 2), sold from fixed premises. The grocers, drapers, innkeepers and booksellers did, but many butchers, bakers, ironmongers and gardeners sold their products in the market place, whilst some, such as the shoemakers, milk sellers and vegetable dealers, hawked in the markets and in the streets.

The fairs of town and country were some of the most notable features of community routine in pre-industrial days. Many villages that had no regular market held an annual fair – there were no fewer than 180 in Somerset in the early eighteenth century, yet there were only 39 market towns. Fairs always caught the eye of commentators. Defoe described the workings of Stourbridge Fair, set up each year in August in a field outside Cambridge, in great detail – 'not only the greatest in the whole nation, but in the world', he wrote. Many London traders had stalls here: 'goldsmiths, toyshops, brasiers, turners, milleners, haberdashers, hatters, mercers, drapers, pewtrers, china-warehouses', all selling to the public, and to other shopkeepers and dealers from all over the Midlands and the north. The central part of the fairground was given over to wholesalers of wine, groceries, irongoods and to textile dealers and manufacturers 'with vast quantities of Yorkshire cloths, kerseyes, pennistons, cottons with all sorts of Manchester ware, fustians, and things made of cotton wool. . . . Western goods had their share here also . . . serges, Devonshire kersies . . .' 'But all this is still outdone', he wrote, 'by two articles which are the peculiars of this fair . . . the Wooll and the Hops'. (*Tour* vol. 1 pp. 80–5). These were products for which Stourbridge was a great wholesale distribution centre, the wool being sold to East Anglian manufacturers by Lincolnshire dealers, the hops to northern buyers by growers from Essex and Kent.

The trade at Stourbridge, though on a greater scale than at other fairs, gives a good idea of the nature of transactions and the variety of products exchanged at these great and lively occasions. Nevertheless, these general fairs were in steady decline after 1750, although many struggled on into the 1840s, a shadow of their former selves. St Bartholomew's Fair in London had already degenerated into a pleasure ground in the early eighteenth century. The wholesale trade at Stourbridge collapsed in the second half of the century. Chester and Liverpool Fairs, formerly focal points of commerce in the north, were in rapid decline by 1800. The reason was straightforward. A growing market required a more regular means of distribution, whilst a developing economy provided the improved transport system and information services that would support it. In manufacturing, significant economies of scale could be achieved with year-round sales, so that as communications improved, the proportion of industrial goods channelled through regular, fixed modes of distribution increased. In agriculture, in response to the growing needs of the urban markets, an elaborate but rather different system of distribution developed.

Increased frequency and regularity of distribution was achieved in a variety of ways. Some manufacturers developed their own distribution systems with warehouses or showrooms, Crowley and Wedgwood being examples. Many, like Boulton and Watt, appointed agents of their own, or engaged the services of a general agent. Samuel Oldknow, the Stockport muslin manufacturer, relied on his London agent to forward orders and distribute goods to customers in the city, whilst the agent himself provided vital information on the state of the market, about latest fashions, and frequently comments on the standard of Oldknow's consignments. London had long had a central cloth hall, Blackwell Hall, as well – a place where producers or the agents could deal directly with merchant buyers. Many of these wholesale dealings were transferred closer to source of production in the late eighteenth century. The Manchester Directory for 1772 listed 119 'country' manufacturers with warehouses in the town, some having their own and others being run by wholesalers acting for a number of firms. Increasingly, the merchants and traders buying for home and overseas markets gathered in Manchester. In the West Riding, nearly all the cloth made was sold through the Cloth Halls in Leeds, Bradford and Wakefield.[1] The wholesaling functions of Chester Fair, the major outlet for Irish linen, were supplanted by the erection of a Linen Hall in the town in 1778, and a Cloth Hall in 1809, built by Manchester and Yorkshire dealers.

Many firms, however, established direct links with their customers, circumventing middlemen and merchants. The most notable example of this was the use of 'Manchester men' (the prototype commercial traveller) by the Lancashire cotton firms. Aikin, the region's historian, provided an excellent description of the changes in distribution of local goods as trade increased. 'For the first thirty years of the present century', he wrote in 1795, 'the old established houses confined their trades to the wholesale dealers in London, Bristol, Norwich, Newcastle and those who frequented Chester Fair. . . . When the Manchester trade began to extend, the chapmen used to keep gangs of pack-horses and accompany them to the principal towns with goods in packs, which they opened and sold to shopkeepers, lodging what was unsold at small stores at the inns. . . . On the improvement of turnpike roads waggons were set up, and the pack-horses discontinued; and the chapmen rode out only for orders, carrying with them patterns in their bags. It was during the forty years from 1730 to 1770 that trade was greatly pushed by the practice of sending these riders all over the Kingdom, to those towns which before had been supplied from the wholesale dealers in the capital places before mentioned'. Matthew Boulton used a similar system, having a pattern book carried by his outriders with 1,470 designs in it in 1772. Josiah Wedgwood had three travelling salesmen in the 1780s. The ironmasters used representatives to call on small manufacturers and shopkeepers. But many firms also made use of itinerant dealers who hawked their products direct to the public. In 1785, when a bill was put before Parliament to outlaw the activities of itinerants, supposedly to protect the interests of shopkeepers, it met with considerable opposition from manufacturers in many towns, including Manchester, Liverpool, Wakefield, Wigan, Halifax and Paisley, and was subsequently withdrawn.

The pattern of distribution of agricultural products changed in some important respects during the eighteenth century as well. Livestock fairs, such as the great sheep fair at Weyhill outside Andover, and the cattle fairs at St Faiths in Norfolk and Falkirk in Scotland, retained their importance often well into the nineteenth century. Periodic trading was well suited to the disposal of animals, which were sold at fairs not to retailers, but to graziers for fattening, or to drovers. The sale of animals to the butcher took place at town markets, and in London twice weekly at Smithfield (for cattle and sheep) (plate E1), Newgate and Leadenhall (for poultry, calves and pigs.) Wholesale buying was often dominated by a few particularly large dealers. Regular markets became the main means of disposal for other agricultural products, with the fairs rapidly losing ground. The food requirements of London and the growing provincial towns had to be met by more frequent buying. London factors had become a common sight in country markets by mid-century, whilst loaded waggons of corn became more unusual. Increasingly, trade was carried out by sample, just as the manufacturers were doing. Many of the bigger inns were providing 'market rooms' where such trade could be conducted in greater comfort. Corn dispatched direct to London was sold at one of the two great markets of Bear Key and Queenhithe. In the 1750s these were supplemented by a Corn Exchange in which samples were displayed and lots sold. The trade was again concentrated: the exchange was a private enterprise, divided into 80 shares held by factors, the Kentish hoymen and buyers (such as brewers, millers and mealmen). By 1800 it was almost completely controlled by only 14 factors.[2] The intervention of London factors raised prices substantially throughout south and western England. In the Midlands, 'Birmingham prices' ruled, in the north, Newcastle and Edinburgh prices. The logical development of the growing presence of the middlemen was the circumvention of the market place altogether. London factors began to buy directly from the farm, and by the early nineteenth century, every town had its corn merchant or two. Hardy's Mayor of Casterbridge was one such.

With changing patterns of wholesaling came changing patterns of retailing. Here as well the fairs lost ground, but both the urban market and the itinerant dealer increased their trade, whilst fixed shops grew in number. Most townsfolk, both middle and poorer classes, could satisfy their basic needs in the market place (plate E2). The country women came to sell their eggs, butter and cheeses, gardeners sold their greenstuffs and fruit, and there the butchers and itinerant dealers in manufactures were to be found. The main markets in neighbouring towns were usually held on different days: not for the buyers' convenience, but so that farmers, itinerants and middlemen could easily move around. In the bigger towns, an array of permanent shops developed in those trades with a big volume of sales: groceries, clothing and textiles. The gaps in this retailing network were filled by street traders, the numbers of which boomed as urban growth proceeded rapidly in the late eighteenth and nineteenth centuries. In 1850, there were about 41,000 in London, most selling fish, fruit, vegetables or milk.

The most numerous types of fixed retail premises were the inns and general groceries. Maitland estimated that of London's 96,000 houses in 1732, some 16,000 were drinking places, including 8,659 brandy shops, 5,975 alehouses, 447 taverns, 207 inns and 551 coffee-houses. Many of the brandy shops would have stocked a wider range of groceries too. Groceries dealt mainly with a middle-class custom, and were to be found in big and small towns alike (table 7:2). They sold some ordinary foodstuffs and imported goods obtained from merchant wholesalers (or in the smaller towns, from London shops): wines, sugar, tea, coffee, lemons, currants, spices and such requisites as soap, candles and simple medicines. In the smaller towns, their wares covered a far wider range, and the grocery was more like a general store. Abraham Dent, the grocer of Kirkby Stephen, was also a vintner, stationer, bookseller, chemist and mercer. The complexity of supply was a basic reason for the development of fixed premises in the grocery trade: Dent bought goods from about 190 suppliers scattered all over the north of England in the years between 1756 and 1777.

Only the larger towns had a well developed shop retail trade in 1800. It was a feature of London, Edinburgh and long established regional centres such as Newcastle, York and Bristol, and of a small number of new resorts with wealthy clienteles, Bath being a good example (plate E3). Edinburgh, in 1774, had 169 grocers, 52 tailors and 45 milliners, 21 booksellers and four stationers, 21 jewellers or goldsmiths, 20 ironmongers, 15 chemists, 12 tobacconists, eight confectioners and two music shops. In London a distinct differentiation was emerging between the well-lit and paved West End, with many of its shops and showrooms open till ten at night, and the older, muddled shops of the City, which did their trade with the capital's ordinary inhabitants and with village shopkeepers and gentry who ordered direct through the carriers. But everywhere new and traditional forms of organisation continued side by side. The Liverpool Guide of 1797 proudly described the view from the Exchange, 'where the spacious street before one; perfectly uniform; all shops, containing everything useful and ornamental, to indulge the taste and gratify the necessities; presents a view not to be excelled, perhaps in the Capital'. Around the corner, by the church, was the fruit and vegetable market, selling oranges and lemons from Spain and Portugal in season. But 'pursuing the course down Pool-Lane, the eye should not be turned to either side, as it would be offended at the very indecorous practice of exposing the shambles meat in the public street'!

*Communications*

A second group of tertiary services was that concerned with *transport and communication.* Throughout the eighteenth century, carrying was often a subsidiary occupation for farmers, small tradesmen or innkeepers. However, the small numbers that were permanently engaged in transport services grew significantly. They had an importance far beyond their total size as the lynchpin of smooth transfers of goods and information. Trends similar to those in the distributive trades became evident. Transport services assumed more regular, frequent and sophisticated forms of organisation. Fixed capitals increased as the demand for transport grew, and business became concentrated in a relatively small number of hands.

In 1836, some 342 coach services were operating out of London, 275 of them being provided by the three largest proprietors, William Chaplin, Benjamin Horne and Edward Sherman. Chaplin, the biggest operator, owned five inns in central London, and employed altogether 2,000 people and 1,800 horses. Such concentration was to be found in the provincial towns and was typical of the immediate pre-railway era, although the pattern becomes common after 1760. The Turner brothers operated nearly all of the coach routes out of Gloucester in the 1760s and 1770s, from a specially appointed Coach Office. In Oxford, William Costar overshadowed all other coach operators. Many coachowners were innkeepers, or else used innkeepers as agents. It was usual for the smaller owners to join in partnership with others, again often innkeepers, along the route. This not only provided a series of booking offices, but enabled the horses to be changed frequently. Goods carriers normally operated from inns as well, and used innkeeper agents on the route to collect goods, and transfer packages to other carriers. The bigger carriers built their own warehouses, often next to their own homes, and employed several waggoners and clerks. By the 1770s, most parts of Britain were well served by a network of independent carriers and coachmen that was both integrated and regular.

Water-based carrying was not separate from the road services, and some carriers operated both. Ownership was relatively concentrated. A survey carried out in 1795 revealed that one third of all the canal boats in the Midlands were owned by ten canal companies and nine big independent carriers. Three fifths of the Midlands boats were owned by carriers, partnerships or individual concerns with more than five boats apiece.

One of the larger enterprises was the firm of Pickford's, still a big national carrier. In the 1790s it was operating between Manchester and London with ten canal boats and 50 waggons; by 1822 it had no less than 83 vessels. The small, independent canal boatman was a rare figure – nearly all were employed. They were also not a numerous group. Pickford's had 40 boatmen in 1795, yet there were no more than 900 'masters of boats', in charge of crews of three or four, throughout the Midlands in that year. But, again, the importance of their function far outweighed their numbers.

*Utilities*

The *public utilities* can be classed together as a third group of tertiary services. This group, too, was never large, but it became very much more numerous with the growth of towns after 1750, and has special significance as the forerunner of today's extensive array of public services. For centuries, rudimentary public service provision was the common law obligation of the individual parishioner, and was enforced by the annual election of unpaid Officers, who served as Highway Surveyors, Scavengers, Overseers of the Poor, Churchwardens, and constables. These officers were empowered to require parishioners to clear their own frontages, keep up the street in front of their homes, and work six days each year on the roads. Such obligations persisted for a very long time. Townsfolk had to maintain the streets of London (outside the City) and hang out their own lights until 1762. In Bristol, they had to do this until 1806.

Rapid urban growth however, overwhelmed a system that had been conceived for small and stable communities. In the latter half of the eighteenth century, town after town applied to Parliament to set up an Improvement Commission to take over street maintenance and the provision of a night watch on a more professional basis. Between 1748 and 1835, nearly 300 were established, in incorporated and unincorporated towns alike. These Commissions were appointed or elected bodies, with powers to levy a household rate to pay for their services. In London, most parishes and many turnpike trusts were also given rating powers for the same purposes.

London's streets, outside the City, were taken over by the Westminster Paving Commission in 1762. (A Commission had been operative in the City itself since the redevelopment after the Great Fire). It made an energetic job of replacing the householders' uneven pavements with a new surface of Aberdeen granite, using the proceeds of an 18d rate, and an extra Sunday toll levied at turnpike gates, as well as a special £5,000 Parliamentary grant. Most of the newer suburbs were outside its jurisdiction, however, and gradually many parishes within its area applied for their own Commissions. St Marylebone, which had a very active Vestry, employed between 50 and 100 paviours in the early nineteenth century. It also had nearly 100 watchmen in its force. The neighbouring Islington Turnpike Trust, which maintained the roads to Highgate and Hampstead, had five watch supervisors, 11 horse patrols and 64 foot patrols in 1787. Birmingham, a fairly typical provincial Commission, was retaining 60 watchmen for the winter nights in 1801. Manchester had 42. These watches were embryonic police forces, as is evident from the description in the Manchester Directory of 1802. The watchmen were 'not only to use their best endeavour in preventing mischief by fire, as well as felonies and misdemeanours, but also to secure night walkers, malefactors, disorderly and suspected persons, and to lodge and detain them in any place of security appointed by the General Commissioners, or in the lock up rooms at the New Bailey, until they can be brought before a Justice of the Peace'.

Manchester's Commission also provided a fire service: Isaac Perrins was the Inspector of Engines, and he controlled 12 engines, manned by 31 conductors and firemen. Its gas works were brought into use in 1817. In this respect, Manchester was very go-ahead, and was renowned at the time for having one of the most active Improvement Commissions. In 1797, it bought 1,000 lamps for the streets, contracting the maintenance and lighting of them. London likewise was well lit by the end of the century. An Act of 1662 had required householders to hang lamps outside their homes during the winter months, but only till midnight. In 1736, the City Corporation obtained lamp rating powers, followed by Westminster in 1761. Most of the turnpike trusts lit their routes too. Foreign visitors were greatly impressed by this service. Monsieur D'Archenholz found 'in Oxford Street alone', in 1791, 'there are more lamps than in all Paris. The great roads within seven or eight miles of town are also illuminated in the same manner; and as they are very numerous, the effect is charming'.

### Clerks

A final group of tertiary services were those provided by the unenumerated, easily forgotten *clerks*, who paradoxically made so many of the records that survive about the early Industrial Revolution. Clerks were petty officials, the forerunners of today's lower grade office workers, responsible for simple tasks of organisation and administration. The increasing volume of business and service activity created more need for keeping accounts, writing and answering letters, documents, notices, working out pay-rolls, accepting and processing orders. Clerks were employed by manufacturing concerns, by transport and distribution services, by professional men, and by public bodies ranging from turnpike trusts to cathedral chapters.

## THE QUATERNARY SERVICES

It is the development of a distinct group of specialist quaternary services that is one of the most characteristic features of economic advance. Britain had long had its educational institutions and lawyers, but the eighteenth century saw the blossoming of a whole range of 'modern' professions to meet the needs of growing business and industry. Banking and insurance developed from within the ranks of the merchants; estate management, auctioneering and accountancy from the attorney's trade. Engineering and surveying became respectable full-time professions, and education changed course to meet the commercial and scientific needs of the times.

### Banking
One of the most distinctive quaternary professions to emerge during the early Industrial Revolution was that of banking. There was nothing particularly novel about the bankers' function, as he did little that big traders and merchants did not do themselves. His uniqueness lay in his specialisation, introducing efficiency, simplicity and economies of scale into the financial world, all particularly important for the smaller trader and industrial firm. In England and Wales, a three-tier banking system developed, with the Bank of England, the monopolist of joint-stock banking south of the Border, at the centre. Around it were the private London banks, and by 1800, a large number of partnership country banks. It was in Scotland, however, that many of the elements of the modern banking system were worked out, the Scots being the pioneers, amongst other things, of banking on the limited liability principle. Formal banking in both countries has had a long history. The Bank of England was founded, as the Government's banker, in 1694; the Bank of Scotland in 1695, but as a joint-stock company to make a trade of banking, wholly unconnected with the State, except for the Act that created it. The most rapid extension of banking throughout Britain, however, came in the years after 1750.

The Bank of England was established for the convenience of the Government at a time when it was desperately short of finance for war. A group of wealthy London merchants and traders, in return for the rights to take in money on deposit from the public, and to create paper loans at will, agreed to lend the government £1.2 million. This remained its main function until the end of the Wars of Spanish Succession in 1713. Of the original loan, £720,000 was in cash, and the rest in printed 'promises to pay' (i.e. bank-notes). The Bank was given other government business, including the handling of overseas remittances, selling Exchequer bills, and buying gold and silver for the Mint. Its private business lay initially with merchants, making loans and discounting bills of exchange, although these functions it increasingly left to the private bankers, becoming itself in turn the banks' banker. Its paper money issue represented credit creation to the extent that the issue exceeded its bullion reserves. However, until 1797, Bank of England notes were convertible to cash on demand, so that stocks of bullion and silver had to be kept to cover a run on its notes in a panic. The embryonic banking system was severely shaken by the events of 1745, when the Bank was forced to pay out in sixpences, but a declaration of faith in its notes by a group of leading merchants during the crisis effectively sealed the stability of Bank of England paper from then on.

The London private bankers developed from merchant houses and long-established goldsmiths. In 1750, there were about 20, in 1770 about 50 and by 1800 – 70. There was some specialisation. Those in the West End (such as Hoares, Coutts and Childs) dealt with the wealthy market of the landowners and gentry, much as did the West End shops. They accepted deposits of money, dealt in government securities and lent long on mortgage. The City banks, which grew rapidly in numbers after 1750, were interested in a different class of business. Unlike the West End banks, they actively issued their own bank notes and discounted bills of exchange for merchants and industrial firms. They also acted as London agents for the Scottish bankers and the great network of country bankers that developed in England and Wales after 1750. Country bankers – the general term given to those outside the capital – needed a London bank to supply them with gold and silver (or Bank of England notes) during local crises, to act as discounters of local and London bills of exchange, and to handle payments in the capital on behalf of their provincial clients.

The development of the banking system in London created a great fountain of credit to support trade and industry. Before the growth of the country bank network, however, there were few well-defined channels along which this credit could flow into the provinces. This problem was compounded by a perpetual shortage of coin, particularly acute in the north and west. No new copper coins were issued by the Mint between 1702 and 1717, or between 1754 and 1794, except for 200 tons of Tower farthings and halfpennies in 1771–5. Silver coin was short because the metal was undervalued in Britain relative to gold, with the result that much was illegally exported. Only half a million pound's worth of silver was offered to the Mint between 1717 and 1760. In the 1790s a lot of gold was exported too with the rising price of bullion overseas. The official coinage of the realm was therefore deficient in quantity and those pieces that remained were, after perpetual filing, somewhat deficient in form and weight.

The shortage of coin was circumvented by the creation of private money. Several manufacturing firms minted their own coins, or trade tokens, with which to pay wages. John Wilkinson and Thomas Williams both made copper tokens, which achieved wide circulation during the economic boom of the last years of the century. Others adopted the truck system in part payment of wages (above, p. 94). Some manufacturers issued notes, thereby creating not coin but their own credit. Wilkinson did this too. Some of these actually became formal bankers. The great cotton printers of Blackburn, Livesey, Hargreaves and Co. collapsed in 1788 with debts of £1.5 million. As a proportion of these were held in their own notes ('promises to pay'), a number of other firms collapsed too, holding worthless paper. After this even bank notes were for long distrusted in Lancashire, and many of the local banks, unlike country banks elsewhere, never issued them. The life blood of trade however, was the 'bill of exchange' or 'trade bill', a simple means of credit creation. The creditor drew a bill on the debtor, which the debtor accepted by signing it. He then returned it to the creditor, who either held it till it matured, or passed it on to cover his own debts, or discounted it with a banker or merchant. Bills achieved very wide circulation throughout the country, and were the essential means of long distance transfers of money. As late as the 1820s, 90 per cent of the business done in Manchester was in bills, and only ten per cent in gold or Bank of England notes.

One of the main functions of the new country bankers was to facilitate the smooth operation of this system of payment by bills. The banker was a man whose credit was trusted, whose credit people were prepared to accept when they took his bank notes in exchange for a discounted bill. He could arrange for payments to be made in London through his agent there, holding a bill drawn against the customer until maturity, or debiting the customer's own bank account. The banker would discount bills held by his customers and drawn against London (i.e. payments by London people to the provinces). These 'London bills' became a very widely circulating medium of exchange, because of the trust generally placed in the capital's credit. The bill was thus a major instrument of credit locally, and a means of payment between London and the provinces. It was also an important inter-regional and international means of transfer. Bankers in the agricultural areas of the east, south and west of England, and south-eastern Scotland, with surpluses of money to invest (deposited by their farmer customers when agricultural prices and incomes rode high after 1750), bought local bills from London bankers as investments. These were bills, not yet at maturity, deposited in London by bankers from Lancashire, the West Riding and the Midland counties, who had discounted them with their London agents in order to raise cash to meet the persistent demand for credit from their own industrial and trading customers. The London private bankers hence acted as intermediaries in the transfer of money from plentiful to deficient areas and for this reason the London banks' Clearing House was created in 1773. They played, therefore, a vital role in articulating a financial system that enabled development to occur relatively smoothly, by channelling funds where they were most needed.[3] Long distance transfer of credit was of far greater significance in the early Industrial Revolution than formal long-distance investment between agricultural and industrial areas. Nearly all firms, as well as enterprises such as turnpike trusts, canal companies and harbour boards, used the services of bankers, some raising considerable amounts of money from them. Banks generally lent 'short', thereby financing circulating capital (raw materials and stocks), but many would extend the period of the loan, or give a series of short-term loans, which effectively meant that they were prepared to underwrite fixed capital investment.

The great expansion of formal banking activity outside London came in the second half of the eighteenth century. In 1750, there were no more than a dozen country bankers. In 1784 the number was 120, in 1800 – 370 and in 1810 at least 650. Expansion was particularly rapid in periods of easy credit as in the early 1750s, 1789–93 and 1797–1800. Country bankers came from all avenues of trade: maltsters and millers in the Home Counties, drovers in Wales, mining partners in Cornwall, big merchant families in the ports. Lloyds of Birmingham were Quakers in the iron industry, Gurneys of Norwich had long been in the worsted business. They were men of substantial means, sufficient for their credit (bills or bank notes) to be trusted and accepted. Most issued notes, with the exception of the Lancashire bankers (and some of the London bankers, who used Bank of England notes instead). From their role of extending credit, the country bankers became deposit holders, being entrusted with people's savings and firms' reserves. These deposits increased the reserves of the banks themselves, and enabled them to increase their credit extension, although there was no generally understood relationship between the two. In times of crisis, when loss of confidence in bank notes resulted in many being presented for payment, country bankers frequently had to call on their London bank for support. The London banks in turn sometimes had to call on the Bank of England as a lender of last resort. Merchants who could get no accommodation from their own banker in a crisis turned to the Bank of England as well. Despite no formal change in the policy of the Bank, it came to assume many of the responsibilities of a central bank. Given the status of its reserves, the volume of its note issue, and its relationship to government, this was inevitable. The Bank became the only major holder of gold in the banking system, other bankers depositing their reserves with it to earn interest. The Bank was the anchor in liquidity crises, supplying bullion abroad to meet balance-of-payments deficits, or to the private bankers to bolster their position. When the Bank was released from its obligation to exchange its notes for gold during the crisis of 1797, its paper currency became the anchor for other banks' currency. Bank of England notes, rather than gold, became the private banker's means of holding his reserves. This remained so even after convertibility was restored to Bank of England notes in 1821.[4]

The Scottish banking system was more advanced in many respects than that of England. The extension of limited liability to a number of banking concerns north of the Border encouraged its development. The Bank of Scotland had been founded as a trading enterprise in 1695. Most of its business was with merchants. The Royal Bank of Scotland received its charter in 1727, founded by Walpole to handle the Equivalent Money – funds given to Scotland under the terms of the Union in 1707.[5] The Royal's main business was with lawyers and landlords, however, and it invented the overdraft system for the convenience of its customers. Both banks were centred in Edinburgh, as was the third major Scottish banking enterprise. In 1746, the British Linen Company received a Crown Charter to set up a limited liability company to engage in the mercantile side of the linen trade and to ease some of the problems of the rapid development of that industry. The British Linen Company sold cloth, issuing notes to weavers and manufacturers in exchange. Its notes – many being as low as ten shillings in denomination – achieved very wide circulation, thereby meeting a real need for credit amongst linen manufacturers.

The Scottish bankers were not limited to large denomination notes as was the case in England, where anything less than £5 was illegal. Note circulation was therefore very wide, in central Scotland at least. By mid-century gold coin had virtually disappeared and notes predominated. In this respect, Scotland was far ahead of England and Wales. Note circulation was assisted by the establishment of a number of private banks, run as partnerships. There were 15 or 20 in Edinburgh in 1761, and two in Glasgow. In 1763, others were founded in Ayr and Dundee, in 1766 in

Dumfries and Perth, and in 1767 in Aberdeen. The three big banks, however, pioneered another first. In 1766, the British Linen Company appointed agents in Perth, Dundee, Aberdeen, Petershead and Cromarty, and the Bank of Scotland began to set up branches: in 1774 in Dumfries and Kelso, in 1780 in Kilmarnock, Ayr, Stirling and Inverness. By 1810, it had 20.[6]

These Scottish bankers all had London connexions, on whom they were reliant in much the same way as were the English and Welsh country banks. They channelled funds through Edinburgh from the agricultural surplus areas of the south-east to the industrialising communities. They lent widely to industry and trade. The Carron Ironworks was loaned £13,000 by the Glasgow Thistle Bank, and Mansfield's, an Edinburgh banker, in 1769. In 1772, the Royal loaned a further £12,500, which was taken over by the Bank of Scotland two years later and increased to £20,000. The Forth & Clyde Navigation was advanced £20,000 by the Royal in 1771, and the Crinan Canal had a £5,000 loan from the British Linen Company in 1795, as did the Ardrossan Canal in 1810. The big banks lent £10,000 'at longish term' for the new Leith docks in 1799, and the Aberdeen bank had lent £1,000 to the Town Fathers towards building the new harbour there in 1774. Everywhere banks were important as sources of short-term credit for the payment of wages and bills. In fact, the development of the banking system must be recognised as a major cause of Scotland's rapid industrial advancement in the second half of the eighteenth century.

In Scotland however, as in England, the system was vulnerable. This was forcibly illustrated by the financial crisis of 1772 during which a number of private bankers collapsed. The most spectacular victim was the Ayr Bank, a partnership of wealthy landowners, which had carried out a vigorous policy of extension, opening branches and pushing its notes widely. It was, in fact, suspected of over-extension, and during the panic in Edinburgh that followed the collapse of a London house with extensive Scottish dealings, it was subjected to heavy pressure which brought it down. Because of the Ayr Bank's widespread connections throughout the economy, the shock was severe, and it was compounded by the collapse of many of the Edinburgh private bankers as well: of the 25 operating before the crisis, only five survived.[7] Scottish trade immediately contracted with the loss of credit. Its exports in 1775 were only 61 per cent of the 1771 level, the linen industry's output fell by 2.3 million yards in a year, the Carron Company found itself in difficulties, the construction of Edinburgh's New Town was halted, and work on the Monkland and Forth and Clyde Canals eventually had to stop. This temporary check on Scottish development well illustrates the vital role that the banks had assumed in the early Industrial Revolution.

*Insurance*

Another aspect of the development of financial services was the rise of the insurance business. Rudimentary marine insurance was probably introduced in London as far back as the fifteenth century, and by 1720, there were about 150 underwriters working in the port. Edward Lloyd's Coffee House in Lombard Street had been used as a clearing house and centre of commercial information by these underwriters since the 1690s. In 1720, two corporate bodies, the Royal Exchange and London Assurance Companies, received charters for transacting marine insurance. Business grew rapidly with the expansion of overseas trade, but it remained predominantly in the hands of the private underwriters. Although the two companies had £6 million-worth of risks in 1809, the private underwriters had an estimated £140 million-worth. They were active in all the ports: a Liverpool Underwriters Association was set up in 1802, reflecting the growing market for transatlantic insurance. London was very much the centre of the system, however. It was London that fixed rates. The new Lloyds was opened in 1789.

Fire insurance was the first to receive corporate status. A fire office called the Phoenix was set up in 1681 as a scheme for house insurance covered by a property investment fund. The famous Sun Fire Office was started in 1710, and in 1721, both the Royal Exchange and London companies were permitted to extend their business into fire risk. Fire insurance was rapidly brought to the provinces, with the companies – unlike the country banks – quick to set up agencies. The Sun appointed agents from the outset. They were generally tradesmen of some standing, such as grocers or booksellers, and received a five per cent commission. Their advertisements are to be found in all provincial newspapers of the period. The Sun had 123 agencies in 1786, the Royal Exchange had 200 in 1800. Their business throughout the country was predominantly with houses and shops, but became increasingly industrial. A new Phoenix Fire Office was formed in 1782 by the owners of London sugar refineries after they had been refused adequate cover elsewhere. This new Phoenix company took a considerable amount of industrial business, and the contrast between it and the original Phoenix scheme epitomises the transformation that overtook the insurance industry in the eighteenth century. The Sun, Royal Exchange and Phoenix were the biggest companies by 1800, but there were quite a number of provincial offices too. The Bristol Crown had been founded in 1718, the Friendly Society of Edinburgh in 1720, the Bath Fire Office in 1767, and Offices in Manchester and Liverpool in 1771 and 1777 respectively. Many new ones were opened in the boom years around the turn of the century, among them the Norwich Union in 1797, the Caledonian and the North British, both in Edinburgh in 1805 and 1809.

Life assurance policies had been available from limited subscription societies in Britain since the late sixteenth century. These societies simply divided their annual subscriptions amongst the estates of those members dying during the year. In 1721, both the Royal Exchange and London companies moved into the market, but in neither case were life policies more than an insignificant part of their total business. The modern history of life assurance does not begin until 1762, when the Equitable Life Assurance Society was founded, the first to base its policies on statistical life tables.

### Education

Education is rather more than a service. Just as the early Industrial Revolution was dependent upon a gradual extension of capital investment in machinery, power sources, and buildings, so it was dependent on the development of human skills. Education – both in the schools and as a technical training within firms – was a vital process of 'human capital formation'. Increasing economic complexity required that different sectors of the workforce be literate, numerate and competent in technical matters. Increasing articulation of the market depended upon a certain degree of literacy to allow information about prices, products and services to circulate freely.

The general level of literacy in the eighteenth century *was* relatively high. In England in 1750 about 60 per cent of males and 35 per cent of females could read fluently, and those with a basic reading ability were probably half as numerous again. Until the 1840s, the level of male literacy stayed remarkably stable, whilst female literacy rose slowly to about 50 per cent. A high proportion of the population had access to elementary education in the parish schools, often run by clergymen, and the Charity Schools, started by the Society for the Promotion of Christian Knowledge (SPCK) in 1695. In the market towns and bigger centres, there was a wide range of 'secondary education'. Schooling was not uniformly available, some parishes having no school at all, except in Scotland where vigorous attempts were made by the Scots Parliament to implement universal schooling in the 1690s. Here the literacy figures were probably rather higher.

Literacy levels were best in the market towns and old regional centres where commercial trades, dependent on numeracy and fluent writing ability, were concentrated. They were lower in rapidly industrialising communities, actually falling in the late eighteenth century in

Lancashire as the growing population outstripped the schooling available. In such areas the vacuum was filled in part by the Sunday Schools, which starting in the 1770s, had an enrolment approaching 250,000 by 1787. Many taught reading and writing. Those firms, such as Owen's New Lanark and Arkwright's at Cromford, that provided their own schools also made a contribution. There were also sharp educational differences by occupation. Literacy was almost universal amongst the gentry, professional classes and retailers, it was lower (about 60 per cent) amongst those in the transport and textile industries, and lowest (between 35 and 50 per cent) in the ordinary ranks of soldiers, husbandmen, and amongst miners, labourers and servants. These differences show that a high literacy attainment amongst *all* groups was not a prerequisite to industrialisation. New factory jobs, and employment in farms and mines did not (except for overseers, engineers, etc.) require much reading or writing ability. The great fall in levels of illiteracy that took place after 1840, giving an almost totally literate population (male and female) by 1890, was more one of the beneficial results of industrialisation than a cause of it.

Rather more important as a causal factor in economic development was the increasing quality of education available to those bound for middle or higher-rank jobs. The role of some of the village schools should not be underestimated in this respect. Often the teaching of the '3Rs' was of a sufficient standard to enable poor children to obtain a free place at one of the grammar schools or academies, or to be apprenticed to a craftsman or trader, so opening up an essential avenue of social mobility. Wedgwood, Arkwright, Strutt, McConnell and Garbett were all successes of the early Industrial Revolution who had followed the latter path. The village schools of parts of the north of England were particularly renowed by the end of the century: they have 'become quite a manufactory for Bankers' and Merchants' Clerks', according to one authority in 1796.

There were about 500 endowed grammar schools in the towns of England and Wales, and every big Scottish burgh had its own. A classical education had long been the standard form of instruction in these schools, but it came under increasing attack for its lack of relevance to contemporary needs from the 1690s onwards. Campbell, in his directory of professions (*The London Tradesman*) in 1747, expressed an opinion common amongst the commercial communities when he wrote that seven years of 'cramming a Boy's Head full of a Dead Language, of useless words, and incoherent terms, satiates his memory and confounds his judgment'! Many grammar schools did respond, however, to the modern educational needs of the age. Two new streams of subjects were widely introduced – the 'commercial' (modern languages, book-keeping, commercial law, geography, navigation) and the 'scientific' (mathematics, physics, chemistry, astronomy). This was a financially-motivated move. Schoolmasters were dependent on their pupils' fees for a reasonable income, as their stipends were low and remained virtually unchanged throughout the century. The pressure of competition from the private schools and new academies, and the prospect of holding children who would otherwise have left for a 'useful' training in trade, was the basic reason for the modernisation of the curriculum. Not all grammar schools changed, and those that did generally taught the new subjects in addition to the classical ones. However, the move towards relevance was widespread, and certainly not limited to Scotland as has so often been assumed.

The range of educational opportunity beyond the grammar schools was wide. The use of private tuition spread from the upper into the middle classes. Some of the foremost scientists of the day (e.g. Joseph Priestley, Charles Hutton) were private tutors. Private schools, often run by clergymen, were numerous – some in the van of curricula improvement, some bastions of the genteel classical education. Their fees – around £12 to £20 a year, including board – were well within the reach of the trading and employing classes. Samuel Whitbread and Matthew Boulton were both educated at such institutions. In some of the bigger towns there were private teachers, instructing in 'modern subjects' such as mathematics, French and handwriting (rather than printing). In Glasgow and Edinburgh these teachers were supported by the burgh councils. A tradition of evening lectures for the public developed in London, Edinburgh, Oxford and Cambridge, and quickly spread to provincial towns. A Mathematical Society was founded in Manchester in 1719, and public science lectures may have been presented in Newcastle as early as 1715. By the last third of the century, there were evening classes in London and throughout the provinces designed entirely for adult mechanics and craftsmen.

The eighteenth century's 'own distinctive contribution to education', however, was the academy, an institution where the classical education was supplemented by a two or three year course in scientific and practical subjects. Often they were founded and staffed by the private teachers of the big towns. Some were very specialist, such as the naval academies at Chelsea (1777) and Gosport (1791), and a number of mathematical schools, concerned mainly with engineering and commercial subjects. Some were clear attempts to provide an alternative to the universities (which students could enter at 14) where, it was argued, youth would be in far less moral danger. This was particularly true of the non-conformist academies, but dissenters were anyway barred from official study at Oxbridge (although they could still attend the Scottish universities). Many famous names emerged from the non-conformist academies, including John and William Wilkinson, Josiah Wedgwood's son John and his partner Thomas Bentley, and Samuel Galton, and they were certainly at the centre of the teaching of the new subjects. Their role should not be exaggerated, however, as the economic stimulus to 'relevant' teaching was felt across the whole spectrum of education. The nonconformist academies were far outnumbered by the 200 private academies in 1800, many of which, along with many of the grammar schools, were teaching equally laudable courses.

The universities were not left out of the modernising current. The traditional view of Oxbridge as moribund (derived essentially from Adam Smith and Gibbon) was hardly true, with both universities introducing many new science subjects in the late seventeenth and early eighteenth centuries. However, they did lag in the second half of the century behind the five Scottish universities, all of which made a conscious effort to popularise new scientific courses. Again, this was related to the low level of stipendiary allowances for Scots professors, and a deliberate policy in Edinburgh and Glasgow of appointing the best teachers available. Theirs were the biggest universities in Britain. Glasgow had about 1,000 students in 1800, and Edinburgh had 2,000 by the end of the Napoleonic wars. In both places almost half of these were medical students, the Scots varsities being the only ones to make serious provision for them. Throughout the eighteenth century the most important role of the two English universities was to train men for the old professions of the Church and law. A school or academy career followed by practical training in an industry or service was the more usual route into one of the newly emerging occupations of the early Industrial Revolution.

*Law*

Law was one of the oldest professions. Along with the Church, medicine or the Armed Forces, it was a natural destination for the younger sons of upper class families, or aspirant middle class youths. Yet in each of these professions there was a yawning difference in status and numbers between the upper and lower echelons. The early eighteenth-century attorney had little social position, being regarded generally as merely a technical clerk, whereas the barristers were very respected gentlemen.

The barristers ('advocates' in Scotland), were rarely seen outside London or Edinburgh, except at Assizes. The legal profession was strongly represented in both capitals. In Edinburgh in 1774 there were

188 advocates, 171 writers (or solicitors), 141 clerks to His Majesty's Signet (who dealt with Crown business and conducted cases before the Court of Session), and 94 Lords' and advocates' clerks. Yet in Glasgow there were just 52 members of the Faculty of Procurators (i.e. ordinary attorneys) (table 7:1). The attorney was to be found in most towns, performing a necessary economic function in guiding his clients through the legal maze. He dealt with the sale and purchase of property, worked out settlements, drew up wills, and acted as agent in legal disputes, sometimes representing his clients in the lower courts. The eighteenth-century 'Law Society', the Society of Gentlemen Practisers, was established in London about 1739. Although primarily convivial, it set professional standards and brought cases of malpractice before the courts. It was a conscious attempt to upgrade the status of the profession. In the second half of the century, a number of provincial societies were set up too: in Bristol (1770), Yorkshire (1786), Somerset (1796), Sunderland (1800), Leeds (1805), Devon (1808), Manchester (1809). Certainly by this time the attorney was a familiar professional figure in all the small market towns (table 7:2).

### The New Professions

It was not a long step for the attorney into a number of related areas that developed as new professions in the early Industrial Revolution. Those dealing with the legal affairs of corporations or partnerships sometimes became more specialised as *accountants* or *company secretaries* (a trend apparent first in Scotland) although both these professions were fed through the banks and merchant houses as well. Country attorneys who dealt with land formed the core of the new *estate management* profession. Some operating in the land market became specialist *auctioneers*. There were enough leading London men in this profession to form the Select Society of Auctioneers in 1799. There were fewer in the provinces – two in Sheffield in 1797, five in Glasgow in 1784.

A number of other new professions developed, related directly to the technical needs of industrialization, manned by the growing ranks of those with a 'commercial' or 'scientific' education. *Chartered surveying* emerged from the old tradition of estate mapping, and was greatly boosted by the need to employ a surveyor for every enclosure award. Surveying developed rapidly from a low status occupation for gifted or untrained amateurs into a respected profession. By the 1770s, many turnpike trusts were demanding the services of a surveyor who could construct roads on 'scientific principles', rather than merely direct labour to fill up holes. Canal schemes called for large and accurate surveys, both before and after an Act of Parliament was obtained. Many of the late eighteenth century topographical maps are of a considerable technical standard (plates A1 and B2). The real indicator of the advance of the surveying profession was the establishment, in 1787, of the Ordnance Survey. Its great theodolite set on the baseline on Hampstead Heath was 'as near perfect as makes no matter', capable of measuring angles to within five feet accuracy over distances of up to 70 miles.

The companion of the surveyor was the *engineer* (above, p. 150), the most numerous group of which were the millwrights. Many, such as Smeaton and Watt, were both civil and mechanical engineers. Many, by the nature of their key position, were also managers. Of this sort of engineer, there seems to have been a perpetual shortage in the early Industrial Revolution, particularly during years of rapid expansion. Watt was said to have been 'overburdened with detail' and had 'exceptional difficulty in finding intelligent managing clerks' (i.e. resident middle-order engineers). The canals were only built by pluralism, with a limited number of top engineers working on several projects at once. McAdam, the great road engineer, had to operate in the same way. By 1819, he had been consulted by or worked for 34 turnpike trusts in 13 counties and his sons on many more. Between them, they had trained a whole generation of new road surveyor/engineers. Industrial *management* as a separate profession, is rather a advanced concept for the early Industrial Revolution. A class of managers, as distinct from entrepreneurs, partners, accountants or engineers, did not really emerge until after 1830.

## PERSONAL SERVICES

The third group within the service sector was the personal services – those that existed primarily for the welfare of the individual rather than the convenience of business. This group includes occupations that equate with tertiary 'trades' as well as quaternary 'professions'. It contains three very old occupations, the Church, medicine and domestic service, and a number of new ones, such as institutional entertainment.

### Medicine

Medicine was divided into upper and lower branches, much as was law. The physicians, the doctors of the nobility and wealthy gentry, were to be found in numbers only in London and Edinburgh. No more than 350 were admitted as fellows or licentiates by the Royal College of Physicians in London between 1771 and 1833. Thirty-nine were listed in the Edinburgh Directory for 1774. The vast majority of people had means or cause only to consult the 'trade' end of the medical profession – the surgeons or apothecaries. Their origins are betrayed by their ancestry. In London, the apothecaries were attached to the grocers until they formed their own separate company in 1617. The surgeons were linked to the barbers until 1745, as their poles still remind us. In the early eighteenth century, the apothecary was seen as a shopkeeper, the surgeon as a craftsman.

With the limited state of medical knowledge in the eighteenth century, the modern identity of the medical profession emerged but slowly. But the growing output of university-trained doctors from Edinburgh and Glasgow gradually increased their status. Apothecaries, who visited and prescribed for their patients (thereby distinguishing themselves from 'druggists' and 'chemists' who were retailers) were the first to follow the physicians and establish a system of qualifications and registration, under the Apothecaries Act of 1815. This really marked the start of the profession of general practitioner, of whom the Society of Apothecaries estimated there were by then about 12,000 in England and Wales.

At the end of the century, all towns had at least two or three representatives of the medical profession (table 7:2). In the bigger places both private and institutional facilities were to be found in some numbers, although by present standards, by no means adequately. Sheffield, with a population of about 32,000 in 1797, had 14 surgeons, ten druggists and three doctors. Manchester, a town of 30,000 inhabitants listed only two physicians, eight surgeons, and nine apothecaries or druggists in its Directory for 1772. It did however, have an Infirmary, a Lunatic Asylum, a House of Recovery and a Lying-in-Hospital. These institutional facilities were more extensive in Liverpool, a town with an active Corporation and merchant community. Its Infirmary, with 200 beds, was established in 1749 and supported by subscription. Next to it was the Seamens' Hospital, started in 1752 to maintain 'decayed' seamen and their widows. The Blue Coat Hospital (1720) cared for 280 orphans and fatherless children, the Blind Asylum (1790) for those who had lost their sight, mostly through smallpox. Its inmates were actively employed in basketry, weaving, etc. The Lunatic Hospital took the poor at parish expense, and the rich at their own. The Institution for Restoring Drowned Persons (1775) was maintained by the Corporation. There was also a Public Dispensary (1778) and a Ladies Charity (1796) which provided for childbirth at home. Both were supported by public subscriptions. Liverpool was undoubtedly one of the luckier towns.

*The Church*

The eighteenth-century Church was viewed as an obvious occupation for the educated man, or the younger sons of landed families, rather than a social service or spiritual calling. This was as it had been for centuries. However, the road to improvement through education for the poor scholar often ended in a poorly paid curacy, in a niche as 'not quite a gentleman'. The well-endowed parishes, and the Church's higher offices, provided a considerable income for their holders. But the majority of church posts were very poor, and most priests and curates were in a status position within the Church similar to that of the apothecary and attorney in medicine and law. In the early eighteenth century, of 10,000 English parishes, over 5,000 were worth less than £80 a year and over 3,000 less than £40. The most prevalent criticism of the eighteenth-century Church, that it was racked by pluralism (and by implication hence inefficient in its service), must be seen in this perspective. Pluralism was indeed widespread. In Exeter diocese in 1779, 159 livings out of 390 were held by non-resident priests. In York diocese, the figures were 218 of a total of 836 in 1788. Yet the cause of pluralism, in the main, was simply the need to combine parishes to give the incumbent a living wage. In many cases, plurally-held livings were adjacent – where they were not, it was a normal requirement that a resident curate be appointed.

On the whole, the Church seems to have done its job well, particularly in the rural areas and older towns. Many churches were rebuilt, extended or fitted with balconies, although much of the evidence was swept away in Victorian times. In industrialising areas, it was undoubtedly overtaken by the challenge of rising numbers. Few new parishes were founded and usually the problem was met by building outlying chapels. This again, has to be understood in the context of the times. Before 1818, an Act of Parliament (an expensive business) was needed to create a new parish, and as the incumbent was directly dependent on the endowments of his parish for income, there was little incentive to forfeit part of his territory. The way was left wide open for Methodism and the nonconformist sects.[8]

In many places, however, the clergyman was the only professional and well-educated man in the parish. His function was far broader than that of pastor alone. Many acted as pillars of local government in their neighbourhoods, sitting as Justices, and turnpike trustees; a lot were schoolmasters, or acted as private or voluntary tutors; many were involved in benevolent work amongst the poor, and in raising subscriptions for local works such as hospitals and charity schools.

## Entertainment

Much in the way of entertainment was as ever before: spontaneous, local and non-institutional, the preserve of fair, alehouse or home. There were significant trends however towards institutionalisation within the towns, as well as a filtering-down into the middle-classes of cultural activities that had formerly been aristocratic pursuits alone.

Most towns had their own library by the 1770s and many had a Coffee House ( a fad that started in Restoration London – there were 500 there in the early eighteenth century). The Coffee Houses stocked local and London newspapers, and the magazines: the tip of a swell of secular literature that brought novels, poetry, scientific books and encyclopaedias into the reach of the literate. Institutional music gained ground in the churches and new concert halls. Liverpool's Public Concert Room could seat 1,300 people, and it was in London that Handel composed his oratorios, and for London audiences that Haydn wrote some of his best music. Music was becoming less of an elitist preserve of the chamber. Sadlers Wells was opened in 1765, and stage theatres were to be found in most big towns. The Olympic and Adelphi Theatres opened in London in 1806, the Lyceum in 1809 and the Old Vic in 1815. It was John Palmer, the theatre manager in Bath, who successfully demonstrated to Pitt in 1784 that a mail coach was a better proposition than a mailboy. He was elevated to Postmaster-General, and put in charge of organising a national system of mailcoaches that was so important in maintaining the information flows that sustained the service sector and producers. Nearly all towns had museums, and some even art galleries. The National Gallery in London was founded in 1824.

Organised sport was an eighteenth-century invention. The bigger towns had dancing and fencing masters. Angelo's fencing academy in Bond Street was a well known London institution, opening in 1763 and surviving till 1897. Lord's cricket ground was opened in 1787 and the MCC founded in the following year. Regular race meetings began at Epsom in the 1730s, and the Derby was instituted in 1780. The Honourable Company of Edinburgh Golfers laid down the basic rules of the game in 1744 – the famous Royal and Ancient Club at St Andrews was founded in 1754. Undoubtedly, however, the epitome of institutionalised entertainment was the entire leisured routine of the spa towns and seaside resorts, fashionable retreats for the upper classes and aspiring wealthy middle class. (plate F2). But Bath, Tunbridge Wells, Scarborough, Weymouth and Brighton were 'fashionable': they were hardly open to all. They symbolised the gradual transformation in the supply of entertainment for the upper levels of the market: for the rest it remained much as it always had been.

*Domestic Service*

The least conspicuous but most numerous group within the whole service sector were the domestic servants. In 1801, there were 600,000 – in towns, country houses and on farms – in a population of only nine million, and the number rose continuously through the nineteenth century. Again, it was a growing middle-class demand, rising incomes encouraging a trickle-down effect of a very old upper-class habit. For many girls and not a few boys too, domestic service was the only hope of a station in life other than that of pauper. Servants, along with labourers, remained the least literate and most socially immobile group in eighteenth-century Britain.

Addison, in the early eighteenth century, had written of 'the three great professions of divinity, law and physic'. By 1800, the term had widened to include a whole range of newly emergent 'modern' professions, themselves one of the clearest indicators of economic advance in the early Industrial Revolution. These, together with the tertiary and personal services, constituted a vital sector in the industrialising economy of eighteenth-century Britain.

## NOTES

1 Nevertheless, direct ordering from merchant or agent to clothier eventually overtook this system too: 'probably the majority of cloths before 1800, especially in the Leeds area, was bought in the cloth halls. After 1800, their position declined rapidly. One clothier in 1821 estimated that even around Leeds not more than one in five broad cloths ever passed through the doors of the Leeds cloth halls' (Wilson (1971) p. 75).

2 This process of concentration is evident in other branches of the wholesale trade. London's sea coal was sold at the new Coal Exchange (1768), owned by 64 shipowners, factors and buyers. By the end of the century, it was practically controlled by only nine factors. Overseas trade was dominated by the big merchant firms. There were more than 100 merchants in Hull throughout the eighteenth century, but never more than 20 counted for much.

3 In the 1790s, a specialist class of bill-brokers developed in London. They took over much of the business of finding buyers for bills that other banks wished to discount.

4 Nevertheless, the notion of a 'central bank' in this period must be used cautiously. The Bank did not operate monetary policy in any modern sense, nor did it manage exchange controls, and even in the late nineteenth century, it expressed some doubts over whether it was a lender of last resort. That is, most of the functions basic to the modern central

bank's discretionary control of the money supply were not developed in this period.

5 But not paid until 1727. It was used to support the Commission 'for Improving Fisherys and Manufacturers', whose activities in the linen industry were discussed in chapter five. (above pp. 139–42).

6 The Bank of Scotland had twice tried to set up branches before: both attempts (one at its start in the 1690s, the other in 1731) were short-lived. Most English country banks however, were too small to have branches, although some of the bigger ones appointed an agent or two in neighbouring towns. The Bank of England did not open any branches for many years. The first was in Manchester in 1826, the second in Liverpool in 1827.

7 A similar contraction of banking facilities followed the 1793 crisis in England. Although it is impossible to be definite about the figures, there were about 280 country bankers open at the end of the year, compared with about 400 a year earlier. By 1797, there were about 230.

8 The Liverpool Guide of 1797, for example, listed the following: 13 established churches, one Church of Scotland, 3 dissenter chapels, one Quaker Meeting House, 4 Methodist chapels, 2 Baptist chapels, 3 Roman Catholic chapels and a Jewish synagogue.


## FURTHER READING

The importance of the service sector was first recognised by the economist A. G. B. Fisher in an article 'The Economic Implications of Material Progress' in the *International Labour Review* Vol. XXXII, (1935). His ideas were taken up by Colin Clark in *The Conditions of Economic Progress* (1940), but only one historian has attempted to assess the role of services in the British Industrial Revolution: see chapter ten of *The Industrial Revolution and Economic Growth* (1971) by R. M. Hartwell.

### TERTIARY SERVICES

The classic work on middlemen, yet to be bettered, is R. B. Westerfield's: *Middlemen in English Business, particularly between 1680–1760* (1915). Although mainly concerned with the sixteenth and seventeenth centuries, Alan Everitt's chapter on 'The Marketing of Agricultural Produce' in the *Agrarian History of England and Wales, vol. IV 1500–1640*, (ed.) Joan Thirsk (1967), is valuable. So too are the short but stimulating essays in T. S. Willan: *The Inland Trade* (1976) The role of the inn is examined in another essay by Everitt 'The English Urban Inn, 1560–1760' in a book edited by him: *Perspectives in English Urban History* (1973). A good reference on trading activities in the ports is Gordon Jackson's: *Hull in the Eighteenth Century* (1972).

The most analytical work on retailing, although mainly concerned with the nineteenth century, is David Alexander's: *Retailing in England during the Industrial Revolution* (1970). A simple narrative text is Dorothy Davis: *A History of Shopping* (1966). An excellent little book compiled from the papers of a country grocer, and of far wider significance than the title suggests is T. S. Willan's: *An Eighteenth Century Shopkeeper: Abraham Dent of Kirkby Stephen*(1970).

For references to the transport services, see chapter six. There is little on public utilities, although there is some material on Improvement Commissions in S. and B. Webb: *Statutory Authorities for Special Purposes* (1922).

QUATERNARY SERVICES

There is quite an extensive literature on banking and finance. Good general coverages of the field are to be found in Hamilton (1963) and T. S. Ashton: *An Economic History of England: The Eighteenth Century* (1955). The authorative works in the field are:- Sir John Clapham: *The Bank of England* (1944), L. S. Pressnell: *Country Banking in the Industrial Revolution* (1956), and S. G. Checkland: *Scottish Banking, A History 1695–1973* (1975). It is well worth consulting some regional essays, such as T. S. Ashton on 'The Bill of Exchange and Private Banks in Lancashire, 1790–1830', in *Papers in English Monetary History*, (eds.) T. S. Ashton and R. S. Sayers (1953); the relevant sections of Gordon Jackson's *Hull in the Eighteenth Century* (1972; and D. M. Joslin: 'London Private Bankers, 1720–1780', *Ec. H.R.* vol. VII (1954). H. Hamilton: 'The failure of the Ayr Bank 1772', *Ec. H.R.* vol VIII (1956) is of general relevance, placing the rise and fall of the Ayr bank in the economic context of Scotland at the time. Humphrey Lloyd: *The Quaker Lloyds* (1975) discusses the origins of the famous Birmingham firm. A valuable guide to insurance records, and a brief history of the service is given by H. A. L. Cockerell and Edwin Green: *The British Insurance Business, 1547–1970* (1976). Useful business histories are those by P. G. M. Dickson: *The Sun Fire Office* (1960) and B. E. Supple: *The Royal Exchange Assurance* (1970).

Again, there is an extensive literature on education, not all of which is particularly useful. There are two good articles on levels of literacy, one by R. S. Schofield: 'Dimensions of Illiteracy, 1750–1850', in *Explorations in Economic History*, vol. 10 (1973), the other, about industrialising Lancashire, by M. B. Sanderson: 'Literacy and Social Mobility in the Industrial Revolution in England', *Past and Present* no. 56 (1972). The book that demonstrated how general was the modernising current in eighteenth-century education is N. Hans: *New Trends in Education in the Eighteenth Century* (1951). But a particularly good essay relating this current to the contemporary economic climate is Donald J. Withrington's 'Education and Society in the Eighteenth Century', in *Scotland in the Age of Improvement*, (eds.) N. T. Phillipson and Rosalind Mitchison (1970). On the role of Sunday Schools, see T. W. Lacquer: *Religion and Respectability: Sunday Schools and Working Class Culture, 1780–1850* (1976). Sidney Pollard's: *The Genesis of Modern Management* (1965) has a useful chapter on the formal and practical training of managers.

There are few good references on the other professions. *Professional Men: The Rise of the Professional Classes in 19th Century England* (1966), by W. J. Reader has some relevant material on the eighteenth century lawyer and doctor. See also Robert Robson: *The Attorney in Eighteenth Century England* (1959), and B. Hamilton: 'The Medical Professions in the Eighteenth Century', *Ec. H.R.* vol. IV (1951), which goes into some detail. The only new profession to receive full length treatment is that of surveying: F. M. L. Thompson: *Chartered Surveyors – the Growth of a Profession* (1966). A short article on Scottish surveyors is 'The Land Surveyor and his Influence on the Scottish Rural Landscape', by Ian H. Adams, in *Scottish Geog. Mag.* vol. 84 (1968). There is a vast literature on the eighteenth century church. A good starting point is Anthony Armstrong's book: *The Church of England, the Methodists and Society, 1700–1850* (1973).

PRIMARY SOURCES

The information in table 7:1 is taken from surviving trade directories. These are listed in Jane E. Norton's excellent handbook: *Guide to the National and Provincial Directories of England and Wales* (1950). Table 7:2 is compiled from the *Universal British Directory*, published in the 1790s and a mine of information. *The London Tradesman* (1747) by R. Campbell is a useful contemporary description of trades and professions. (repr. 1967).

# 8 The Role of Towns and Urban Change

'No, Sir, when a man is tired of London, he is tired of life; for there is in London all that life can afford.'

*Samuel Johnson ( 1777 ).*

London certainly played a dominant role in national life. 'Soon London will be all England' King James I had declared a century and a half before Johnson's time. Its population then was about 200,000: by 1801 it was little short of a million, the largest city in Europe, very nearly double the size of Paris and ten times as big as the largest provincial British town. For ten per cent of the population of England and Wales, London was life. And throughout the rest of the country, it exerted a powerful influence as an engine of change. The growth of London encouraged the development of agriculture and transport networks, it was the focus of commerce and the finance system, it was a major industrial centre and market, and just as important but less tangible, it was a great economic and social flux: the promoter of modernisation and the solvent of traditionalism.

But London was not quite all England, still less all Britain. There was a well-developed urban hierarchy, notwithstanding the immense primacy of the capital. Every centre, from the smallest market town of only a few hundred people to the bigger regional centres, ports and industrial towns, had a role to play. Moreover, this urban hierarchy was far from stable in the eighteenth century. It is symptomatic of the changes taking place that in 1700 Norwich and Bristol were the biggest English provincial towns, but that by 1800 Liverpool and Manchester occupied these positions. In Scotland, Glasgow had grown as large as Edinburgh. Expanding towns such as these were centres of economic influence and change comparable with London, albeit on a smaller scale.

It is the emergence of large provincial towns that is the most notable feature of eighteenth century urban change. There were only three provincial towns with 20,000 people or more in 1700. By 1800, there were 20, including five in Scotland. The biggest of these were over 80,000 in size.

Overall, the urban population of England and Wales (comparable figures for Scotland are not available) had grown from about 1.2 million to 3 million. Yet the degree of change should not be exaggerated. The eighteenth century did not see massive urbanisation: the urban population rose only from 22 or 23 per cent to about 33 per cent of the total, with most of this change taking place after 1750.[1] Neither was urban growth uniform. Most of the larger centres were growing, some very rapidly, but others – notably some of the long-established industrial towns subject to the competition of the rising centres – were stagnant or even declining. Amongst the lesser urban places, change was far from even. Trade was becoming increasingly concentrated in the more accessible market towns, leaving small and intermediate places to sink. The eighteenth century, then, is a period of urban change, rather than of massive urban growth.

Where urban growth was occurring, it was by a combination of the two demographic processes: natural increase and immigration. The large, rapidly expanding towns, and London in particular, grew mainly by immigration. They were consumers rather than producers of population until the 1750s, London till the early nineteenth century. These migrants were drawn from wide fields (fig. 2:4), although the majority came from the surrounding area, the Home Counties in the case of London. Natural increase was important as a mechanism of urban growth in the smaller towns, and with the gradual conquest of disease, it began to contribute in the larger ones as well by the last two decades of the century (above, p. 33).

## THE ROLE OF TOWNS

It was function, rather than status, that was the distinguishing characteristic of the eighteenth-century town. The nominal labels of urban status had long ceased to bear much relation to reality. There were about 200 municipalities in England in 1700, but some of these were so small that they numbered populations of only a few score. Some did not even exercise market functions. Yet there were many urban centres that were not incorporated, including some very important ones. The tiny town of Queensborough on the Isle of Sheppey and the skeletal foundation of Pevensey in Sussex were both incorporated, unlike Birmingham, Manchester or Sheffield. Parliamentary representation was little guide. Uninhabited Old Sarum and the 400 townsfolk of the decayed port of Seaford each had two MPs, Weymouth had as many as four – yet the thousands in Manchester and Sheffield had none. Neither was a cathedral any indication of city size or function. Several cathedral 'cities' were very important regional centres, notably York, Norwich, Worcester and to a lesser extent, Carlisle, Lincoln and Salisbury. But some were little more than villages, of less note locally than neighbouring market towns: Wells, Ely, St Asaph, St David's.

Towns – those centres of population that performed urban functions – had long played an important role as central places. As market centres, they were the commercial nodes of the countryside providing, alongside the regular fairs, facilities for the sale of agricultural produce. They were also suppliers of basic services and distributors of imported goods and manufactures from elsewhere. Some were administrative centres, county towns or burghs, seats of Quarter Sessions and Assizes. They were foci of transport services, and an essential link between the local area and the world beyond. These central place functions became better articulated during the early Industrial Revolution, as agriculture and trade expanded, and marketing facilities and transport services modernised. But the central place role was essentially a static one, a role that towns had played through several centuries in pre-industrial Britain. It was one that sustained and maintained economic and social life.

The rapidly growing large towns of the second half of the eighteenth century began to play a far more dynamic role than this. They began to act as engines of growth and centres of change alongside London. It is this role that deserves close attention, as the large towns of the early Industrial Revolution were far more than symbols of change; they were, to a substantial degree, the cause of it.

*The Economic Role*

Urban growth exerted considerable influence in the development of each of the main sectors of the economy. The importance of the London market in stimulating agricultural production was a frequent contemporary theme. As the metropolis grew, not only did it spread its net wider and wider, but it also encouraged regional specialisation: 'all the counties of England contribute something towards the subsistence of the great city', according to Defoe. The important provincial centres likewise exerted a wide influence. The intrusion of urban middlemen into country markets raised prices towards city levels. Arthur Young noted that 'in respect of the influence of great cities, I was never out of it. London affects the price of wheat everywhere, and though veal and butter were very cheap in Wales, yet the prices of them were by no means those that arose from a home consumption alone, as I plainly perceived by the great quantities of provisions bought up in all the little ports of the Severn, by the Bristol market boats'. Growing urban demand and improving communications encouraged farming enterprise. Long before the railways, the Vale of Evesham was growing 'garden plants, onions, cucumbers and asparagus' for the markets of Birmingham, Bath and Bristol. The most progressive farming region in Scotland lay in the counties around Edinburgh.

For industry, London and the big towns were both important markets and producing centres. London wages, including those of the labourer, were higher than elsewhere. It was a relatively wealthy, as well as a large market. Its growing middle-class population, and its season for gentry and nobility, made it a centre of conspicuous consumption of great potential for aspiring industrialists. Wedgwood and Boulton established showrooms there, and many textile firms retained agents, or warehouses. It was the demands of the capital that led to the development of large-scale coal-mining in the north-east. The constant call for fuel meant deeper mines and the expansion of the collier marine, and directly contributed to the success of the steam engine and railway.

As industrial producers themselves, towns had many advantages. The large centres offered a wide range of scale economies: ancillary industries, specialist services, regular transport, a labour force, and not least, competition (and with it, often, innovation). The well developed structure of industrial Sheffield (table 5:4) and the complex interlinkage of industries on the south bank of the Thames illustrate the advantages of specialisation to be gained from location in a large urban community. It was industry that was the foremost force of urban growth in the eighteenth century. Although a considerable amount of industrial enterprise was rural (above, pp. 79–82) most was urban-based, to be found either in established centres, or creating its own urban communities in areas of closeknit thriving domestic trade, such as the West Riding, east Lancashire and south Staffordshire.

Thirdly, the growth of towns encouraged the development of transport networks and service activities. The nodal position of London in the turnpike road network (fig. 6:2) reflects its centrality in the system of inland trade, but it was also the biggest port in shipping tonnage, and the focus of marine mineral and agricultural traffic (fig. 5:4). It was Birmingham that became the hub of the canal network, however, being an inland centre remote from natural water transport. The urbanising communities of northern England also built dense networks of waterways. But transport was only one part of the service sector. It was in the towns, with their high market thresholds and educational facilities, that specialist services and professions developed, ranging from fixed forms of distribution to banking and insurance (above, chapter seven).

*The Modernising Influence*

Closely tied in with their economic role, in part cause, in part effect of it, was the modernising influence of the bigger towns. This is something that has been particularly associated with London, but it was by no means its monopoly. As concentrations of population, towns were more than locations of scale economies. They had a social, and hence economic, function that went beyond this. They were centres of discussion, generators of ideas, transmitters of knowledge, creators of fashion: especially those with expanding groups of well-educated professional men, entrepreneurs, industrialists and tradesmen. It was here that the forces of reason and empiricism took hold, here that the modernising trend in education developed and where the philosophical societies, renowned for their meetings of general cultural and scientific interest, were to be found. London's Royal Society, Birmingham's Lunar Society (to which Watt, Boulton, Wedgwood and Priestley all belonged) and the Manchester Philosophical Society were but the most renowned of these. Significantly too, the Agricultural Societies, dedicated to the propagation of more rational farming methods, were located, in the main, near the growing industrial centres (fig. 3:7).

This 'modernising' atmosphere was responsible for hastening many trends in production, consumption and life-styles in general. It was an atmosphere of flux and mobility, one that encouraged the change and development that underlay the early Industrial Revolution. It was the big towns that were the centres of innovation in production. The fertility of competition and collaboration within and between firms, in machinery and cloth design, in finishing and marketing, led Manchester and Glasgow to the top of the cotton trade – rather than remote Cromford or tiny Tamworth, just as it led Sheffield there in steel, and Birmingham, 'the grand toy-shop of Europe'. Proximity to innovating manufacturers and, in London and the ports, to sources of foreign products, influenced market behaviour and sustained the deepening of demand. It was in London in particular, with its society season, that tastes and fashions were created. By mid-century, many provincial shopkeepers advertised groceries from London importers and clothes in the latest London styles. John Byng, in the 1770s wished 'with all my heart that half the turnpike roads of the Kingdom were ploughed up, which have imported London manners – I meet milkmaids on the road, with the dress and looks of Strand misses'. A sure consequence of the extension of urban influence was the erosion of traditional rural ways.

The most notable aspect of the modernising influence for the bulk of the urban population, however, was the evolution of new life-styles. Mass production introduced specialisation of work-roles. It relied upon more rigid work-patterns. The factories, workshops and services required a regular discipline that was not a feature of domestic activity. Inevitably, home and workplace became separated too, with consequences for the pattern of urban growth. It was in the towns that payment in money wages, rather than wholly or partly in kind, was first firmly established. Families had to buy their everyday requirements in the market place. Towns were the creators of the modern market economy, and it is because they were centres of monetary exchange that a wide range of industrial and service enterprises could develop and flourish within them.

It was also in towns that the new social order began to emerge. There is a danger in attaching the term 'class' to the social groups of the day, either to the 'working' or 'middle' classes, as it suggests that they possessed a cohesiveness, an identity which they did not: not in individual towns, and certainly not nationally. But it was the years of the early Industrial Revolution that saw the beginnings of a mass urban proletariat, engaged in town mills, factories and workshops. And it was then that an influential band of urban middle-income earners emerged, a 'middle-class', but one made up of loose groupings of individuals. It included those in positions of control in trade and industry, those in the old and new professions, and the 'urban gentry' – those of independent means but without country estates, retired from business or the Army, or living off family fortunes. These social groups were not self contained. There was some mobility between them as debtors sank from the ranks of middle income and the more fortunate amongst the 'lower order' rose through education or self enterprise. But it was essentially the urban 'middle-class' groups that were of such significance in economic development. It was these that provided many of the leaders, innovators and organisers in business, and as a collective force, created the market deepening process that underlay growing demand.

Some perceptive contemporary commentators recognised the important role that thriving towns could perform. Edinburgh in the first half of the eighteenth century was a poor, overcrowded, underserviced community. It lacked the vitality and air of comfortable progress of the larger English centres. One Mr Fletcher of Salthoun writing 'a discourse on the affairs of Scotland' in 1698, considered this. 'As the happy situation of LONDON', he said, 'has been the principal cause of the glory and riches of ENGLAND; so the bad situation of EDINBURGH, has been one great occasion of the poverty and uncleanliness in which the greater part of the people of Scotland live'.

## THE CHANGING URBAN HIERARCHY

*In 1700*

England was well endowed with towns in 1700, a reflection of the relative development and market orientation of its agriculture. However, many of them were very small. There were about 500 market centres, nearly all with very local spheres of influences, with populations of between about 500 and 2,000.[2] However, there were only 40 or 50 towns with a population in the range of 2–5,000, many of these having a local industry or small port, and acting as regional marketing centres with far larger hinterlands than the average market town. There were 31 towns with more than 5,000 people, and only seven of these were over 10,000 in size. These were: Manchester and Yarmouth with just over 10,000 each, York with about 11,000, Exeter with 13 or 14,000, Newcastle with 14 or 15,000, Bristol – the metropolis of the west – with about 20,000, and the greatest provincial centre, Norwich, with 30,000 people. Nevertheless, none of these was more than a middling town in the shadow of London, with its 550,000 inhabitants.

It is less easy to be so definite about the urban hierarchies of Wales and Scotland in the early eighteenth century, but in keeping with their many acres of barren or marginal upland, both were considerably less well endowed with towns than England. Only in the Scottish Lowlands, the Vale of Glamorgan and fringes of north Wales was an urban fabric comparable to that of most of England to be found. Glasgow had a population of 12,766 in 1708, Aberdeen – the regional centre of the north – was about the same size, Dundee was appreciably smaller, whilst all the other Scots burghs, with the obvious exception of Edinburgh, were under 5,000 in size. Edinburgh exhibited primacy in Scotland as did London in England, but not to such a great degree. Its population was about three times that of Glasgow. However, in Wales there were no centres at all of any size. The more prosperous south looked to Bristol as its regional focus and there were as yet no real industrial towns. Carmarthen, not Swansea or Cardiff, was the biggest settlement, yet it had no more than 3,000 inhabitants.

Industrial towns were by no means absent in England. Just as many industries had had a long history before the eighteenth century, so the industrial town was not a creation of the early Industrial Revolution. London was an industrial centre as well as much else, so too were Norwich and Bristol. Manchester, Colchester, Exeter, Shrewsbury, Worcester, Coventry, all were prosperous industrial towns of between 7 and 14,000 people in 1700. But it is significant that with the changing distribution of industry in the eighteenth century, the industrial towns of

1700 were not, with obvious exceptions, the booming industrial centres of 1800.

## Changes, 1700–1801

The degree of urbanisation in the eighteenth century was not great. The most significant development was the growth of large provincial centres. Over half the increase in the urban population of England and Wales was accounted for by the 15 English towns that were over 20,000 in size when the first Census was taken in 1801. Industry and trade were the most potent forces of urban growth. Including London, 12 of these 15 were major industrial towns, two – Plymouth and Portsmouth – were Navy ports and shipbuilding centres, six others were big commercial ports, and one – Bath – had become a fashionable resort town. It is the importance of these industrial centres that confuses any underlying network of central places. The hierarchy and distribution of towns reflects the process of industrialisation and not the theoretical regularity of service centres (fig. 8:1).

The pattern of change was not even amongst these larger centres however. This point is best illustrated by the experience of Bristol and Liverpool. Both prospered but one more so than the other. In 1750 Bristol had 50,000 inhabitants and ranked second only to London. In 1801, Liverpool occupied that position, its numbers having grown from 22,000 to 88,000 in 50 years. Bristol had only increased to 64,000. It had been relatively eclipsed. The reasons for this were complex. Liverpool had a rapidly developing industrial hinterland, not only in south Lancashire, but through the canal network into the west and east Midlands. By 1795 it had overtaken London as the leading cotton importer. Bristol did not have such a hinterland. The Midlands producers were better served by their canal links to Liverpool than by the long course of the Severn River. The new industries of south Wales had their own ports. Bristol's harbour was inconvenient, being situated several miles up the tidal Avon, whereas Liverpool had direct sea access, with a deep water frontage that it developed throughout the century. In port improvements, Bristol lagged, too late. This in itself was symbolic of the differing attitudes of the two communities. Bristol was well established as the country's second port in 1700, with its Irish trade and triangular run between the coasts of Africa, the Indies and home. It became a little complacent. Liverpool merchants had no difficulty in breaking into the system, which they were doing by the late seventeenth century, using their own traditional Irish links and salt trade to supply the Indies with food, and themselves with sugar and other groceries. Liverpool entered into the African slave trade as well, and by 1750 was second to London in the

Anglo-American trade, sending Sheffield steel, Midlands iron products, Yorkshire heavy woollens and Lancashire cloth mixtures in exchange for

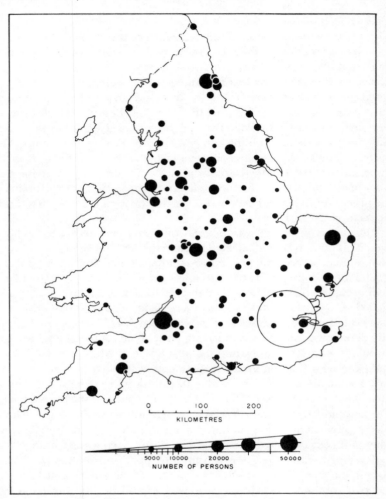

Fig. 8:1   *The Distribution of the Urban Population of England and Wales, 1750.*
*Source*: redrawn from Law (1972).

tobacco, cotton and timber. Liverpool's more northerly trading routes were safer from French privateers in the long wars after 1789 than were those of either London or Bristol. This, with the boost to trade after the American peace, and the rapid development of its hinterland, gave exceptional prosperity to Liverpool, and its population shot up from 41,600 in 1786 to 88,358 by 1801.

The importance of the nature of the hinterland was reflected in the growth of the east coast ports as well. In 1700, Hull and Kings Lynn were about the same size, with roughly 6,000 inhabitants. Both had extensive agricultural hinterlands. Yarmouth, a great herring fishing centre and outport of Norwich, was bigger, with about 10,000. Yet in 1801 Hull was by far the largest of the three with a population of over 27,000. Within its hinterland it counted not only the West Riding textile area and Sheffield cutlers, but Nottingham hosiers and Manchester cotton manufacturers as well. The journey over the Pennines and Yorkshire by turnpike and waterway to Hull was the quickest route from Lancashire to the north European markets. Hull merchants had extensive relations in the Baltic too, importing grain and timber, linseed (the basis of an important processing industry, providing materials for soap and paintworks) and Swedish steel. Lynn, by contrast, had barely reached 10,000 in size by 1801 and Yarmouth grew more slowly still to a total of 14,845.

Another port which did not realise its apparent promise was Whitehaven in Cumberland. It was a new town built around a harbour in the 1670s and 1680s by Sir John Lowther to exploit the coal on his estates. The town grew from 2,222 in 1693 to 9,063 in 1762, a prosperous community engaged in coal export to Ireland and in the colonial North American trade. At mid-century Whitehaven was second only to London in tonnage cleared from its wharfs and it was the second or third tobacco port in the country. Yet being so far from the main centres of population, it was little more than an entrepôt. It did not develop a range of industries and became increasingly uncomfortable located between Glasgow and Liverpool. Its population barely grew after 1750 – it was 10,628 in 1801 – yet it remained a port of considerable importance until well into the nineteenth century. Its fortunes were tied up with those of Glasgow. The Scots were technically excluded from English colonial trade by the Navigation Laws before the Union of 1707, but quickly took advantage of their relaxation to expand their own embryonic trade after this. As early as 1709, Whitehaven merchants were complaining of a loss of trade to Glasgow, but ironically much of that trade was carried in chartered Whitehaven ships. In 1722, a Commons Committee was told that most of Glasgow's trade still relied on the use of Whitehaven vessels. The annual import of tobacco to the Clyde then averaged four million pounds, having increased from less than 250,000 in the 1680s. With tobacco came sugar and raw cotton – the other pillars of Glasgow's prosperity. Glasgow exhibited a combination of Liverpool's trading and Manchester's industrial enterprise, and grew as fast as them. In 1801, it had a population of 83,769.

As well as some ports, some industrial centres were stagnant or even losing population. The seventeenth century's great provincial city of Norwich is the prime example. Between 1700 and 1801 it slipped from second to ninth in the ranking of English towns. In 1752, a local census counted 36,196 inhabitants, another in 1786 – 40,051, but the national census of 1801 only 36,832. Even allowing for inaccuracies in the local counts, Norwich's population was at best stagnant after 1750, it may have declined in the 1780s and 1790s as West Riding competition intensified. Leeds, the finishing and marketing centre of the Yorkshire industry, grew to a population of 53,000, rising from about thirtieth to sixth rank. In fact, Norwich did recover some of its lost momentum in the early nineteenth century. After several years of prosperity, its population in 1821 was 50,288.

Other old cloth centres shared the experience of Norwich. Colchester, the focus of the Essex–Suffolk baize industry, and an important centre of 10,000 people in 1700, was stagnant throughout the century as its industry shrank with the loss of overseas markets. This decline was cushioned only by Colchester's regional role as a central place and fashionable resort town for the increasingly wealthy Essex countryside. In 1801, it had 11,500 inhabitants. A similar regional role counteracted the industrial decline of Worcester, Shrewsbury, Salisbury and Exeter. But the smaller cloth centres of 1700, which did not have an alternative function to fall back on, were badly hit. Tiverton, only 15 miles from Exeter, lost inhabitants, and not till 1821 did its numbers recover to those of a century before.

Conflicting fortunes were not limited to the larger centres. There were marked patterns of growth and stagnation amongst the rural central places. Improving communications by turnpike road increasingly channelled trade towards the larger of them, those with a wider range of facilities and customers. Many developed an important coaching trade, the length of the stages (15–20 miles) corresponding to the spacing of the larger market centres. In Dorset, for example, the most rapidly growing towns were the port of Poole, the resort of Melcombe Regis (now part of Weymouth) and Blandford, all nodal communications centres. There was a ring of market towns from Bridport to Shaftesbury, each growing a little faster than the county population as a whole. Yet in between were several low-growth centres eclipsed by their proximity to successful neighbours. One of these was the county town of Dorchester, its rural hinterland containing much poor heath, and its role as a county resort usurped by fashionable Melcombe (fig. 8:2). A similar story of differential growth is repeated from county to county. In Essex, trade was concentrated in the well-spaced centres of Colchester, Chelmsford, Dunmow, Witham, Maldon, Epping and Romford. The smaller towns

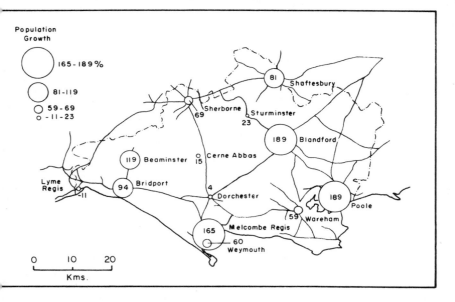

Fig. 8:2 *Population Change in Dorset Towns between the 1660s and 1801.* *Source:* Pawson (1977) p. 326.

of Rochford, Rayleigh and Chipping Ongar stagnated as their markets declined, whilst those at Kelvedon, Thaxted and Harlow had even been discontinued by 1800.

*In 1801*

The rank-size distribution of urban places at the time of the first national census was no less skewed than at the start (fig. 8:3). London remained the supreme metropolis: the most important port, financial and professional centre, a major industrial city and seat of government. Its primacy and its influence were not diminished. Below London, however, came a relatively even distribution of manufacturing centres and seaports, the fastest growing provincial towns that ranged in size from just under 90,000 to just under 30,000. Below them there was a distinct break in the distribution to a group of towns between 12 and 17,000 in size. This group included many of the old industrial centres whose base had contracted or was adjusting but slowly, several old regional centres as well as some textile boom towns such as Stockport and Ashton-under-Lyne.

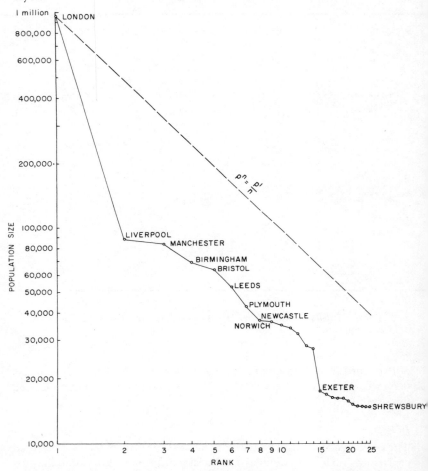

Fig. 8:3   *Rank-Size Distribution of English Towns, 1801. Source*: based on table 8:1.

With the exception of Middlesex, no county was predominantly urban in 1801. Only there, and in Lancashire, Nottingham, Warwick and Durham, did the urban population exceed 40 per cent of the county total (fig. 8:4). Despite the prominence of the big towns, most settlements were still small. In the West Riding and Staffordshire, as well as over large parts of Lancashire, industrial activity was still carried on in a web of villages, 'a countryside in the course of becoming industrialised' (and urbanised) (plate B2). Many of these were not big enough to be labelled 'towns' as yet. In 1801, the large provincial centres were a very prominent feature of national life, but there were not many of them. Fully two-thirds of the British population still lived in the countryside, on farms, in straggling hamlets, or in villages.

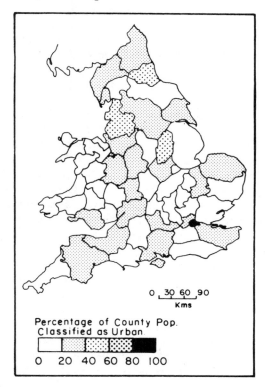

Fig. 8:4    *Levels of Urbanisation by county in England and Wales, 1801. Source:* redrawn from C. M. Law: 'The growth of urban populations in England and Wales, 1801–1911', *T.I.B.G.* no. 41 (1967) p. 133.

## INTRA-URBAN CHANGE

### The Urban Infrastructure

Industry, investing in machinery and buildings, and the services, adopting fixed forms of organisation, were both gradually moving towards a greater degree of permanence. It was this quality that enabled them to meet not only the increasing demands of the present, but to prepare and build for the future too. For these same reasons urban infrastructure was reorganised in similar ways. Town buildings of the eighteenth century were altogether more solid, permanent and (with the obvious exception of housing for the poorer workers) better appointed than those of earlier periods; town plans were slowly being rationalised to cope with the needs of urban affairs. It was a trend that began with the architectural renaissance of the early seventeenth century, it started naturally in London, but spread throughout Britain between 1660 and 1800.

London's Great Fire of 1666 raged for three days. The City was razed, the Guildhall and St Paul's destroyed, 89 churches burnt, along with innumerable public buildings. No less than 13,200 houses were lost. Wren's ambitious plan for rebuilding was not adopted: it was impractical in view of the intricacies of both landownership and topography. Instead an Act of Parliament was passed, raising a tax on coal for the reconstruction of public buildings and laying down a building code to standardise aspects of house reconstruction. Only brick and stone materials were allowed. The City was rebuilt with great speed, many streets being widened and straightened in the process. A Paving Commission was established, and lamps provided. Work started on a new St Paul's and Wren rebuilt another 51 churches.

The Great Fire and its results were symbolic. There were few towns in Britain (at least outside the limestone areas where wood was the normal building material before 1700) that were not partially or wholly destroyed by fire at some stage. Northampton was burnt down in 1675, Builth Wells in 1691, Buckingham in 1725, Blandford Forum had to be completely rebuilt in 1731 (and preserves an almost perfect Georgian centre today). Heytesbury, also in Wiltshire, was burnt in 1765, 'the wind blowing very briskly from the West and the weather very dry. . . .'. Most townsfolk had at least one such experience in a lifetime, and in each case, solid brick or stone buildings were erected as a better insurance against a recurrence. Brick and stone were also used in the more piecemeal building and reconstruction that accompanied the gradual accretion of wealth in urban communities as the numbers of well-off traders, professional people and urban gentry increased. Brick was becoming the most common construction material in southern and Midland towns in the 1660s. The fields of Islington and Marylebone to the north of London were pock-marked by clay and gravel pits and dotted with brick kilns. Stone was in less frequent use for house construction (except in upland and limestone areas such as the Cotswolds and Pennines where good building stone was abundant), but it was widely used in public buildings. The plasterwork stucco front was very much in vogue. It gave a finish of distinction to a brick house at far less cost than a facing of stone. Whole towns were transformed, modernised in these ways. Those that were not rebuilt were altered 'cosmetically', with fashionable fronts being added to older houses. Today the urban Georgian architecture of the smaller towns (where it has been allowed to survive) is the most conspicuous reminder of the prosperity of the period. It is also a witness to the force of fashion and the spread of ideas in a society of rapidly improving communications. Towns as far removed as Farnham (Surrey), Bath, Woodstock (Oxon), Welshpool and Louth (Lincolnshire) still retain almost complete Georgian facades (plate F1).

There was also a considerable amount of new public building outside London. Wren was consulted about the new County Hall in Abingdon and the town hall at Windsor. The Mid Steeple in Dumfries was built in 1707, and the Court House in Kelso a little later. A new Shire Hall was completed in Monmouth in 1724, and later others in Warwick, Aylesbury, Hertford, Nottingham and Caernarvon. The Shire Hall at this date was usually used as an Assize Court, not as a county administrative building. This was one of the many functions of the urban inn, one in the big towns providing a room for Quarter Sessions. Inns were also social and political centres for different groups in urban society and many of the more fashionable ones were remodelled or rebuilt. There was a conspicuous amount of new church building, and in many old ones galleries were added. A dozen new churches were built in London under an Act of 1711, and there are some notable provincial examples: All Saints, Oxford, St Chad's, Shrewsbury, St Philips in Birmingham – now the Cathedral (1715). Derby's Parish Church was completely remodelled in 1725 by James Gibbs – it too is now the Cathedral, and St Andrews in Edinburgh New Town was finished in 1787. Alongside these were new or rebuilt schools, hospitals, Cloth Halls, Exchanges, Assembly Rooms and theatres.

After the Great Fire, although London's street plan was modified, few new streets were built. It was similar elsewhere. Whole new areas of building were developed, but within existing town centres, there were few radical changes, yet commonly many minor improvements. Obstructions such as old market houses and crosses, conduits and overhanging eaves were removed. Many towns lost their medieval gates. Nottingham's last one was taken down in 1743, Glasgow's in 1751, Gloucester's North and East Gates in 1781. A few new streets were built. New Road (today Marylebone, Euston, Pentonville Roads) was staked out around the northern edge of London in 1756. It was the first urban by-pass, providing an unpaved route into the heart of the City for the droves of cattle and sheep marching to market. Oxford's New Road provided a direct link from the town centre to the new Botley Causeway, the main route westward. However, the great central replanning exercises, such as Nash's Regent Street (1817–23) in London, or Dobson and Grainger's plan for Newcastle, executed in the 1830s, belong to the next century. But by 1801, many towns had less congested street plans and the Improvement Commissions had begun their work.

The general effect of improving urban infrastructure was summarised by John Britton, in his description of Gloucester in the early nineteenth century. 'Its old gate-houses, walls, castle, bridge and most of the timber-houses that formerly abounded . . . . have disappeared, and given place to formal brick elevations, expanded streets and a bridge of one wide arch across the river'.

## Urban Growth

The pace of urban growth was determined by population change, but its nature and direction were essentially moulded by land ownership patterns and the relative wealth or poverty of the market. Initially growth took the form of the intensification of building in the core of the town, but in the faster growing places in particular, it spilled over into surrounding gardens and fields, often leading to a considerable expansion of the built-up area. Urban growth is best considered under these two headings of *intensification* and *expansion*.

The groundplan of the eighteenth century town reflected its origins. Land adjacent to the main thoroughfares was often held in long, narrow strips, at right angles to the street, known as burgages. These burgages represented the original holdings of the enfranchised members of a medieval borough. The pattern can still be seen in country towns little disturbed by growth: Battle or Lewes in Sussex, Tewkesbury in Gloucestershire, Alnwick in Northumberland. Passageways from the street give access between or through buildings to the long yards or gardens behind, often occupied now by a chapel, workshop or new house. It was these gardens, or burgage heads, that provided the space for intensifying town centre land use. The process can be clearly traced in contemporary maps.

It began early in London. Ogilby's 1677 map of the City shows a large number of courts, of houses and workshops, in the back gardens of properties. As early as 1731, there were 150 courts in Birmingham (Westley's map). In 1786, more than one third of the dwellings in the town were described as 'back-houses'. A typical sale notice in the Birmingham Gazette advertised 'three freehold tenements, one of which is fronting to Park Street and the other two in the yard at the back. There is good room in the said yard to erect three or more other tenements at very easy expense'. (19 May, 1788). Tuke's map of Leeds (1781) shows the same central infill of burgages, and by 1815 it was virtually complete there. In Glasgow, the burgages were large, on average 220 yards long and five and a half yards wide. In the western part of the town, several were combined to form new streets after the old frontage houses had been demolished: Queen St., Virginia St. (named for one of the city's trades), Miller and Buchanan St. (building speculators!). Elsewhere in Glasgow, these long burgages proved ideal for back building.

It was the development of the back house, combined with certain other conditions, that led to the spread of one of the worst abuses of the Industrial Revolution, the back-to-back. It was a short step from the tenement or cottage, wedged against a garden wall with no back door, to the court of houses built around a narrow alley and abutting directly against the next court. Frequently just 'one-up, one-down' affairs, no more than five yards square, these new hovels were little more deficient than the burgage tenements and many rural cottages with respect to water supply, drains or sanitation. It was lack of light and through ventilation (often houses were even built across the front of the courts) combined with intense proximity that were their real evils.[3] The back-to-back sprouted in the rapidly growing industrial centres of the Midlands and north, including Glasgow, particularly in those towns where land was sold off in small plots around the edge of the core area, so ruling against more spacious planning. Houses for the new industrial proletariats had to be let at low rents, hence building and land costs had to be low. For building speculators in the housing booms that accompanied urban growth in the 1780s and 1790s, the back-to-back was the most economical, rational form of housing for the poorest end of the market. The better paid artisans were able to rent slightly larger houses in more generously proportioned streets, built in terraces, sometimes with small back yards (plate F3). The higher wage levels in London may well explain why back-to-backs were never built in great numbers there.

Nottingham, a pleasant gentry town in Defoe's time, was infamous by the 1840s for its slums and overcrowding. The roots of this lay in a building boom in the 1780s, as the town's cotton industry expanded, and another between 1812 and 1825, with the rapid growth of the lace industry after the introduction of the bobbin-net machine. Building land in Nottingham was sold off in small parcels, mainly to the east and south of the centre. Overall expansion was restrained by the town's open-fields, which were not enclosed to be made available for building until the mid-nineteenth century. Although the new houses were often three-storey, many were backs, or back-to-backs, the first courts appearing in the

1780s. Similar economic pressures in Leeds brought similar results. With the infill of burgage plots, housing spread out in ribbons along the main roads, leaving empty fields between the tentacles. These fields were typically 200 yards long, and between 40 to 70 yards wide, an ideal shape to accommodate several elongated courts of housing. In the building boom of 1790–5 (200 houses per annum) and 1800–5 (900 per annum), the fields to the north, east and south of Leeds were filled with new streets and alleys, nearly all of them of back-to-backs.[4] Most of these were erected by speculative builders (attorneys and small businessmen were very active in this), but some were put up by terminating building clubs, funds in which families pooled their resources. Family expediency as well as speculative greed produced the back-to-back.

The home of the building club was Birmingham, where many artisan homes were erected by this means. There was a rapid expansion of housing from the mid-1760s onto the big Colmore and Gooch estates to the north, north west and west of the town. The estates staked out their land in rough grid-iron street patterns, but very little effort was made to control the type of buildings erected. Furthermore, most of the land was disposed of in small lots, resulting in a pattern of development little different to that in Nottingham or Leeds. Although some handsome houses were erected for more prosperous buyers, plots were often sold as long strips, specifically to permit the building of back houses. In Liverpool, over half of the land developed belonged to the Corporation. However, it did not plan its estate as a whole, dealing instead through developers, and because the housing demand was mainly for the low-paid as the port blossomed, Liverpool again was little different. Although the Corporation took some interest in the type of buildings erected, and employed inspectors to ensure that its covenants were carried out, the rapid urban expansion proved too much to control. In 1790 – before the great boom of the last decade – 20 per cent of Liverpool's houses were back-to-backs, although the Corporation had been successful in ensuring that most houses were built in terraces, with a yard behind and street in front. But they had not been able to control cellar dwelling – 12.5 per cent of the population was estimated to be living in these subterranean and unhealthy habitations then, and the problem worsened considerably after. Manchester, too, was notorious in this respect. The multi-occupation of houses, and the construction of separate cellars, offered an alternative to the back-to-back, which did not become numerous in Manchester till two decades after its appearance in Leeds and Nottingham. The cellars had 'a kitchen and a back room with one small window near the roof'.

In all these towns there were middle-class housing schemes, but they were rather limited. Several squares were erected in Liverpool, and the western part of Leeds (held in larger estates than the rest of the town fringe) was developed for better-class housing in the 1780s and 90s. But theirs was nothing to match the grand schemes of the capital cities, the West End of London and Edinburgh New Town, and the resorts that they spawned: Bath, Brighton, Scarborough and Tunbridge Wells (plates F2 and F4). London and Edinburgh, with their concentration of wealth, provided a rich as well as a poor housing market. This was also the case in Bristol, where the great Clifton development of the 1780s and 1790s represented an investment in conspicuous consumption that, compared with the modest middle-class housing provision of Liverpool, symbolises the differences of attitudes in these two great ports.

London's West End was well removed from the trading activities of the City. It was close to Court and Parliament and was built on large estates by wealthy, mainly titled, landowners. These were the essential reasons why it developed as the fashionable quarter. Into London came the seventeenth century's rediscovery of the square. The Earl of Bedford built Covent Garden in the early 1630s, designed by Inigo Jones in Italian piazza style, a revolution for Stuart London. It was followed by a succession of squares after the Restoration – Bloomsbury (Earl of Southampton) – 1665, Soho – 1681, St James' (Earl of St Alban's) – 1684, Grosvenor – 1695, Berkeley – 1698. Although strict covenants were used, the houses were built by developers under a system of building leases. Plots were let at a low rent on the understanding that the houses erected became the property of the ground landlord at the end of the lease. Initially 42 years long, the 60-year lease was introduced about 1700. By 1800, the 99-year lease was almost universal. The developer needed little money to finance his speculations, and the profits were potentially great. Many of substantial and insubstantial means became building speculators, but as Richard Campbell wrote in 1747, 'it is no new thing in London for these Master-Builders to build themselves out of their own houses and fix themselves in jail with their own materials'.

The West End was not built to an overall plan, the squares spreading as little communities of their own. Not until the development of the Crown Estate of Regents Park by Nash, and his master stroke with the building of Regents Street, was there any attempt to develop a grand design. In Edinburgh, however, matters were altogether more clear-cut. The decision to build a New Town was a political one, the realisation of the hopes of several Lord Provosts, to improve the city, to attract the Scots gentry back from London, and to turn it into a modern social and economic centre. Plans were called for in 1767, and one submitted by Robert Craig accepted. It was a bold gridiron, with a square at each end connected by three parallel avenues: Princes, George and Queen Streets. It was a plan completely lacking in the subtle romantic sweeps of contemporary Bath, yet one that forces order upon a very solid and imposing site. The first plots were soon taken up for building, but with the general depression in the wake of the Ayr Bank collapse in 1772, little more was done for over a decade (above, p. 177). House construction resumed vigorously after 1784 and by the end of the century, Craig's streets were practically all built up. The Council feued the sites individually (let them in perpetuity) and regulated the design of houses in a very general fashion. It did not attempt to impose any sort of architectural uniformity until the great Scots architect Robert Adam was commissioned to design the frontages for Charlotte Square in the 1790s. After 1800, the New Town was extended both north and west with the addition of many new squares, circuses and avenues. Building enjoyed a considerable boom until 1830 (plate F4).

One immediate and lamented effect of the development of the New Town was the social separation it produced. The nobility, urban gentry, wealthy merchants and professional people moved, leaving the traders, shopkeepers, artisans and poor in the Old Town. A feature of the Old Town had always been the closeness in which rich and poor lived, often dwelling in the same tenement. It was characteristic of pre-industrial towns in general. In the Stuart City of London, the prosperous lived in the big houses fronting the streets, the poor in the back houses behind. With the development of the West End, this changed. The intensification of building in town centres with rapid urban growth, combined with the increasing prosperity of the middle classes, encouraged those who could afford to move to do so. But they did not only move to select quarters such as the West End. Around many of the bigger towns, and London in particular, the eighteenth century saw the evolution of more dispersed suburban settlement. 'Scattered villas and genteel houses, in the manner of a continued, and rather elegant village, are erected on one or both sides of the road, for three, five or seven miles out of London', it was said in 1798. Neele's (1798) and Paterson's (1802) maps clearly show this. Some of the earliest turnpike roads from London (all pre-1720) connected popular residential villages with the city: Hampstead, Highgate, Kentish Town ('where the air being exceedingly handsome, many of the citizens of London have built houses'), Tottenham, Greenwich, Clapham and Peckham. Improving transport permitted an increasing separation of home and workplace, today one of the most obvious features of towns and cities. The effect of this suburban growth, and the building of discrete fashionable urban estates, was to modify with increasing starkness the former pattern of socially-mixed residential town cores.

The distinction between rich and poor was certainly apparent in pre-industrial towns. But as the ranks of the prosperous grew, and working-class numbers swelled, the two became more socially and physically separate. This separateness became increasingly conspicuous throughout the eighteenth century as it was sealed into the building fabric of towns. But no matter who it was for, rapid urban expansion in the capital cities and big provincial towns was very much a reality by 1800.

> 'The richest crop for any field,
> Is a crop of bricks for it to yield,
> The richest crop that it can grow,
> Is a crop of houses in a row'.

TABLE 8:1    *The Urban Hierarchy*

|  | ENGLAND AND WALES | | |
|---|---|---|---|
| *Rank in 1801* | *1700* | *1750* | *1801* |
| 1. London | 550,000 | 657,000 | 960,000 |
| 2. Liverpool | 6,000 | 22,000 | 88,358 |
| 3. Manchester | 10,000 | 18,000 | 84,020 |
| 4. Birmingham | 5–7,000 | 23,700 | 69,384 |
| 5. Bristol | c20,000 | 50,000 | 64,000 |
| 6. Leeds | 5–6,000 | 16,000 | 53,000 |
| 7. Plymouth | 6,500 | 13–14,000 | 43,194 |
| 8. Newcastle-on-Tyne | 14–15,000 | 29,000 | 37,000 |
| 9. Norwich | 30,000 | 36,196 | 36,832 |
| 10. Sheffield | 3,500 | 12,000 | 35,344 |
| 11. Bath | | 7,000 | 34,160 |
| 12. Portsmouth | 6,000 | 10,000 | 32,166 |
| 13. Nottingham | 7,000 | 13,000 | 28,861 |
| 14. Hull | 6,000 | 6,250 | 27,609 |
| 15. Exeter | 13–14,000 | 16,000 | 17,398 |
| 16. Leicester | 5,500 | 8,000 | 16,933 |
| 17. Stoke-on-Trent | | | 16,414 |
| 18. York | 11,000 | 11,400 | 16,145 |
| 19. Coventry | 6,900 | 12,850 | 16,049 |
| 20. Ashton-under-Lyne | | | 15,632 |
| 21. Chester | 9,000 | 13,000 | 15,052 |
| 22. Great Yarmouth | c10,000 | 10,000 | 14,845 |
| 23. Dover | | | 14,845 |
| 24. Stockport | | | 14,830 |
| 25. Shrewsbury | c9,000 | 13,328 | 14,739 |

TABLE 8:1    *Continued*

|  |  | SCOTLAND |  |  |
|---|---|---|---|---|
|  |  | 1700 | *1755* | *1801* |
| 1. | Glasgow | 12,600 | 23,546 | 83,769 |
| 2. | Edinburgh | c40,000 | 57,000 | 82,560 |
| 3. | Paisley |  | 6,799 | 31,179 |
| 4. | Aberdeen |  | 22,000 | 26,992 |
| 5. | Dundee |  | 12,477 | 26,084 |
| 6. | Greenock |  | 3,858 | 17,458 |

*Sources:* Chalklin (1974), Law (1972) and the 1801 Census.

The pre-1801 figures are based on local censuses and estimates: most can be regarded as informed approximations. The 1801 Census figures for each place vary, sometimes considerably, according to the boundaries adopted. For instance, Burslem, contiguous to Stoke, had a population of 6,578, so that the size of the Potteries might be more properly regarded as 23,000. Coventry had a population of almost 22,000 if the surrounding parishes are included; Shrewsbury's total likewise was 16,631.

## NOTES

1  The exact figures depend upon the urban definition used. Law (1972) gives a proportion of 24.1 per cent in 1750 and 33.8 per cent in 1801, using a minimum urban size of 2,500. Chalklin (1974) gives ranges of 22–23 per cent in 1700 to 28–33 per cent in 1801, apparently including all market 'towns', some of which had as few as 400 people. The exact figures do not matter. It is their relative magnitude and degree of change that is significant.

2  But some of these places had an importance as markets out of all proportion to their size, for example, Farnham (Surrey) Haddington and Dalkeith (the Lothians) – great grain marts; Market Weighton, in the East Riding, the major sheep market in the north of England.

3  Often these courts shared one standpipe, from which water was available for only a few minutes a day. Sometimes there was no immediate supply. One of the most notorious cases, the Boot and Shoe yard in Leeds, was said to have no water supply within a quarter of a mile in the 1840s. In some towns, water was sold from carts. The bog houses were open-pits, cleared periodically by bog-men. Flushing closets with traps were not invented till 1775, and although rapidly adopted for middle-class housing, it was a century before they penetrated

many working class areas. The middle classes likewise had their own water supply in many towns, piped to cisterns by the water companies – although it was turned on for only a limited period each day.

4 Leeds continued to build back-to-backs longer than any other town: the last being erected as late as 1937.

## FURTHER READING

Urban history has become very popular in the last few years and is well served by an annual review of themes and recent research, *The Urban History Yearbook*, (ed.) H. J. Dyos. Accessible references for this period are not numerous, but much of the available work is of high quality. Two such contributions are *The Early Modern Town*, (ed.) Peter Clark (1976), a collection of key articles with a very useful bibliographical introduction, and *The Provincial Towns of Georgian England, 1740–1820*, by C. W. Chalklin (1974). This work is a study of the building process, but has two good general introductory chapters on the urban system as a whole. There are several useful chapters in *Rural Change and Urban Growth, 1500–1800*, (eds.) C. W. Chalklin and M. A. Havinden (1974), and in Alan Everitt (ed.): *Perspectives in English Urban History* (1973). Estimates of population totals of the bigger towns are given in C. M. Law's article: 'Some Notes on the Urban Population of England and Wales in the Eighteenth Century', *Local Historian* vol. 10 (1972).

ROLE OF TOWNS

On the role of towns as market centres, see Alan Everitt: 'The Marketing of Agricultural Produce' in Joan Thirsk (ed.): *The Agrarian History of England and Wales vol. 4 1500–1640* (1967), and John Patten: *English Towns 1500–1700* (1978).

A useful framework of the examination of the role of cities is Alan Pred: 'The External Relations of Cities during Industrial Revolution', *Dept. of Geography, University of Chicago, Research Paper 26* (1962). And see two chapters in Philip Abrams and E. A. Wrigley (eds.): *Towns in Societies* (1978), one by Wrigley: 'A Simple Model of London's Importance in Changing English Society and Economy, 1650–1750', the other by M. J. Daunton: 'Towns and Economic Growth in 18th Century England'.

THE CHANGING HIERARCHY

The best overview is in Chalklin (1974) (above). The eighteenth century was not an important period of urban growth in Wales, so there is little literature, but see Harold Carter: *The Towns of Wales* (1965). Hamilton (1963) provides a basic outline of trends in Scotland.

There are several useful references on individual towns, but few comprehensive treatments as yet. See P. G. E. Clemens: 'The rise of Liverpool, 1665–1750', *Ec. H.R.* vol. XXIX (1976), J. E. Williams: 'Whitehaven in the eighteenth century', *Ec. H.R.* vol. VIII (1956); Gordon Jackson: *Hull in the Eighteenth Century* (1972); and T. M. Devine: *The Tobacco Lords* (1975) for a study of one of the pillars of Glasgow's growth. Two useful studies of declining industrial centres are: W. G. Hoskins: *Industry, Trade and People in Exeter, 1688–1800*, 2nd edn. (1968) and A. F. J. Brown: 'Colchester in the Eighteenth Century' in Lionel Munby (ed.): *East Anglian Studies* (1968).

For changes at the lower end of the hierarchy, see Alan Everitt: 'Urban Growth and Inland Trade, 1570–1770', in *The Local Historian* vol. 8 (1968) and Roy Millward: 'The Cumbrian Town between 1600 and 1800' in Chalklin and Havinden (1974).

INTRA-URBAN CHANGE

A useful reference for many of the points in this section is Sir John Summerson's classic: *Georgian London* (rev. 1962). A short, well illustrated book is Gerald Burke's *Towns in the Making* (1971). The evolution of several towns is examined in *The Atlas of Historic Towns* (ed.) M. D. Lobel (vol. 1, 1969, vol. 2, 1975).

The pioneer of work on the intensification of town-centre building is M. R. G. Conzen. His study of Newcastle is useful in this respect: 'The plan analysis of an English city centre', in *Lund Studies in Geography*, Series B, no. 24 (1962).

The most important work on urban expansion in this period is Chalklin (1974). He discusses the building process in the growing towns, as well as landowners, builders, house types and the course of building through time. On working-class housing, see S. D. Chapman (ed.): *The History of Working-Class Housing: A Symposium* (1971), which concentrates on the process of building, and Enid Gauldie: *Cruel Habitations: A History of Working-Class Housing, 1780–1918* (1974) which has more to say about social conditions. There is a valuable chapter by Beresford on Leeds in Chalklin and Havinden (1974).

The higher income housing promotions are discussed by Summerson (the West End), and A. J. Youngson in a lavish book: *The Making of Classical Edinburgh, 1750–1840* (1966). The relationship of suburban development and improving transport is discussed briefly in Eric Pawson: *Transport and Economy* (1977) – chapter twelve. F. M. L. Thompson examines one 'suburban village': *Hampstead, Building a Borough, 1650–1964*

(1974). The spas and resort towns have not been discussed in this chapter, but there are several useful references. Chalklin and Havinden (1974) contain chapters on Bath by Neale, and Chalklin; Everitt (1973) has a chapter on Margate by Whyman; also see E. W. Gilbert: *Brighton, Old Ocean's Bauble* (1954).

The study of the social history and geography of towns in this period is poorly developed, but see an article by Peter Borsay: 'The English urban renaissance: the development of provincial urban culture, c. 1680–1760', *Social History*, 5 (1977). Some of the references above have material of relevance to particular places, e.g. Youngson (1966). For London, there are two books: M. D. George's pre-war classic: *London Life in the Eighteenth Century*, 2nd edn. (1965) and G. Rudé: *Hanoverian London, 1714–1808* (1971).

# 9 External Relations

When Gregory King made his calculations of 'political arithmetick' for 1688, he estimated that the average annual income in Holland was £8 1s 4d, in England: £7 18s, and in France: £6 3s. In 1776, Adam Smith ranked the three countries in the same order. Yet by the end of the eighteenth century, industrialising Britain had pulled ahead of the stagnating Dutch trading economy. In 1800, Great Britain was the richest country in Europe. That this was achieved at the same time as a rapid growth of population was an early indication of the benefits of the Industrial Revolution.

But this was not a position into which British merchants, industrialists, farmers and workers had led the country unaided. The forces of change and growth were not generated completely independently. Two general factors of great importance must be taken into account as well: external relations (that is, overseas contacts, in particular trading partners), and the state. It would be a mistake to assume that Britain's industrialisation owed nothing to places beyond her shores; it would be equally mistaken to assume that the state itself played no part.

These two factors are best appreciated in the context of the general causes of growth discussed in the first chapter (above pp. 15–18). Three broad groups were identified: rising demand; an increasing supply of resources; and increasing efficiency in the use of those resources. Britain's overseas trade assumed an important role in both the first and the second. Some of her trading partners also contributed, through the supply of innovations and special skills, to the third. And the action of the state was important for all three: trade depended on privileges, protection and certainly on colonial power; whilst increasing economic efficiency was considerably furthered by the nature of common and statute law.

## Overseas Trade

The growth of Britain's overseas trade (fig. 4:1) and its role in stimulating demand, have already been discussed. (above, pp. 74–6). The

TABLE 9:1    *The Evolution of Britain's Trading Links*

1    *Imports* (by value, per cent of the total)

| From: | 1700–1 | | 1772–3 | | 1797–8 | |
|---|---|---|---|---|---|---|
| N. W. Europe | 23.8 | | 9.0 | | 10.1 | |
| N. Europe | 9.2 | 61.3% | 12.0 | 34.2 | 13.8 | 29.2 |
| S. Europe | 28.3 | | 13.2 | | 5.3 | |
| Ireland | 4.9 | | 10.6 | | 13.1 | |
| N. America | 6.4 | | 14.5 | | 7.1 | |
| W. Indies | 13.5 | | 23.7 | | 25.0 | |
| E. Indies | 13.3 | | 16.2 | | 24.0 | |
| Africa | 0.4 | | 0.5 | | 0.2 | |

2    *Re-Exports*

| | 1700–1 | | 1772–3 | | 1797–8 | |
|---|---|---|---|---|---|---|
| N. W. Europe | 62.4 | | 55.7 | | 68.3 | |
| N. Europe | 4.0 | 77.3% | 3.0 | 65.4 | 7.7 | 77.5 |
| S. Europe | 10.9 | | 6.7 | | 1.5 | |
| Ireland | 7.4 | | 18.2 | | 10.9 | |
| N. America | 5.0 | | 8.7 | | 3.1 | |
| W. Indies | 6.1 | | 2.5 | | 4.1 | |
| E. Indies | 0.5 | | 1.0 | | 0.6 | |
| Africa | 3.0 | | 4.1 | | 3.7 | |

3    *Exports*

| | 1700–1 | | 1772–3 | | 1797–8 | |
|---|---|---|---|---|---|---|
| N. W. Europe | 43.5 | | 15.1 | | 11.2 | |
| N. Europe | 5.4 | 82% | 3.0 | 39.1 | 4.5 | 21.0 |
| S. Europe | 33.1 | | 21.0 | | 5.3 | |
| Ireland | 3.2 | | 9.9 | | 9.0 | |
| N. America | 5.7 | | 26.0 | | 32.2 | |
| W. Indies | 4.6 | | 12.0 | | 25.2 | |
| E. Indies | 2.6 | | 8.1 | | 9.0 | |
| Africa | 1.8 | | 4.8 | | 3.6 | |

*Source:* Deane and Cole (1967) p. 87. The 1700–1 figures refer to England, those for 1772–3 and 1797–8 to Great Britain.

TABLE 9:2    *The Structure of the Domestic Export Trade, 1700–1800*

| | | 1700 | 1750 | 1770 | 1792 | 1800 |
|---|---|---|---|---|---|---|
| Coal | | 1.7% | 1.6% | 2.7% | 3.2% | 2.0% |
| Grain | | 3.7 | 19.6 | | | |
| Fish | | 3.2 | 1.0 | 1.0 | 1.0 | 1.0 |
| Leather | | 2.2 | 1.4 | 0.7 | 0.9 | 0.5 |
| Iron and Steel Metals and Manufactures | | 2.3 | 4.5 | 7.8 | 8.0 | 6.6 |
| Non-Ferrous Metals and Manufactures | | 7.0 | 5.2 | 7.0 | 6.9 | 5.8 |
| Cotton | ⎫ | 0.8 | 0.2 | 2.0 | 10.5 | 24.1 |
| Wool/Worsted | ⎬ Yarn and | 64.7 | 45.6 | 43.3 | 28.1 | 28.4 |
| Linen | ⎟ Manufactures | 0.2 | 2.4 | 4.5 | 5.2 | 3.3 |
| Silk | ⎭ | 1.8 | 1.2 | 1.4 | 1.6 | 1.2 |
| Refined Sugar | | 1.3 | 0.6 | 1.1 | 3.4 | 4.5 |
| Total – % of all Domestic Exports | | 88.9 | 83.3 | 71.5 | 68.8 | 77.4 |

*Source:* compiled from Mitchell and Deane (1962) and Schumpeter (1960). The table includes only domestic exports, not unprocessed re-exports. The first three columns are for England and Wales alone, those for 1792 and 1800 also include Scotland.

changing structure of overseas trade deserves further attention, however, as it helps both to explain and to amplify some of the main points about the changing nature of the economy as a whole during the eighteenth century.

In the early part of the century, Britain's trade (the vast bulk of which was accounted for by England) lay essentially with Europe (table 9:1). Her exports were dominated by the products of a relatively unspecialised economy: the industrial staple, wool textiles, and a wide range of primary goods (table 9:2). Wool textiles alone accounted for two-thirds of the export total, selling particularly well in the countries of the Mediterranean. Spain and Portugal were good customers for the light English cloths, an increasing amount was being sold to Italy, whilst the Levant Company (one of the great incorporated trading monopolies) exchanged cloth in Asia Minor for silk. Large quantities of fish from England's east coast ports were also sold to the Catholic countries. In northern Europe, English textiles faced stiff competition from the Dutch cloth industry, centred on Leiden. Nevertheless, Holland was then Britain's major export customer (followed by Germany), taking considerable amounts of corn, coal, salt, lead and sugar. Legal trade with France was heavily circumscribed by protectionist policies (it was actually forbidden between 1678 and 1713), although smuggling of course flourished.

In the course of the eighteenth century, trade with Europe expanded substantially. The Irish trade grew in absolute and relative terms, much to the benefit of Bristol, Liverpool and Whitehaven. The Irish, subjugated to the British Crown, sent a considerable quantity of foodstuffs to England, and because they were forbidden to manufacture with their own wool, acted as a captive market for English textiles, as well as coal and salt. British trade with the rest of Europe did not experience relative expansion, however. In absolute terms, exports to the Continent rose three times in value, due largely to the contribution of the thriving re-export trade in colonial commodities, such as sugar, coffee and tobacco. Yet in relative terms, they declined very remarkably from over three-quarters of the total to less than one quarter by the late 1790s (table 9:1). The frequent closure of the Mediterranean to English shipping in war-time, and the loss of Spanish markets in the hostilities of the Seven Years War, did not help. But this was not the essential reason.

The whole structure of British trade matured in the early Industrial Revolution. Its base broadened and diversified, the most rapid growth being in the new industrial products: metal goods, refined sugar, linen and after 1770 – cotton yarn and textiles. The meteoric rise of cotton exports in the 1790s, as the industry turned its attention from home to overseas markets, is particularly notable (table 7:2). But these new manufactures did not find their major markets in Europe: they were goods that European industries, increasingly protected, could produce themselves. They found a readier market in the colonies, especially in America and the West Indies, where they were exchanged for primary products. America provided raw cotton, tobacco, furs, timber and fish, and the West Indies, above all else, sugar – this commodity alone accounting for about one-fifth of all imports at mid-century. The East Indies, a source of silk and spices, tea and coffee, featured prominently in the import trade, but less so in exports. The Navigation Acts (which were not repealed until 1854) tied colonial trade to Britain, but even after the American Revolution, this branch continued to grow very quickly. British exports to America rose from a pre-war annual average of £2.1 million in 1765–70, to £7 million by 1796–1800: woollen goods, cottons and iron tools all found a receptive market.

The evolving pattern of overseas trade thus reflects the changes in Britain's industrialising economy. Exports were able to rise rapidly, by supplying young primary-producer economies that sent raw materials in return. Europe continued to form the major market for re-exports and also provided a wide range of imports. Many of these imported materials, if not indispensible, were extremely important for the progress of industrialisation. Without a high elasticity of supply in overseas cotton production, the cotton textiles industry would have grown very much more slowly. Soda, a vital component of soaps and bleaches, was largely derived from the ash of the saltwort plant (known as barilla) which had to be imported from the Canary Islands and Spain, although Irish and Scottish kelp was used to supplement these supplies. The Sheffield steel industry was dependent on shipments of high quality bar iron from the Baltic. Quite apart from such industrial materials, however, trade supplied foodstuffs – it made up a growing deficiency of corn from the 1760s onwards, and provided a range of tropical products that had long since been regarded as necessities.

*The Exchange of Technology*
Britain's external relations were important in another respect. The supply of ideas, skills and technology from overseas was a potential source of increasing efficiency on the supply side of the economy. That there was such a contribution to Britain's pre-industrial progress has long been accepted. Some of the essential parts of the new husbandry were introduced from the Low Countries, including turnips and the leguminous grasses in the late sixteenth and early seventeenth centuries. It was Dutch and Flemish refugees who, about the same time, established cotton and silk working in England, introduced the 'new draperies' – the light, worsted cloths – and brought over the improved Dutch loom. It was Dutch engineers who drained the Fens in the middle years of the seventeenth century, and afterwards worked extensively on watermill design in England. The blast furnace was introduced into the Wealden iron industry from France in the sixteenth century, and contemporaneously German skills did much to improve the process of smelting and refining non-ferrous ores. Abraham Crowley, the great ironmonger of the early eighteenth century, used skilled workers from Liege in his operations in the north-east.

It has been less readily accepted that this continental contribution continued during the early Industrial Revolution. But there are important fields in which it did. The first factory, Lombe's silk mill, housed machinery drawn up from designs smuggled out of Italy. The great factory industry, cotton spinning, was based on a series of British inventions, but in the textile finishing processes, French expertise was very significant. Eighteenth century France was renowned for its scientific work, actively promoted by the French state. It was a French chemist who first made chlorine bleaching a viable proposition. The process was communicated to James Watt, but it was another Frenchman who set up the first chlorine bleach plant in Britain, on Merseyside, in the late 1780s. This was a vital application for the fast-growing cotton industry: without it, the age-old method of protracted outdoor bleaching would have been a serious production bottleneck. French dyers were also instrumental in the introduction of new methods into Glasgow and Manchester, and it was a French chemist, Leblanc, who in 1790–1 discovered how to produce soda from inorganic materials, although because of the assurance of supplies of barilla and kelp it was 30 years before the Leblanc process was undertaken on a large scale in Britain. There are other examples of the use of continental expertise. Dutch workers were hired to improve the technical side of the Scots linen industry (above, p. 11). Matthew Boulton recruited metal workers from France and wrote to Vienna, Berlin and Sweden in search of engravers. The great new Ravenshead plate glass works, set up near St. Helens in 1783, drew many of its key workers initially from the renowned St Gobain works in Picardy.

This exchange of skills and technology was certainly not one way; in fact, during the whole period of the Industrial Revolution, the net flow was in the other direction. Britain contributed much to the modernisation of industry on the continent (in particular in France and Belgium) and in America. This was in spite of a succession of eighteenth century laws prohibiting the export of British machinery, parts or plans (which were not repealed until 1843), and Acts of 1719 and 1780 forbidding the emigration of skilled workers. This legislation reflected the attitude of many manufacturers who (in the absence of completely effective enforcement of the patent laws) carried on their operations in attempted secrecy. Even Arthur Young 'could not gain any intelligence even of the most common nature (at Birmingham), through the excessive jealously of the manufacturers'. Yet plans and parts were still smuggled out of the country, and skilled workmen were tempted away by lucrative offers. In the later years of the eighteenth century the attitude of manufacturers to foreign visitors seems to have relaxed a little, with the realisation of the possibilities of trade and exchange of information. In these years, many foreigners made journeys round Britain's industrialising regions. Some were sent by their governments, the Prussian and Swedish states regularly dispatching engineers, scientists and other travellers.

The direct introduction of British techniques in Europe was usually by Britons themselves, however. Much of the northern French textile industry was modernised by John Holker, an escaped Jacobite soldier and skilled Manchester worker. He not only managed a royal textile factory in Rouen, but had wide influence through his post as Inspector General of Factories, which he held for 30 years until his death in 1786. Although the best known, he was but one of many British textile workers in France. It was John Wilkinson's brother, William, who established the first modern cannon works in France in the late 1770s, and he was involved in the project that produced the first successful coke iron furnace in France, at Le Creusot in the 1780s. In Belgium, which industrialised more rapidly than France, the Cockerill family played a leading role. William Cockerill moved to Belgium, apparently from Lancashire, in 1798. He took mechanised wool carding and spinning machines, and built up a large textiles business, also dispensing his technical knowledge freely. His sons all ran textiles concerns in Germany, although John, the youngest, gained the greatest renown, starting the great Seraing iron and machine-works outside Liege in 1817.

Nevertheless, overall Britain's assistance to Europe was limited. The prohibitive laws did mean that machinery very often had to leave the country in small parts, as blueprints or even entrusted to memory. (Samuel Slater, who had worked for Arkwright and Strutt, arrived in Rhode Island in 1790 with the details of the water-frame firmly in his head, thus introducing mechanised spinning to New England). This inevitably meant that continental copies were imperfect or did not work at all, whilst time-lags were considerable. Mule spinners were introduced to Normandy in the late 1780s, but it was not until 1803 that a factory to make them was established in France. None were introduced in Saxony or Bohemia until the late 1790s. France was able to secure certain rights to make Boulton and Watt engines relatively quickly, in 1779, but the Cockerills were unable to import one till 1813, and no rotative engines were to be found in Germany until 1822. In the iron industry, diffusion was often very slow. France did not acquire its second coke furnace, or a working knowledge of Cort's process, until 1818. Prussia had an operative coke furnace in 1792, but Cort's process was not successfully introduced till 1824–5. Even John Cockerill did not open a coke furnace until 1823.

Britain's role in Europe's early industrialisation should therefore be kept in perspective. Furthermore, the spin-off effect of the small industrial sector that her technology helped to modernise was not great. With the possible exception of Belgium, the gap between the British economy and the major countries of Europe continued to widen well into the nineteenth century. Overall, the British contribution was far greater in America – not because she was any more free with her ideas, but because she did provide American producers with an immense market: the southern states selling staples direct, the northern states sending grain, fish and timber to the British West Indian colonies.

### The Role of the State

In most European countries, the state attempted to play a very direct economic role. The French government established royal factories which enjoyed fiscal and often monopoly privileges. It maintained a rigid protective customs wall (which in retrospect is seen to have done much to retard the modernisation of French industry by denying her firms competition). The Prussian government sponsored the development of factories in textiles, ironmaking, glass and chemicals. In Belgium, King William I actively encouraged industry, even to the extent of becoming a major shareholder in Cockerill's Seraing works in 1825.[1]

In Britain, state action was much less conspicuous. Examples of direct intervention are few. The funding of the Scottish Board for Fisheries and Manufactures is one. Its political interest in some transport projects is another: for example, the Highland roads schemes of Wade and Telford, its subsidies for the construction of the military road between Newcastle and Carlisle after the Forty Five and of the later reconstruction of the Holyhead and Portpatrick roads; its assistance with the Caledonian Canal. But these were primarily military programmes. There were no state factories, state scientific institutes or state economic plans. This does not mean, however, that the role of the state was unimportant. Its direct role may have been, but its indirect role in establishing a permissive framework for economic development was crucial.

This is not surprising. The governing classes themselves were but part of a nation pervaded by the desire for progress, what Landes has called the 'wealth instinct'.[2] Firstly, the state itself created and defended Britain's great commercial empire and, particularly under Pitt the Elder in the Seven Years' War and Pitt the Younger in the Napoleonic Wars, was ever prepared to protect or add further prizes to this immense free-trade area. The Navigation Laws assured maximum benefit to the mother country, whilst tariffs protected home industry, sometimes, as in the case of East Indian calicoes, to the point of outright prohibition. Secondly, Parliament was extremely active in processing a continuous flood of private legislation: applications to improve harbours and rivers, modernise towns, set up turnpike roads, initiate enclosure schemes. No less than 591 of the total of 3,036 private and public Acts (20 per cent) passed in the 1750s and 1760s were for turnpike road schemes alone. By far the largest amount of Parliamentary time was spent not in discussing monetary or foreign affairs, or in political manoeuvering. It was spent in paving the way for the development of the infrastructure of the Industrial Revolution.

There were, it is true, some state measures that were potentially restrictive. Of these the Bubble Act has excited most attention (above p. 89). Yet the prohibition of joint stock enterprise in no way seems to have prevented progress in a country where capital was plentiful, and where the legality of paper credit and the mortgage were recognised in law. For those schemes for which it might well have proved an inhibition, Parliament was usually prepared to grant an Act confering incorporation: the canal and insurance companies were the obvious beneficiaries. The action – or inaction – of the Mint in starving the provinces of coin was more serious (above, pp. 173–4) but again this merely encouraged the development of other forms of money: in particular the bill of exchange, whose existence and use was considerably facilitated by the operation of the law. It was Lord Mansfield, the great eighteenth-century lawyer, who declared that 'the law should exist to assist, and not to frustrate, the needs of the mercantile community'.

In 1800, the government of Great Britain had embroiled the country in the middle of a long and costly European war, a war that raged, with one short break, from 1793 to 1815. And yet these years were witnessing the most rapid economic and social changes so far experienced. Industry and trade flourished as the factories and ships of Europe were tied down by the hostilities. Agricultural production was rising sharply to meet the demands of a rapidly growing population. Farmers were expanding into previously uncultivated areas. Canal investment was at its height; many of the service professions were booming. To take just one quantitative indicator (but one of the most impressive), the export of cotton yarn and manufactures rose from £1.65 million to £22.55 million between the start and end of the war. All this was not without its costs – in the squalid slums of the industrial towns and the monotonous routine of farms and factories. Two unwelcome and familiar modern foes – inflation and the income tax – had arrived temporarily as well. But by the time the war ended, Great Britain was indeed the richest, the most powerful and the most economically advanced country in Europe. She was fully over the threshold of the workshop from which she was to lead the world for most of the nineteenth century.

## NOTES

1  The King also sold Cockerill the Seraing estate as the site for his factory in 1817 for a 'trifling' price. When the Belgians achieved independence from the Netherlands in the Revolution of 1830, the King's share in Seraing was taken over by the Belgian state.

2  See the discussion in David Landes: *The Unbound Prometheus* p. 77 ff.

# FURTHER READING

The best short summary of patterns of trade in this period is the editor's introduction to W. E. Minchinton (ed.): *The Growth of English Overseas Trade, in the 17th and 18th Centuries* (1969), which also contains the major articles on the subject. Ralph Davis' book: *The Rise of the English Shipping Industry in the 17th and 18th Centuries* (1962) contains informative accounts of the main branches of overseas trade, by region. Specific references: Charles Wilson: *Anglo-Dutch Commerce and Finance in the 18th Century* (1941); Ralph Davis: *Aleppo and Devonshire Square: English Traders in the Levant in the 18th Century* (1967); H. E. S. Fisher: *The Portugal Trade: A Study of Anglo-Portugese Commerce, 1700–1770.* (1971); H. S. K. Kent: *War and Trade in the North Seas: Anglo-Scandinavian Economic Relations in the Mid-Eighteenth Century* (1973).

Statistics of overseas trade can be found in B. R. Mitchell and P. Deane: *An Abstract of British Historical Statistics* (1962). Detailed figures relating to particular commodities were compiled by E. B. Schumpeter, in *English Overseas Trade Statistics, 1697–1800* (1960), although the coverage is not complete. On the problems of interpreting trade figures, see the introductions to both these works, and Deane and Cole, chapter two.

There is much information on European exchange of techniques and skills in A. E. Musson and Eric Robinson's work: *Science and Technology in the Industrial Revolution* (1969). The only concise summary of its topic is the essay by Musson: 'Continental Influences on the Industrial Revolution in Britain', in Barrie M. Ratcliffe (ed.): *Great Britain and Her World, 1750–1914* (1975). This collection is on honour of W. O. Henderson, whose own book: *Britain and Industrial Europe, 1750–1870* (1954) discusses the flow the other way. Chapter 3 of Nathan Rosenberg: *Technology and American Economic Development* (1972) analyses the transfer of British technology to the USA. *Svedenstierna's Tour of Great Britain, 1802–3* (trans. 1973) is a recently published diary of one of the 'industrial spies' from the Continent. For references concerning European economic development as a whole, see the Further Reading section to chapter one.

The role of the state is discussed briefly by Barry Supple: 'The State and the Industrial Revolution', in Carlo M. Cipolla (ed): *The Fontana Economic History of Europe: The Industrial Revolution* (1973). The policy of government intervention in trade and industry, known in this period as mercantilism, is ably discussed in the book of that name, by Charles Wilson (Historical Association, repr. 1971). The collection of articles edited by D. C. Coleman: *Revisions in Mercantilism* (1969) tackles the topic in greater depth. The only book on its subject is L. A. Harper: *The*

*English Navigation Laws* (1939). On the role of law in economic development, see the introductory essay in R. M. Hartwell: *The Industrial Revolution and Economic Growth* (1971), chapter eleven. The only in-depth treatment, however, is by Sir William Holdsworth, in his multi-volume *A History of English Law* (1938), especially volumes X, XI, and XII. Any good general history of the eighteenth century underlines the importance of the state's role in expanding and defending the trading empire: see J. H. Plumb's short but illuminating paperback: *England in the Eighteenth Century* (1950), or a more substantial text such as Dorothy Marshall's: *Eighteenth Century England* (1962). For specialist treatments, see Judith Williams: *British Commercial Policy and Trade Expansion, 1750–1850* (1972) and Paul Langford: *The Eighteenth Century, 1688–1815* (1976, Modern British Foreign Policy Series).

# Index